European Yearbook of International Economic Law

EYIEL Monographs - Studies in European and International Economic Law

Volume 29

EYIEL Monographs is a subseries of the European Yearbook of International Economic Law (EYIEL). It contains scholarly works in the fields of European and international economic law, in particular WTO law, international investment law, international monetary law, law of regional economic integration, external trade law of the EU and EU internal market law. The series does not include edited volumes. EYIEL Monographs are peer-reviewed by the series editors and external reviewers.

Iulianna Romanchyshyna

Technical Barriers to Trade in "New Generation" RTAs and in the WTO Agreements

Conflict or Complementarity?

Springer

Iulianna Romanchyshyna
Brussels, Belgium

ISSN 2364-8392 ISSN 2364-8406 (electronic)
European Yearbook of International Economic Law
ISSN 2524-6658 ISSN 2524-6666 (electronic)
EYIEL Monographs - Studies in European and International Economic Law
ISBN 978-3-031-25790-2 ISBN 978-3-031-25791-9 (eBook)
https://doi.org/10.1007/978-3-031-25791-9

This Springer imprint is published by the registered company Springer Nature Switzerland AG
The registered company address is: Gewerbestrasse 11, 6330 Cham, Switzerland

Contents

Chapter 1
Introduction

In the context of the changing nature of global trade, where tariffs are becoming less relevant and non-tariff measures (NTMs) are gaining prominence, it is important to find ways to fill in the gap in the global trade governance, which would reflect today's realities. In a situation where the WTO is lagging behind in fulfilling this task, regional trade agreements (RTAs) come to the forefront to respond to a demand for new trade rules. However, with a growing number of RTAs, a question arises as regards their interrelation with the WTO system.

This study explores the following **research question**: what is the interrelation between cooperation on technical barriers to trade (TBT) in RTAs and the WTO system? More precisely, the task of this research is to examine in detail whether the TBT facilitation methods in RTAs go in line with the WTO approach, and whether, drawing from the RTAs experience, the WTO could improve its TBT-related disciplines and institutional procedures. A part of this research is dedicated to examining the approach of the European Union (EU) and the United States (US) in disciplining technical barriers to trade in their trade agreements, as these trade agreements, as a rule, contain the most ambitious agenda on the issue, and, therefore, could be instrumental in understanding the trend of TBT rules addressed within RTAs and might also serve as an inspiration for future multilateral rules and procedures.

In general, the subject of a relationship between regionalism and multilateralism is not new in academic literature. It has been explored in earlier works of Jagdish Bhagwati,[1] Jacob Viner,[2] as well as more recent works of Caroline Freund,[3] Thomas

[1] Bhagwati (1992).

[2] Viner (1950).

[3] Freund (2000b).

I. Romanchyshyna, *Technical Barriers to Trade in "New Generation" RTAs and in the WTO Agreements*, EYIEL Monographs - Studies in European and International Economic Law 29, https://doi.org/10.1007/978-3-031-25791-9_1

Cottier,[4] Sungjoon Cho,[5] etc. However, most of the sources on this issue are still focusing on tariffs and other border measures, while sources on regionalism and multilateralism in the context of non-tariff measures are lacking. This study builds on the existing literature on regionalism in relevant parts. It also draws from the studies examining certain particular aspects of the research question. For instance, on the issue of applicability of the regional integration exception to measure beyond tariffs and other border restrictions, studies by Joel Trachtman,[6] Lorand Bartels,[7] James Mathis,[8] Nicolas Lokhard and Andrew Mitchel[9] exploring the particular features of Article XXIV of the GATT provide important insights. Likewise, studies by Bollyky and Mavroidis,[10] Rudolf Adlung and Hamid Mamdouh,[11] and Robert Basedow,[12] are instrumental in analyzing the possibilities to transform the WTO system and adjust it to new realities.

Research methods used when writing this study involve doctrinal research, including study of legal sources, such as the WTO Agreements, panel and Appellate Body Reports, as well as discourse analysis, i.e., study of various opinions of academics and legal practitioners in academic journals, books, and news articles.

The structure of this research is the following.

Chapter 2 sets the scene for the ensuing chapters by analyzing the increasing relevance of TBT for global commerce and the way they are addressed at the WTO. It reflects on the limitations, as well as the benefits of the WTO in addressing TBT measures. Further, it pinpoints that the gaps in global trade governance are often addressed in RTAs and briefly explains the methods, which are used in RTAs. It suggests that RTAs could act as complements to the WTO rules, but to avoid fragmentation, they should also go in line with basic WTO disciplines. Furthermore, considering the benefits of the WTO as a multilateral forum, it could be desirable for some of the RTA provisions to be addressed within the WTO framework.

Chapter 3 examines how TBT cooperation in RTAs fits into the debate on regionalism and multilateralism. To do this, it firstly provides a theoretical underpinning of the analysis by reviewing the historical account on the issue and studying the classic theory. Further, it reviews how TBT in RTAs could fit into this paradigm and what are the RTAs' limitations. This is supplemented by a legal analysis of some of the TBT cooperation methods in RTAs in terms of their consistency with respective WTO disciplines. Chapter 3 also explores another facet of the discussion on regionalism and multilateralism: whether TBT cooperation in RTAs might be

[4] Cottier et al. (2015), pp. 465–496.

[5] Cho (2001).

[6] Trachtman (2003).

[7] Bartels (2005).

[8] Mathis (1998).

[9] Lokhard and Mitchell (2005), p. 236.

[10] Bollyky and Mavroidis (2017).

[11] Adlung and Mamdouh (2018), pp. 93–102.

[12] Basedow (2018), p. 417.

further multilateralized and which institutional instruments and procedures at the WTO could serve this process. It avoids analyzing the political constraints for such process, but rather focuses on the legal instruments and methods.

Chapter 4 focuses more specifically on the TBT provisions in free trade agreements of the European Union and the United States as major rule makers in the area of TBT cooperation. It analyses the most recent EU and US approaches to TBT in their free trade agreements to understand the direction of TBT liberalization, the instruments that countries are using in this regard, and how these instruments interrelate with the WTO disciplines. Also, this Chapter speculates on which issues from the EU and US FTA agenda on TBT could be brought to the multilateral level.

References

Books and Book Chapters

Cottier T, Sieber C et al (2015) The dialectical relationship of preferential and multilateral trade agreements. In: Dür A, Elsig M (eds) Trade cooperation: the purpose, design and the effects of preferential trade agreements. Cambridge University Press, Cambridge, pp 465–496

Lokhard N and Mitchell A (2005) Regional Trade Agreements under GATT 1994: an exception and its limits. In: Mitchel A (ed) Challenges and prospects for the WTO. Cameron May, London, pp. 217-252

Viner J (1950) The Customs Union Issue. Carnegie Endowment for International Peace, New York

Journal Articles

Adlung R, Mamdouh H (2018) Plurilateral agreements: an escape route for the WTO. J World Trade 52(1):85–111

Bartels L (2005) The legality of the EC mutual recognition clause under the WTO law. J Int Econ Law 8(3):691–720

Basedow R (2018) The WTO and the rise of plurilateralism – what lessons can we learn from the European Union's experience with differentiated integration. J Int Econ Law 21(1):411–431

Bhagwati J (1992) Regionalism versus multilateralism. World Econ 15(5):535–556

Bollyky T, Mavroidis P (2017) Trade, social preferences and regulatory cooperation. The new WTO-think. J Int Econ Law 20(1):1–30

Cho S (2001) Breaking the barrier between regionalism and multilateralism: a new perspective on trade regionalism. Harv Int Law J 42(2):419–465

Freund C (2000b) Multilateralism and endogenous formation of Free Trade Agreements. J Int Econ 52(2):359–376

Mathis J (1998) Mutual recognition agreements. Transatlantic parties and the limits to non-tariff barrier regionalism in the WTO. J World Trade 32(6):5–31

Trachtman J (2003) Towards open recognition? standardization and regional integration under Article XXIV of the GATT. J Int Econ Law 6(2):459–492

Chapter 2
"Deep" Trade Agenda and Multilateralism

2.1 Changing Paradigms of Global Commerce: Towards a "Deep" Trade Agenda

The paradigms of global commerce are changing at a great pace with production and distribution processes being unbundled across countries via global value chains (GVCs), facilitated through rapid technological growth modifying the channels of communication, manufacturing and trade leading to greater interconnectedness between countries and creating a demand for closer cooperation, including not only on tariffs—traditional trade barriers, but also on NTMs.[1] The significance of tariffs is decreasing, since they have already been reduced to a large extent globally following the trade liberalization efforts of the last couple of decades, while NTMs often present new trade barriers.

There have been numerous studies that tried to capture the effects of NTMs. For instance, a study performed jointly by the United Nations Conference in Trade and Development (UNCTAD) and the World Bank (covering 109 countries and 90 per cent of world trade) essentially confirmed that NTMs affect around 80 per cent of trade and in most sectors their restrictiveness is higher compared to tariffs.[2] Moreover, the study emphasized their growing impact on international trade and indicated that they will have a direct effect on the future economic growth overshadowing tariffs and other restrictions applied at the border.

[1] See Gereffi et al. (2005), Baldwin (2014), Baldwin (2016), pp. 79–110 (See paragraphs arguing for the fundamental importance of information and communication technologies in the new dynamics of globalization).

[2] UNCTAD and World Bank (2017) The Unseen Impact of Non-Tariff Measures: Insights from a New Database, p. iv. http://unctad.org/meetings/en/SessionalDocuments/ditc-tab-MC11-UNCTAD-NTMs.pdf. Accessed 1 Nov 2022.

I. Romanchyshyna, *Technical Barriers to Trade in "New Generation" RTAs and in the WTO Agreements*, EYIEL Monographs - Studies in European and International Economic Law 29, https://doi.org/10.1007/978-3-031-25791-9_2

Technical barriers to trade have a particular significance. The UNCTAD and World Bank study demonstrates that TBT measures are by far the most widely used type of NTMs having the most profound effects in terms of trade value and product coverage affecting around 65 per cent of world trade and 35 per cent of product lines.[3] These technical measures cause compliance costs for producers, which may be far more burdensome than tariffs. They may inhibit trade in various ways. For example, producers have to comply with regulations on product design and packaging in different destination markets and thereby spend additional verification costs for mandatory labelling,[4] as well as for procedures such as testing and certification to assess the conformity of products with environmental and health regulations. Differences in regulations may also induce producers to establish separate production lines leading to higher costs and preventing economies of scale. Procedures of assessing the conformity of products with environmental and health regulations may be duplicative and unduly burdensome. Moreover, these measures are less transparent than tariffs and therefore produce uncertainty and additional costs for importers. There is an important development dimension of these policies too as TBT are by far mostly applied by developed countries—three times as much as by least developed countries. For the most part, they negatively impact low-income countries.[5]

Issues related to domestic regulation in a broad sense are a subject of international cooperation at various levels and at multiple fora. For instance, the Organisation for Economic Cooperation and Development (OECD) and the Asia - Pacific Economic Cooperation forum (APEC) are especially proactive fora for fostering good regulatory practices and dialogue.[6] In fact, regulatory policy is among the key areas of their work, within which they produce multiple intergovernmental initiatives. In one of its research papers, the OECD takes stock of multiple methods to deal with regulatory divergences and classifies them into eleven categories—from soft law instruments, such as regulatory dialogue and subscription to the OECD guidelines and principles of good governance, to binding instruments, such as intergovernmental agreements on harmonization and mutual recognition.[7]

It is important to note that because of the link between trade and regulatory areas, more and more regulatory issues are addressed specifically within the context of trade. In its study, the OECD elucidates the link between trade and regulation and, by

---

[3] Ibid., p. 6.

[4] Hobbs (2007), p. 397.

[5] UNCTAD and World Bank (2017) The Unseen Impact of Non-Tariff Measures: Insights from a New Database, p. iv. http://unctad.org/meetings/en/SessionalDocuments/ditc-tab-MC11-UNCTAD-NTMs.pdf. Accessed 1 Nov 2022, p. 10.

[6] The OECD and APEC also have a joint initiative. It is called "The APEC-OECD Cooperative Initiative on Regulatory Reform", https://www.oecd.org/gov/regulatory-policy/apec-oecd-initiative-regulatory-reform.htm. Accessed 1 Nov 2022.

[7] OECD (2013) International Regulatory Cooperation: Addressing Global Challenges. OECD Publishing, Paris, p. 21. https://read.oecd-ilibrary.org/governance/international-regulatory-co-operation_9789264200463-en#page25. Accessed 1 Nov 2022.

referring to various economic papers on specific aspects of regulatory heterogeneity, pinpoints a significant untapped potential that reducing technical barriers might have for economic growth.[8] Especially, it is relevant for global value chains (GVC) trade, where regulatory divergences in various jurisdictions significantly add to the cost of the final product. The regulatory heterogeneity may lead to accumulation of behind the border measures along the supply chain meaning that their "trade-distorting effects are greater for goods produced in a fragmented manner than goods with simple production processes".[9] The case-study performed by the OECD focusing on the example of selected Latin American countries, demonstrated the negative correlation between the NTMs restrictiveness (mainly TBT and sanitary and phytosanitary measures (SPS)) and GVCs participation. It estimated that the costs of NTMs overall could add around 20 per cent of the tariff equivalent to the price of primary intermediate goods and twelve per cent for processed ones.[10] Therefore, it is fair to assume that these measures would represent an avenue where future trade liberalization efforts will be focusing on. One of the WTO annual trade reports specifically stresses out the growing relevance of regulatory measures in the globalized world and a need to incorporate them in future trade liberalization efforts.[11]

Another issue relevant in the context of the changing paradigms of global commerce is the expanded regulatory need to protect consumers, the environment and other societal values.[12] Increasing production and trade via GVCs creates increased sensitivities in these areas, exposing the risk of a "race to the bottom" (when regulators weaken the levels of protection to maintain competitive advantage).[13] Therefore, it is clear that future trade agreements also have to address those public policy issues in a more comprehensive manner.

---

[8] OECD (2017) International Regulatory Co-operation and Trade. Understanding the Trade Costs of Regulatory Divergence and the Remedies. OECD Publishing, Paris. https://www.oecd.org/gov/international-regulatory-co-operation-and-trade-9789264275942-en.htm. Accessed 1 Nov 2022.

[9] Ferrantino M (2012) Using Supply Chain Analysis to Examine the Costs of Non-Tariff Measures and the Benefits of Trade Facilitation. Staff Working Paper of the WTO Economics Research and Statistics Division, p. 1. https://www.wto-ilibrary.org/content/papers/25189808/121/read.

[10] OECD (2016) Participation in Global Value Chains in Latin America. Implications for Trade and Trade-Related Policy. OECD Publishing, Paris, p. 54. https://www.oecd-ilibrary.org/trade/participation-in-global-value-chains-in-latin-america_5jlpq80ts8f2-en. Accessed 2 Nov 2022.

[11] WTO (2012) World Trade Report: Trade and Public Policies: A Closer Look at Non-Tariff Measures in 21st Century, p. 161.

[12] Ibid., p. 174.

[13] See Bull et al. (2015), p. 24.

2.2 The Diversity of Technical Barriers to Trade

Before discussing the international legal framework for technical barriers to trade in more detail, it is due to make clear which forms these barriers take. This research follows an understanding on technical barriers to trade, as identified in the WTO Agreement on Technical Barriers to Trade (TBT Agreement). The TBT Agreement defines the following three categories of TBT measures:

i. Technical regulations
ii. Standards
iii. Conformity assessment procedures

2.2.1 Technical Regulations

Technical regulation, as clarified in the Annex 1 of the TBT Agreement, is defined as follows:

> Document which lays down product characteristics or their related processes and production methods, including the applicable administrative provisions, with which compliance is mandatory. It may also include or deal exclusively with terminology, symbols, packaging, marking or labelling requirements as they apply to a product, process or production method.

In other words, technical regulations are technical prescriptions of mandatory force regarding the characteristics of the products themselves or the way they are produced, including labelling, packaging, etc. They are usually adopted by governments, although Article 3 of the TBT Agreement also foresees that technical regulations might come from non-governmental bodies, if granted mandatory force.

As a rule, such regulations have a certain public policy objective and, although their effects could be trade restrictive, it might be justified by the public policy goal in question. The examples of such measures could be found in WTO case law: prohibition of the products containing asbestos (*EC – Asbestos*), a requirement to provide plain packaging for tobacco cigarettes (*Australia – Tobacco Plain Packaging*), etc.[14] These examples of the measures were aimed to deal with public health concerns.

2.2.2 Standards

"Standards" are oftentimes conflated with "technical regulations" and both terms are often used interchangeably. However, it is crucial that, according to the TBT

[14] Appellate Body Report, *EC – Asbestos*, para. 72; Panel Report, *Australia – Tobacco Plain Packaging*, paras. 7.142 and 7.145.

Agreement's definition, standards have a distinctive feature: they do not have mandatory force.[15] The following definition of a "standard" applies:

> Document approved by a recognized body, that provides, for common and repeated use, rules, guidelines or characteristics for products or related processes and production methods, with which compliance is not mandatory. It may also include or deal exclusively with terminology, symbols, packaging, marking or labelling requirements as they apply to a product, process or production method.

In fact, standards are technical specifications that may be produced by a variety of actors (as follows from Article 4 of the TBT Agreement): governmental or non-governmental organizations, international standardizing bodies such as the International Standardising Organisation (ISO), International Electrotechnical Commission (IEC), International Telecommunication Union (ITU) and others, or regional standardizing bodies.[16]

It is relevant to note that in certain cases the lines between standards and technical regulations may be somewhat blurred when governments endow standards with a certain degree of legal force—for instance, by way of their direct reference in legislation, in which case they may have a *de facto* similar trade affect as technical regulations. Although industry standards *a priori* have nothing to do with government regulations, governments might use them as a means to regulate (or co-regulate) certain relations. The basic idea is to have flexible guidelines that, in contrast to rigid laws, would easily adjust to fast-growing technological changes and innovative solutions reflecting primarily certain business preferences. However, when a standard is used as the so-called "exclusive reference" (compliance with the given standard is the one and only means to meet the requirement of a technical regulation[17]), it is particularly restrictive. This might be illustrated with the example of the *US – Tuna* case, where the US government restricted dolphin safe labelling to compliance with a specific technical standard. Despite that the government did not prevent market access for tuna without a label, it nevertheless constituted the only way to display the "dolphin safe" status of tuna products, which put imported tuna in a less competitive position as it could not be marketed as "dolphin safe" unless a prescribed standard is strictly followed.[18] Therefore, it limited significantly marketing opportunities of imported tuna and was found a *de facto* "technical regulation". Therefore, according to the understanding provided in the *US – Tuna* case, as soon as standards are endowed with mandatory force by the government, they shall be treated as technical regulations.

However, even without being used in legislation, standards *per se* may have a powerful impact on the market. From the business perspective, a wide adoption of certain standards leads to increased interoperability between technologies that would facilitate business operations and increase trade within supply chains. Increased

---

[15] See also Romanchyshyna (2019), p. 4.

[16] Appleton (2017), p. 412.

[17] ISO and IEC (2004) ISO/IEC Guide 2. Standardisation and Related Activities, p. 17.

[18] Panel Report, *US – Tuna*, para. 7.144.

interoperability could also have positive implications for innovation and development. For instance, a number of studies show that standards bring about economic growth by codifying technological know-how. [19]

This could also impact the competition in the market, for instance, in a situation when companies using different technical solutions find themselves in a competitive disadvantage being *de facto* forced to adjust to a given standard. Standards might have a significant effect on supply chains. One of the examples could be competition between video standards VHS and Betamax: since the former became more commonly used, despite the availability of Betamax video recorders on the market, consumers would prefer VHS as most of videotapes they could buy or rent implemented this format.[20] Another example could be a direct prescription of some market actors to use a certain standard as a condition for a contractual relationship—for instance, a supermarket chain requiring its suppliers to use a certain label.[21]

It is also important to point out that standards include certain technical specifications to reduce a variety of production processes which prevents economies of scale. A large extent of standards (which distinguishes them from technical regulations) are not even concerned with public policy objectives such as health, safety, environment, etc. They simply deal with technical and business aspects.[22] Nevertheless, in many cases, those issues are directly or indirectly related to matters of public policy.

There is another angle of standardization, which is related to strategic concerns. Peter Swann draws attention to the "competitive advantage" rationale, which is built on the premise that with the diffusion of standards, domestic companies "use their home market base to build international market share".[23]

The benefits of international standardization have been widely recognized, as a way to attain interoperability, economic growth, ensure the use of best technologies and to elevate the protection of certain values.[24] This is a variety of organizations, such as the International Standardisation Organisation (ISO), International Electrotechnical Committee (IEC), International Telecommunication Union (ITU), the work of which is dedicated to promotion of international standards around the world.

---

[19] Blind et al. (2000) The Economic Benefits of Standardization, German Institute for Standardization (DIN). https://www.din.de/blob/89552/68849fab0eeeaafb56c5a3ffee9959c5/economic-benefits-of-standardization-en-data.pdf. Accessed 1 Nov 2022; Blind and Jungmittag (2008); Menon Economics (2018) The Influence of Standards on the Nordic Economies. https://www.menon.no/wp-content/uploads/2018-31-Nordic-market-study-influence-of-standards.pdf. Accessed 1 Nov 2022.

[20] Appleton (2005), p. 379.

[21] Wouters et al. (2008), p. 15.

[22] Correia de Brito et al. (2016), p. 22.

[23] Swann (2000), p. 17.

[24] Wagner (2013), p. 241.

2.2.3 *Conformity Assessment*

Finally, as regards conformity assessment procedures, Annex 1 of the TBT Agreement defines them as measures to assess whether requirements of technical regulations and standards are met.

> Any procedure used, directly or indirectly, to determine that relevant requirements in technical regulations or standards are fulfilled.

The explanatory note also clarifies the following:

> Conformity assessment procedures include, inter alia, procedures for sampling, testing and inspection; evaluation, verification and assurance of conformity; registration, accreditation and approval as well as their combinations.

As we could derive from this definition, the infrastructure of conformity assessment could have multiple levels and forms. There are, first of all, activities, which deal with assessing the characteristics of a product itself:

(1) *Supplier's declaration of conformity*: an assurance issued by the manufacturer or importer that a product conforms to specified requirements. It is based on either the supplier's own testing, or the results of third-party institutions and is admissible, as a rule, where there is no significant risk involved.
(2) *Testing and inspection*: a set of procedures to determine the characteristics of a product, often based on random samples that may be performed by the supplier, regulatory authorities or commercial bodies at the request of a supplier.
(3) *Certification and quality systems registration*: Certification is a set of procedures to evaluate whether process or product characteristics conform to a certain standard, which is not necessary for testing and inspection, and it is usually performed by a third party independent from the supplier. Apart from certification of products, there is also a quality systems registrations, which is the audit of the conformity of supplier's systems, such as the quality management system, to ensure that there is no variation in the quality of the production.[25]

In addition, there is such an element of conformity assessment infrastructure as *accreditation*, which is, according to the ISO/IEC Guide 2:1991, a "[p]rocedure by which an authoritative body gives formal recognition that a body or person is competent to carry out specific tasks".[26] In other words, accreditation is the authorization of conformity assessment bodies. In contrast to testing, inspection and certifications that are more commonly performed by commercial bodies,

[25] WTO (2005) World Trade Report: Exploring the Links between Trade, Standards, and the WTO, pp. 97–100.

[26] ISO/IEC Guide 2:1991: General Terms and Their Definitions Concerning Standardization and Related Activities, para. 13.7. The TBT Agreement (Annex 1) incorporates the terms of this guide.

accreditation is a government responsibility.[27] At the same time, it is relevant to mention that the definition of accreditation could also refer to the work of international bodies, which promote more uniform principles for accreditation criteria. In this respect, the work of such international organizations as the International Laboratory Accreditation Cooperation (ILAC) and the International Accreditation Forum (IAF) could be relevant.

Conformity assessment procedures are necessary elements of the regulatory process, which aim to ensure that the respective goals of technical regulations and standards are achieved. At the same time, it could be imagined that the conformity assessment requirements themselves might have a protectionist motive or simply be inefficient and more burdensome than necessary to demonstrate the conformity of certain products with regulatory requirements, which might contribute to processing time and costs.

It is important to point out the above definitional clarification at the outset, as we will see further that a distinction between variety of forms reflects on the legal disciplines in the TBT Agreement, as well as has an impact on further international cooperation manifested in different roles for the countries' engagement.

2.3 WTO as a Forum to Address a "Deep" Trade Agenda

The original GATT 1947 was designed in the era when tariffs and other border measures were the primary target of the trade liberalization agenda and thus they are more apt to deal with these kind of restrictions, rather than non-tariff measures. Over the years, the GATT/WTO system has demonstrated its ability to adapt towards the realities of global commerce, however in within the recent decades, the progress has been quite slow. This section reflects on the development of the GATT/WTO system, how the non-tariff measures appeared on the agenda and what are the constraints for further progress on disciplining these kind of measures.

2.3.1 Cornerstone of Trade Liberalization at the WTO

Since its inception in the aftermath of the Second World War, the idea of the GATT system (and afterwards the WTO) has been to promote trade liberalization to end the "beggar thy neighbour" trade policies that were causing economic instability. The context of the early GATT years prompted the multilateral rounds of negotiations to be focused primarily on tariffs, although it is fair to state that the GATT from the

[27] It is also relevant to note that conformity assessment relies on *metrology*, which is the work of special calibration laboratories to develop reference standards for measurement to be used by conformity assessment bodies. See WTO (2005) World Trade Report, p. 97.

outset was not only a tariff deal. Aside from disciplining tariffs and other border measures, like quotas (Article XI GATT) or anti-dumping duties (Article VI), it applied to a broad range of measures of discriminatory nature by incorporating the MFN (Article I) and the national treatment (Article III) principles. Significantly, it also accommodated public policy concerns by putting forward a list of exceptions (Article XX and XXI). In the GATT era, however, addressing non-tariff measures was mainly aimed at ensuring that they would not be used as a back door for protectionism frustrating the contracting parties' market access commitments.[28] The non-discrimination provisions to which regulatory measures were subject to would constitute "negative" or "shallow" forms of integration, which do not require specifically that the parties cooperate, but proscribe discrimination of WTO Members.[29] Going deeper into the domestic policy arena with the objective of providing regulatory coherence was not yet on the radars at the time of GATT creation.

At the time, however, the multilateral system proved to be prone to adjustments to reflect the realities of global commerce. The Tokyo Round (1973–1979) of trade negotiations became in a way a game changer in setting up additional rules for regulating non-tariff measures in several key areas, such as TBT, subsidies and public procurement. It resulted in the adoption of the so-called "codes" that were applied on a plurilateral basis meaning that they were binding only upon a certain group of the GATT contracting parties. In fact, the first substantial calls for regulating some of these areas appeared before at the Kennedy Round (1964–1967) where the contracting parties recognized that "trade negotiations should cover not only tariffs but also non-tariff barriers" and identified the main topics for discussion where domestic regulations used to hinder trade.[30] A shift of attention towards NTMs, as Billy Melo Araujo points out, was explained by a variety of factors, including the changing patterns of global commerce resulting from transportation and telecommunication developments, but also the fact that tariffs had already been reduced significantly throughout the previous GATT negotiating rounds putting a spotlight on other measures undermining free trade.[31] The Tokyo Round's codes materialized the solutions on NTMs into the substantive legal instruments.

With regard to TBT, the Tokyo Round produced the so-called "Standards Code", the predecessor of the TBT Agreement. Building on the GATT, it also incorporated provisions on non-discrimination, but went deeper into the domestic policy domain. Non-discrimination remained at the core of the Standards Code (and later the TBT Agreement) covering both the MFN and national treatment principles. However, some new additions emerged. In particular, the signatories were proscribed from adopting regulations that were more trade restrictive than necessary to achieve legitimate regulatory objectives, and they had to base their regulations on relevant

[28] WTO (2012) World Trade Report, p. 41.

[29] On "deep" and "shallow" integration, see, e.g., Lawrence (1996), p. 17; On "negative" and "positive" integration, see Tinbergen (1954), p. 4.

[30] GATT (1963) Kennedy Round of Trade Negotiations - Forthcoming Meetings, GATT/873.

[31] Melo Araujo (2016), p. 14.

international standards unless these standards were inappropriate for them (both additions transitioned to the modern TBT Agreement).[32] These aspects constituted in fact an evolvement from a "negative" or "shallow" towards a "positive" or "deep" integration agenda at the GATT. Although the basic reasoning for the Standards Code was still to prevent measures used to circumvent tariff liberalization, these particular provisions created a possibility to target trade-distorting regulations even if they were not discriminatory.[33] It should be acknowledged that the Standards Code was an effort to harness unfettered regulatory discretion and to summon the parties to collaborate in order to improve regulatory coherence. However, obviously, the main weakness of the Standards Code was its limited application only to a set of the GATT contracting parties.

Later, the Uruguay Round (1986–1994) of multilateral trade negotiations has become a major step in the development of the global trade governance. Apart from establishing the WTO, it resulted in groundbreaking developments of trade rules—in services (GATS), intellectual property (TRIPs), dispute settlement and a number of areas with regard to goods regulation. As a result of the Uruguay Round, the Tokyo Round codes were multilateralised. The provisions of the Standards Code, with a number of amendments, became a basis of the Agreement on Technical Barriers to Trade (TBT Agreement).[34]

Throughout the negotiation rounds preceding the creation of the WTO, one could observe how the agenda had been changing to adjust to the new realities of global commerce, however, it is also worthwhile noting that the driving force behind this process was coming mostly from the developed world.[35] Although the Uruguay Round was already an expression of diversified interests of countries with different levels of development, the developed countries were the ones to advocate for a deep trade agenda at the negotiating table. This fact would have significance for further trade negotiations. As explained below, one of the arguments for an ensuing halt in multilateral negotiations and a resulting proliferation of regional trade agreements was the North-South divide in prioritizing certain issues post-Uruguay. The inability to account for interests of developing countries led to practical impossibility to get them on board with a deep integration agenda.

Furtherance of the multilateral liberalization of NTMs came to a halt within the Doha Round of negotiations that commenced in 2001. The DDA had ambitious goals with regard to agricultural market access, developmental policies, services, intellectual property, the environment, and trade facilitation. However, to date, with some exceptions like disciplining agricultural subsidies, compulsory licensing and

---

[32] Agreement on Technical Barriers to Trade ("Standards Code"), 1979. http://www.worldtradelaw.net/tokyoround/standardscode.pdf.download. Accessed 1 Nov 2022.

[33] Lester et al. (2018), p. 685; See the language used within the negotiations: "*It merely seeks to minimize the effect of such actions on international trade*" (GATT Drafting Group on Standards, Proposed GATT Code of Conduct for Preventing Technical Barriers to Trade, 30.12.1971. https://docs.wto.org/gattdocs/q/GG/SPEC/71-143.pdf. Accessed 1 Nov 2022).

[34] Marceau and Trachtman (2014), p. 355.

[35] Melo Araujo (2016), p. 21.

the Trade Facilitation Agreement, mostly did not deliver on its promises. Among many issues raised in Doha were the non-agricultural market access (NAMA) negotiations including the area of NTMs (paragraph 16 of the Doha Declaration), where WTO Members recognized the significance of measures of regulatory nature and noted the insufficiency of the current WTO framework with regard to those issues.[36]

When it comes to TBT measures, differences in domestic regulation of food, environmental standards, and labeling requirements remained to be trade concerns continuing to prompt Members to seek ways to limit their effects. Although the rules provided in the TBT Agreement were progressive at the time of their adoption, it was clear that the new realities demanded somewhat deeper forms of cooperation to catch up with global commerce developments. Notably, in an effort to develop the existing rules, some of the Members provided certain sectoral proposals to promote the regulatory coherence at the multilateral level. For example, harmonization of information requirements on labeling of textiles and clothing products,[37] conformity assessment of electronics,[38] labeling and conformity assessment of chemicals,[39] conformity assessment in the automotive sector[40] or creating a general framework for sector specific TBT proposals.[41] These proposals were never given traction.

Nevertheless, the experience of the Standards Code and the TBT Agreement, as well as the later endeavors to develop disciplines within the Doha Agenda demonstrated the ability and aspiration of the GATT/WTO system to adapt to the new trade context and to create rules that were not within the ambit of the original idea of the GATT. This is an important point for the later discussion on how the WTO provisions and institutional structure could be further transformed.

2.3.2 *Overview of WTO Legal Disciplines Related to TBT*

The purpose of this subsection is to give an overview of the legal disciplines that apply to TBT measures within the WTO framework in order to provide a clear picture of the approach to TBT already existing at the WTO. It does not aim to make a full comprehensive analysis, but rather to give an overview of the general features of the legal provisions and to emphasize the aspect of interrelation between trade liberalization and policy space. It demonstrates that the TBT Agreement has become an important advancement in comparison to the GATT, however, still, the changing

---

36 WTO, Doha WTO Ministerial Declaration, WT/MIN(01)/DEC/1, 20.11.2001.

37 WTO, EU Proposal TN/MA/W/93/Rev.1 and Add.1, 15.09.2009.

38 WTO, EU Proposal TN/MA/W/129, 7.12.2009; US Proposal TN/MA/W/105/Rev.2, 15.09.2009.

39 WTO, Argentina and Brazil Proposal TN/MA/W/135, 04.02.2010.

40 WTO, EU Proposal TN/MA/W/118/Rev.1, 4.12.2009; WTO, US Proposal TN/MA/W/ 120,15.09.2009.

41 WTO, Brazil EU and India's Proposals TN/MA/W/136, 15.03.2010.

nature of global trade calls for deeper forms of cooperation. Mostly, the WTO Agreements' law and practice in this area is focused on distinguishing legitimate measures from protectionism and it is quite limited in terms of further integration, including regulatory dialogue and cooperation.

2.3.2.1 The TBT Agreement and the GATT

At the outset, it is relevant to note that the WTO Agreements that are targeting technical barriers to trade are the TBT Agreement and the GATT. In this respect, it is worth to clarify the interrelation between the GATT and the TBT Agreement's disciplines when it comes to technical barriers to trade. In *EC – Asbestos* the Appellate Body explained that both agreements apply cumulatively and that the TBT Agreement is furthering the objectives of the GATT "through a specialized legal regime that applies solely to a limited class of measures". This legal regime is "different" and "additional" to the disciplines of the GATT.[42] At the same time, in case of conflict, as follows from the General Interpretative Note to Annex IA of the Marrakesh Agreement and further clarified in the *US – COOL* case, the provisions of the TBT Agreement should prevail, as the TBT Agreement is a more specific agreement on trade in goods.[43] If, however, there are similar claims under the TBT Agreement and the GATT, panels tend to examine firstly the claims under the TBT Agreement.[44] Panels in principle may exercise judicial economy with regard to a similar claim under the GATT, in case the measure at issue has been already found inconsistent with a similar provision of the TBT Agreement.[45] A different situation exists if a panel did not find inconsistency with the provisions of the TBT Agreement. Here, additional scrutiny may be required under the similar GATT disciplines, as was, for instance, made clear by the Appellate Body in *US – Tuna II (Mexico)*.[46]

The TBT Agreement has become a major advancement in comparison to the GATT in terms of disciplining technical barriers to trade. In the text of its Preamble, the two main lines of purpose could be identified. Firstly, it is the prohibition of "regulatory protectionism", which, in comparison to the GATT approach consists of not only prohibiting discriminatory measures, but also all other measures

---

[42] Appellate Body Report, *EC – Asbestos*, para. 80.

[43] Panel Report, *US – COOL*, para. 7.233.

[44] Panel Reports, *US – COOL (Article 21.5 – Canada and Mexico)*, paras. 7.2–7.6; *US – Tuna II (Mexico) (Article 21.5 – Mexico)*, paras. 7.3–7.8; *EC – Seal Products*, paras. 7.57–7.69; *US – COOL*, paras. 7.70–7.73; *US – Tuna II (Mexico)*, paras. 7.39–7.46; *US – Clove Cigarettes*, paras. 7.7–7.19; *EC – Sardines*, paras. 7.14–7.19; and *EC – Asbestos*, paras. 8.15–8.17.

[45] See, e.g., Panel Report, *EC – Sardines*, paras. 7.147–7.152.

[46] In *US – Tuna II (Mexico)*, the Appellate Body noted that the panel exercised a "false judicial economy" by failing to assess the measure at issue under the non-discrimination provisions of the GATT after having found that the non-discrimination provisions of the TBT Agreement have not been violated (para. 405).

disadvantaging foreign firms in a manner that is unnecessary to achieve a truly legitimate objective.[47] Secondly, it is the promotion of international standards, which stands very prominent throughout the whole text of the Preamble:

> *Recognizing* the important contribution that international standards ... can make ... by improving efficiency of production and facilitating the conduct of international trade,
>
> *Desiring* ... to encourage the development of such international standards,
>
> *Recognizing* the contribution that international standards can make to the transfer of technology from developed to developing countries.

All these references testify that the TBT Agreement reflects a choice to address technical barriers to trade in a more comprehensive fashion by making a step towards so-called "positive integration".[48] In which way this intention is reflected in the legal disciplines and WTO case law is discussed further.

2.3.2.2 The Relevance of Production Methods

There is a specific area of technical barriers to trade that is contentious in terms of TBT coverage—processes and production methods that do not have a trace in product characteristics (in TBT Agreement's parlance, non-product related PPMs), such as, environmental requirements, the prescription not to use child labour, etc. The current position of the Appellate Body in *US – Tuna II (Mexico)* appears to be that the TBT Agreement does apply to those non-product related PPMs that deal with terminology, symbols, packaging, marking or labelling requirements, which are explicitly mentioned in the second sentence of the technical regulation's definition (see Sect. 2.2.1).[49] The panel's clarification in *US – Tuna II (Mexico)* implies that such a contentious issue as eco-labelling now has been effectively placed under the ambit of the TBT scrutiny.[50] However, whether non-product related PPMs that are not reflected in terminology, symbols, packaging, marking or labelling requirements are covered by the TBT Agreement or not remains unclear. The panel in *US – Tuna II (Mexico)* deliberately declined to rule on this issue.[51]

It is important to note that this category of PPMs, despite that it might not fall under the TBT Agreement and thus might not be subject to its "positive integration" disciplines, would still be subject to the GATT non-discrimination scrutiny.

---

[47] See such a definition of "regulatory protectionism" in Sykes (1999), p. 3.

[48] Howse (2013), p. 1.

[49] Appellate Body Report, *US – Tuna II (Mexico)*, para. 199. See also Panel Report, *EC – Trade Marks and Geographical Indications*, para. 7.449.

[50] Ankersmit and Lawrence (2012), p. 137.

[51] Panel Report, *US – Tuna II (Mexico)*, para. 7.79.

2.3.2.3 Non-discrimination

From its very inception, one of the basic principles of the GATT system, and later on the WTO, has been the principle of non-discrimination: most-favoured nation (MFN) (meaning equal treatment for like products coming from all WTO Members) and national treatment (equal treatment between like products coming from a WTO Member and those produced domestically). This principle is embedded in the WTO Agreements, in particular, the GATT and the TBT:

- Articles I (MFN) and III:4 (national treatment) of the GATT, and
- Articles 2.1 (non-discrimination with respect to technical regulations), 5.1.1. (non-discrimination with respect to conformity assessment), and paragraph D of Annex 3 "Code of Good Practice" (non-discrimination with respect to standards)

The legal test for non-discrimination in the TBT Agreement, in essence, mirrors the legal test for MFN and national treatment in the GATT. As the Appellate Body in *US – Clove Cigarettes* observed, in respect of technical regulations, for the violation of the national treatment obligation of Article 2.1 of the TBT, similarly to Article III:4 of the GATT, the products at issue (imported and domestic) must be "like" and the treatment accorded to imported products must be less favourable than that accorded to like domestic products.[52] A similar legal test would be applied for standards (paragraph D of Annex 3 "Code of Good Practice"), as well as for conformity assessment procedures (Article 5.1.1), except that for the latter the "less favourable treatment" has to be established with respect to the access conditions for the suppliers of like products.

The following analysis focuses on the issue how the legitimate policy considerations could be addressed within the above legal test, in particular, whether these considerations might be a basis for determining that the products at issue are not "like", and what are the specific disciplines in the GATT and the TBT Agreement that deal with this issue.

2.3.2.3.1 "Likeness"

Similar to the GATT, with regard to the analysis of "likeness" between the products at issue (between imported products in case of MFN and between imported and domestic products), the Appellate Body in *US – Clove Cigarettes* confirmed that such an analysis has to be based on competitive relations between the products at issue and rejected the panel's view that "the text and context of the TBT Agreement support an interpretation of the concept of "likeness"... that focuses on legitimate

[52] Appellate Body Report, *US – Clove Cigarettes*, para. 87. The same could be stated in respect of the MFN violation: it must be established that products from one Member, which are "like" products from another Member, are granted less favorable treatment.

objectives..."[53] Therefore, this decision confirmed a position that has been prominent in the GATT jurisprudence that legitimate policy concerns cannot be a reason to consider products not "like" unless those legitimate concerns are grounded in the physical characteristics of the products themselves, e.g. the health risks that these products at issue present, as was the case, for instance, in *EC – Asbestos*.[54] In case the products are physically identical and the difference between them lies in the production methods that are not reflected in the characteristics of the products, the question on whether these products could be considered like or not is contentious. In this instance consumers' tastes and habits might be a relevant factor to assess "likeness". In *US – Tuna II (Mexico)*, the panel recognized that consumers' tastes and habits might play a role in determining whether tuna caught with fishing methods dangerous to dolphins and tuna caught with dolphins-safe methods are like.[55] This suggests a possibility to provide a different treatment to products based on their production methods if there is a consumer preference for or against these methods. One could imagine environmental concerns, the use of child labour, etc. Such differentiation could be more legally persuasive with the evolvement of strong public preferences. Take, for instance, an ever-increasing concern regarding climate change.

Nevertheless, at the time of writing, there has not been a case where "likeness" was judged purely based on consumer preferences. The interrelation between non-discrimination vs. legitimate policy concerns is traditionally addressed within the framework of the exceptions (Sect. 2.3.2.3.2).

2.3.2.3.2 Non-discrimination vs. Legitimate Policy Considerations

In the GATT, the justifiability of legitimate policy concerns is assessed through the interplay of the non-discrimination obligations with Article XX (general exceptions) of the GATT. It implies that a discriminatory measure may be found justified if it is aimed at protection of certain values, inter alia, human, animal or plant life or health, the environment, or prevention of deceptive practices (paragraphs (a)–(j)), as well as not "applied in a manner which would constitute a means of arbitrary or unjustifiable discrimination between countries where the same conditions prevail, or a disguised restriction on international trade".

In the TBT Agreement, it is slightly different when it comes to a distinction between technical regulations and conformity assessment procedures, although in

[53] Appellate Body Report, *US – Clove Cigarettes*, para. 112.

[54] See Appellate Body Report, *EC – Asbestos*, para. 114–116.

[55] See Panel Report, *US – Tuna II (Mexico)*, paras. 7.249. In this case, however, the panel underlined that the comparison for the purposes of "likeness" concerned Mexican tuna products vs tuna products of US origin and tuna products originating in any other country, and not dolphin-safe and not dolphin-safe tuna. The panel ruled that "to the extent that US consumers would distinguish between different tuna products based on their dolphin-safe status, they would not apply this distinction to all tuna products, whatever their origin" (para. 7.250).

the end, the interrelation between non-discrimination and legitimate policy considerations does not differ substantively, except that technically in the TBT Agreement the legitimate policy considerations are a part of a non-discrimination test, while in the GATT they are addressed within the exceptions.

With regard to technical regulations (Article 2.1), the TBT Agreement reflects a continuity with the GATT and is similarly construed through the interpretation of the sixth recital of the TBT Agreement's Preamble, which essentially copies the language of Article XX of the GATT and which the Appellate Body interpreted as an essential part of the non-discrimination test itself—"less favourable treatment" component.[56]

For the technical regulations, therefore, to establish that a measure provided a less favourable treatment to imported products at issue, one must prove not only the fact that the measure modifies conditions of competition to the detriment of imported products at issue, but also that this measure does not stem exclusively from a "legitimate regulatory distinction".[57] Such a "legitimate regulatory distinction" means, according to the sixth recital of the TBT Agreement's Preamble, that the measures are necessary to protect certain values, and, at the same time, it has to be ensured that the measures "are not applied in a manner which would constitute a means of arbitrary or unjustifiable discrimination" or a "disguised restriction on international trade".

The implementation of the stated "legitimate regulatory distinction" might be called into question. Reflecting the continuity with GATT Article XX practice, as the Appellate Body clarified in *US – Clove Cigarettes*, it is necessary to assess whether the measure is implemented in an "even-handed" manner:

> …[A] panel must carefully scrutinize the particular circumstances of the case, that is, the design, architecture, revealing structure, operation, and application of the technical regulation at issue, and, in particular, whether that technical regulation is even-handed, in order to determine whether it discriminates against the group of imported products.[58]

This approach practically ensures that the WTO Members' regulatory space is respected without undermining the disciplines set forth in the TBT Agreement. For that, the way a measure is applied has to relate closely to a legitimate objective and to be closely calibrated to the risks at hand. The lack of a nexus between a measure and a legitimate objective and the lack of calibration to the risks can be manifested in various ways, and thus, is assessed on a case-by-case basis. For instance, in *US – Clove Cigarettes*, the US failed to demonstrate how the clove cigarettes (mainly imported from Indonesia) ban was rationally related to the

---

[56] See., e.g., Appellate Body Reports, *US – Clove Cigarettes*, para. 173; *US – Tuna II (Mexico)*, para. 213.

[57] See this two-tier test in Appellate Body Reports, *US – Clove Cigarettes*, para. 174; *US – Tuna II (Mexico)*, para. 284; *US – COOL*, para. 271; *US – Tuna II (Mexico) (Article 21.5 – Mexico)*, para. 7.26. See also Panel Reports, *US – Tuna II (Mexico) (Article 21.5 –Mexico)*, para. 7.73; and *US – COOL (Article 21.5 – Canada and Mexico)*, paras. 7.60–7.62.

[58] Appellate Body Report, *US – Clove Cigarettes*, para. 182.

objective of reducing youth smoking, if, at the same time, menthol cigarettes (similarly appealing to young smokers) were exempted from the ban.[59] In *US – Tuna II* (Mexico), the Appellate Body also disagreed with the US that its requirements for access to the "dolphin safe" label stemmed exclusively from the legitimate regulatory distinction to contribute to the protection of dolphins. The US requirements contained stringent compliance standards for tuna caught in the Eastern Tropical Pacific region (ETP), while tuna coming from outside the ETP (if not being caught by a specific fishing method, i.e., setting on dolphins) was eligible to be labelled dolphin-safe without certifying that no dolphins had been harmed.[60] It is worthwhile noting that following this Appellate Body's decision, the US modified its original measure. Its 2016 Tuna Measure was "calibrated" to different risks to dolphins arising from the use of different fishing methods in different areas of the ocean, and therefore, in the course of the Article 21.5 DSU compliance procedure, was found non-discriminatory.[61]

With regard to conformity assessment procedures, the non-discrimination obligation is qualified by the phrase in Article 5.1.1—"in a comparable situation".[62] In *Russia – Railways Equipment*, the panel rejected the transposition of the "legitimate regulatory distinction" from the Article 2.1 interpretation on technical regulations. It noted that the phrase "in a comparable situation" already "confirms that Article 5.1.1 permits differential access conditions where they concern situations that are not comparable", and "preserves a degree of flexibility for the importing Member to design and apply its conformity assessment procedures in a situation-appropriate manner".[63] The decision on a lack of the "comparable situation" has to be based on "objective evidence that sufficiently pertain[s] to the specific suppliers at issue".[64] From the Appellate Body's interpretation in *Russia – Railways Equipment*, one might observe that the legal test for a "comparable situation" resembles the criteria of even-handedness in the context of Article 2.1. The Appellate Body also addressed the rational connection between, on the one hand, Russia's justification for refusing to conduct a conformity assessment in the territory of Ukraine as it feared for the life of its inspectors, and, on the other, the situation of the suppliers of Ukrainian railway products.[65] It found that Russia failed to demonstrate this relation and that the evidence it provided on a general security situation did not show how it related to the suppliers at issue.[66]

---

[59] Appellate Body Report, *US – Clove Cigarettes*, para. 225.

[60] Appellate Body Report, *US – Tuna II (Mexico)*, para. 250.

[61] Appellate Body Report, *US – Tuna II (Mexico) (Article 21.5 – Mexico)*, paras. 6.257–6.258.

[62] Panel Report, *Russia – Railway Equipment*, para. 7.273; See also Appellate Body Report, *Russia – Railway Equipment*, para. 5.110.

[63] Panel Report, *Russia – Railway Equipment*, para. 7.272.

[64] Appellate Body Report, *Russia – Railway Equipment*, para. 5.147.

[65] Appellate Body Report, *Russia – Railway Equipment*, para. 5.146.

[66] Appellate Body Report, *Russia – Railway Equipment*, para. 5.147.

It also needs to be mentioned that the TBT Agreement contains a non-discrimination obligation when it comes to standards (paragraph D of Annex 3 "Code of Good Practice" of the TBT Agreement). This provision repeats the language of a non-discrimination obligation with regard to technical regulations (Article 2.1), except that the obligation is on the standardizing bodies. Also, since the standards have a non-mandatory force, it could be assumed that proving an actual or potential trade effect could be daunting task. In any case, this provision has never been adjudicated, although, as it mirrors the language of Article 2.1, it could probably be assumed that, in essence, the dispute settlement reports would be based on the Article 2.1 jurisprudence.

Therefore, the TBT Agreement permits a legitimate departure from the non-discrimination obligations: through "legitimate regulatory distinction" in application of technical regulations, or judgment that the situation of importing suppliers is not "comparable" when applying conformity assessment procedures. The authorities' decision making such a differentiation based on a "legitimate" ground has to be applied in an "even-handed" manner in order not to circumvent the non-discrimination obligations.

At the same time, it is worth to note that the interrelation between non-discrimination and legitimate policy objectives, that was developed by the practice of the WTO panels and the Appellate Body is not devoid of criticism.[67] The WTO approach is oftentimes accused of a bias towards trade liberalization at the expense of sustainable development considerations. It is true that sustainable development considerations are not clearly pronounced in the WTO Agreements and the WTO remains to be primarily an organization for trade liberalization. While there is a list of exceptions which authorize the legitimate regulatory measures of WTO Members, those measures have to be closely scrutinized, irrespective of the benefits they might bring in terms of protecting certain values. Any solution to this problematic issue is not easy, as the scrutiny with respect to government's measures is necessary to avoid excesses and disguised protectionism. It could be suggested that to address the urge of furthering the sustainable development goals, WTO Members have come to an agreement on new common rules and/or guidelines on how to approach those issues.

2.3.2.4 "Necessity"

As was mentioned earlier in the introduction to this section, the TBT Agreement, in contrast to the GATT, tackles another dimension of "regulatory protectionism"—measures that might not be discriminatory, but which create "unnecessary obstacles to international trade".

A certain variation of this "necessity" evaluation could be found in several other places of the WTO Agreements, including Article XX of the GATT. In fact, because

[67] See, e.g., Conca (2000), pp. 484–494.

of the similarity of the legal provisions, the "necessity" analysis under the TBT Agreement follows relevant interpretations developed within the GATT jurisprudence.[68] However, the "necessity" in the TBT Agreement differs from the one of the GATT in a significant way: it is a positive obligation and not an exception, meaning that the obligation to evaluate "necessity" is a standalone obligation and does not require a prior establishment of another provision's violation. Accordingly, in a dispute, the burden of proof would be on a complainant to show a violation of this provision.[69]

Overall, the inclusion of the "necessity" test in the TBT Agreement has become a crucial development in terms of limiting the regulatory discretion of Members in a way conducive to trade opening, as, before, in the GATT era, only regulatory measures that actually discriminated could be found inconsistent with relevant obligations.

When it comes to technicalities, the legal standard of the "necessity" obligation somewhat differs depending on the type of technical barriers to trade – technical regulations (Article 2.2) and standards (paragraph E of Annex 3 "Code of Good Practice"), or conformity assessment procedures (Article 5.1.2). The following analysis only concerns the relevant legal disciplines for technical regulations and conformity assessment, as the provision on standards mirrors the first sentence of the provision on technical regulations, and there is no reason to believe it would be interpreted in a substantially different way.

The provision concerning technical regulations in Article 2.2 of the TBT Agreement provides that Members have to ensure that their technical regulations are "not more trade restrictive than necessary to fulfil a legitimate objective, taking account of the risks non-fulfilment would create". It further provides a non-exhaustive list of such "legitimate objectives", including national security requirements, protection of human health or safety, protection of the environment, etc. As the list is not exhaustive, it could be assumed that other objectives, not mentioned there, such as the protection of public morals, human rights, labour rights, etc., could also be legitimately targeted by technical regulations.[70]

What is crucial in this provision is that it is for a Member's own discretion to decide on the protection of the values at issue "at the levels it considers appropriate" (sixth recital of the TBT Agreement's Preamble). At the same time, a Member's legislative choice to obtain the level of protection is balanced with the trade liberalization commitment—notably, a Member has to pursue this level of protection in the least trade restrictive manner.

Such an understanding is reflected in the legal test developed by the panels and the Appellate Body, which, by quoting the summary of the Appellate Body's decision in *Australia – Tobacco Plain Packaging,* "involves a "relational analysis" of the following factors: (i) the trade restrictiveness of the technical regulation;

---

[68] Panel Report, *US – Clove Cigarettes*, para. 7.369.

[69] See also Ankersmit and Lawrence (2012), p. 142.

[70] Kudryavtsev (2013), p. 59. See also Neumann and Turk (2003), p. 218.

(ii) contribution that the technical regulation makes to the achievement of a legitimate objective; and (iii) the risks non-fulfilment would create".[71] Moreover, in the course of such an examination, the conceptual tool to evaluate whether the measure at issue is "more trade restrictive than necessary", is the comparison of the measure with available alternative measures that could provide a similar degree of contribution to the legitimate objective while being less trade restrictive.[72]

There are few important points to be made here. The first relates to "trade restrictiveness" of the measure at issue. The general approach is that trade restrictiveness is demonstrated through a "limiting effect on international trade".[73] This, for instance, could be manifested by the modification of conditions of competition to the detriment of the group of imported products (discrimination), however, a measure might have "limiting effects on international trade" without being discriminatory, in which case the "limiting effects" has to be assessed on a case-by-case basis "taking into account in particular the design and operation of the measure, or . . .a qualitative assessment of [the measure's] actual trade effects".[74] It is interesting that in *Australia – Tobacco Plain Packaging,* the panel also noted that in demonstrating trade-restrictiveness, the existence of initial costs related to compliance with a technical regulation would not be sufficient.[75] The Appellate Body in *US – COOL* also noted that the phrasing "technical regulations shall not be more trade restrictive than necessary" actually implies that "some" trade restrictiveness is allowed.[76]

The second important issue to be clarified in the context of the Article 2.2 legal test is the issue of "alternative measures". As the idea behind Article 2.2 is that Members have to apply their technical regulations in a least trade restrictive manner, it follows that a given measure would not be found consistent with Article 2.2 if there has been other less trade restrictive alternatives available to a Member that could achieve the legitimate objective pursued by the contested measure. To qualify as a possible alternative, a proposed measure has to satisfy a number of requirements: (i) it has to be less trade restrictive, (ii) it has to make at least an equivalent contribution to the objective being pursued through the challenged measure, and

[71] Appellate Body Report, *Australia – Tobacco Plain Packaging,* para. 6.3. See also Appellate Body Reports, *US – COOL,* para. 374, *US –Tuna II (Mexico),* para. 318.

[72] Appellate Body Report, *Australia – Tobacco Plain Packaging,* para. 6.4; See also Appellate Body Reports, *US – COOL,* para. 376, *US – Tuna II (Mexico),* paras. 320–322, *US – COOL (Article 21.5 – Canada and Mexico),* para. 5.328.

[73] Appellate Body Report, *US – Tuna II (Mexico),* para. 319; See also Panel Report, *Australia – Tobacco Plain Packaging,* para. 7.1166; Appellate Body Report, *Australia – Tobacco Plain Packaging,* para. 6.389.

[74] Panel Report, *Australia – Tobacco Plain Packaging,* para. 7.1168; On the Appellate Body's reliance on the modification of competitive conditions to demonstrate trade restrictiveness, see, e.g., Appellate Body Report, *US – COOL (Article 21.5 – Canada and Mexico),* para. 5.208.

[75] Panel Report, *Australia – Tobacco Plain Packaging,* para. 7.1235.

[76] Appellate Body Report, *US – COOL,* para. 375.

(ii) it has to be reasonably available.[77] In assessing whether a proposed alternative measure makes an equivalent contribution to the objective in question, the "overall" degree of contribution has to be taken into account and the ways to achieve this contribution could be different.[78] What is essential is to make an assessment in the light of the nature of the risks at issue that would arise from non-fulfilment of the legitimate objective at stake.[79] According to the panel in *Australia – Tobacco Plain Packaging,* "the proposed alternative may not make an equivalent contribution to the challenged measure if the alternative entails greater risks of non-fulfilment of the relevant objective."[80] The proposed alternative measures have been rejected for this specific reason in multiple cases. For instance, in *US – Clove Cigarettes*, to tackle underage smoking, instead of the outright ban on clove cigarettes introduced by the US, Indonesia proposed health warnings and fines for underage smoking. However, the panel found that these proposed measures would not satisfy the level of protection stated by the US measure.[81] Similarly, in *US – Tuna II (Mexico)*, Mexico suggested an alternative to the US measure ("dolphin-safe" labelling subject to specific strict conditions) by suggesting to accept the Agreement on International Dolphin Conservation Program's (AIDCP) provisions regulating "dolphin-safe" labelling in parallel to the US requirements. The Appellate Body disagreed with the panel that the proposed alternative would make a contribution to the US legitimate objective "to the same extent", as under the AIDCP provisions, tuna caught by a method of setting on dolphins would be eligible for a "dolphin-safe", while the US requirements explicitly prohibit setting on dolphins.[82]

Moreover, to be reasonably available the alternative measure shall not create an excessive burden,[83] such as substantial technical difficulties and prohibitive costs,[84] although it does not mean that the alternative measures might not generate any costs and burden.[85]

---

[77] Panel Report, Australia – Tobacco Plain Packaging, para. 7.1364; Appellate Body Report, Australia – Tobacco Plain Packaging, para. 6.461.

[78] Panel Report, Australia – Tobacco Plain Packaging, para. 7.1454.

[79] Appellate Body Report, US – Tuna II, para. 321. See the interpretation of this issue in: Marceau and Trachtman (2014), p. 379.

[80] Panel Report, Australia – Tobacco Plain Packaging, para. 7.1528.

[81] Panel Report, *US – Clove Cigarettes*, paras. 7.422–7.424.

[82] Appellate Body Report, *US – Tuna II (Mexico),* para. 330.

[83] Panel Report, *Australia – Tobacco Plain Packaging*, para. 7.1709. This interpretation also follows the Appellate Body's interpretation in *US – Gambling* in the context of the "necessity" analysis under Article XX of the GATT: "*An alternative measure may be found not to be 'reasonably available', however, where it is merely theoretical in nature, for instance, where the responding Member is not capable of taking it, or where the measure imposes an undue burden on that Member, such as prohibitive costs or substantial technical difficulties.*" (para. 308).

[84] Appellate Body Reports, *US – Gambling*, para. 308, *Colombia – Textiles*, para. 5.74. See also Appellate Body Report, *EC – Seal Products*, where the Appellate Body agreed with the panel that the alternative measure would not be reasonably available, as it would be difficult to implement and enforce (para. 5.279).

[85] Appellate Body Report, *China – Publications and Audiovisual Products*, paras. 326–327.

When it comes to the legal standard of "necessity" for conformity assessment procedures (Article 5.1.2.), it has few differences. The first sentence of Article 5.2.1, similarly to Article 2.1, provides that such procedures should not create "unnecessary obstacles to international trade". The second sentence clarifies that it means, *inter alia*, that they shall not be stricter than necessary to provide "an adequate confidence" to the importing Member that the products at issue conform to the applicable technical regulations. Therefore, it follows from the second sentence and, as the Appellate Body later confirmed in *Russia – Railways Equipment*, the only legitimate objective that could be pursued by a conformity assessment measure is to provide an adequate confidence that a product conforms to a technical regulation at stake.[86] Moreover, the scope of Article 5.1.2 is broader than Article 2.2, as Article 5.1.2 refers to conformity assessment measures that "shall not be more strict or be applied more strictly than necessary" to provide such "adequate confidence". Thus, Article 5.1.2 applies not only to trade restrictive measures, but there could be other ways in which conformity assessment procedures are "strict" and thus "fall afoul" of Article 5.1.2.[87] With these reservations in mind, the rest of the test is similar to Article 2.2. At the core of the analysis is a comparison with an alternative measure, in particular, whether a reasonably available less strict alternative measure could provide an equivalent contribution to giving an importing Member an adequate confidence of conformity.

To date, the only piece of jurisprudence involving Article 5.1.2 analysis is *Russia – Railway Equipm*ent.[88] In this case, the measure at issue was already modifying the competitive conditions with regard to Ukrainian products (suspension of conformity certificates which did not allow market access of Ukrainian products because of impossibility to conduct in-person inspections). Therefore, it was not problematic to demonstrate its strictness.[89] Also, one of the core issues was the establishment whether the alternative measures brought up by Ukraine were "reasonably available". The panel found that all alternatives identified by Ukraine were not reasonably available. For instance, the panel ruled that Ukraine failed to demonstrate that a proposed alternative of designating inspectors from Belarus and Kazakhstan was something that the Russian authority had the power to accomplish.[90]

---

[86] Appellate Body Report, *Russia – Railways Equipment*, para. 5.185.

[87] Appellate Body Report, *Russia – Railways Equipment*, para. 5.185; Panel Report, *Russia – Railway Equipment*, para. 7.422; See also the interpretation of this issue in Appleton (2013), p. 93.

[88] The panel in *EC – Seal Products* also analyzed Article 5.1.2, however, this analysis was found "*moot and of no legal effect*" by the Appellate Body. (See Panel Report, *EC – Seal Products*, paras. 7.511–7.547, as well as Appellate Body Report, *EC – Seal Products*, para. 6.1).

[89] Panel Report, *Russia – Railway Equipment*, paras. 7.453.

[90] Panel Report, *Russia – Railway Equipment*, paras. 7.474. It is important to note that Appellate Body disagreed with the panel that Ukraine has not established a *prima facie* case with regard to one alternative measure—off-site inspections. It noted that it was sufficient for Ukraine to point out that such off-site inspections were foreseen by Russian legislation. Further, it was for Russia to rebut this allegation. Nevertheless, the Appellate Body has not found a violation of Article 5.1.2, as it was

Overall, it appears that the legal test to actually demonstrate that a technical regulation or a conformity assessment procedure creates an "unnecessary obstacle for international trade" is not an easy undertaking. However, a positive "necessity" obligation in the TBT Agreement is an advancement in terms of disciplining domestic regulatory measures and as long as the relevant provisions exist, the Members' measures could be challenged on their basis. When it comes to legitimate measures, the "necessity" requirement provides an additional burden for these measures to be applies in a "least trade restrictive" way, which limits the options for implementation.

2.3.2.5 Harmonization Based on Relevant International Standards

It has already been briefly mentioned that the benefits of formal international standardization have been widely recognized as a way to attain interoperability, economic growth, ensure best technologies and to improve the protection of certain values.[91] The TBT Agreement elevated international standardization from completely voluntary to the level of a legal obligation.[92] As has been mentioned earlier, this is an example of so-called "positive integration", which has become an innovation in comparison to the GATT that is based on "negative integration" rules (essentially, non-discrimination). It requires the Members to take action towards integration rather than just prohibit certain behaviors as non-discrimination provisions do. It has already been highlighted that the TBT Agreement's Preamble puts a strong emphasis on the role of international standards for facilitating trade, innovation and development. Now, it is worthwhile to point out how the intention to promote international standards could be seen in the legal obligations and related panel and Appellate Body jurisprudence.

The legal obligation with regard to international standards is established with respect to technical regulations (Articles 2.4–2.6), standards (paragraphs F–H of the Annex 3 "Code of Good Practice") and conformity assessment procedures (Articles 5.4–5.5). In general terms, these obligations mirror each other. The main obligation is that WTO Members have to use relevant international standards as a basis for their technical regulations, standards and conformity assessment procedures.[93] Also, the Members have to participate—to the extent possible—in the development of international standards.[94]Moreover, with respect to standards, the standardizing bodies

unable to complete a legal analysis based on the evidence on record (Appellate Body Report, *Russia – Railway Equipment*, paras. 5.199–5.200).

[91] Wagner (2013), p. 241.

[92] Ibid., p. 239.

[93] See the following provisions of the TBT Agreement: Articles 2.4, 5.4 and para. F of the "Code of Good Practice".

[94] See the following provisions of the TBT Agreement: Articles 2.6, 5.5 and para. G of the "Code of Good Practice".

have to make every efforts to avoid duplications with the overlapping activities of international standardizing bodies.[95] With respect to technical regulations, Article 2.5 also provides an additional incentive for Members to use international standards: whenever technical regulation "is in accordance" with a relevant international standard, "it shall be rebuttably presumed not to create an unnecessary obstacle to international trade". Therefore, the use of a relevant international standard, to a certain extent, shields a Member from the challenge based on Article 2.2 (although it is not quite clear to date to which extent a technical regulation at issue has to use a relevant international standard to have that advantage).[96]

The following analysis focuses on the legal obligation to use a relevant international standard as a basis. It interprets the legal provisions on technical regulations—Article 2.4, as it is the only provision on this issue that has ever been subject to dispute settlement and other obligations on standards and conformity assessment practically mirror it. However, before going into the legal analysis of this provision, it has to be clarified what is a "relevant international standard" in the meaning of the TBT Agreement.

2.3.2.5.1 "Relevant International Standard"

The TBT Agreement itself does not contain a definition of an "international standard". Neither points it to international bodies that could produce such standards, as is pointed out in the SPS Agreement. It only has a definition of a "standard" (Annex 1.2). However, Annex 1 also makes a reference to the ISO/IEC Guide 2:1991 implying that one could also refer to the definitions therein. The ISO/IEC Guide defines an "international standard" with a reference to its source, i.e., a "standard that is adopted by international standardizing/standards organization and made available to the public".[97] In addition to that, Annex 1.4 provides a definition of an "international body or system", which puts an emphasis on the "openness" of the membership of such body or system to all WTO Members. Notably, later on, in 2000, to clarify the issue of what constitutes an "international standard" for the purpose of the TBT Agreement disciplines, the TBT Committee issued a "*Decision on Principles for the Development of International Standards, Guides and Recommendations with Relation to Articles 2, 5 and Annex 3 of the Agreement*" (The TBT Committee Decision on international standards), which clarified a number of criteria for international standards development, among which the most notable is the openness, i.e.,

[95] See para. H of the "Code of Good Practice".

[96] It is not quite clear how to interpret the wording "in accordance". There is a view that it implies a stronger connection than "based on" in Article 2.4. See Tamiotti (2007), p. 226.

[97] ISO/IEC Guide 2:2004: General Terms and Their Definitions Concerning Standardization and Related Activities (reviewed version of the 1991 Guide), 2004. https://www.iso.org/standard/39976.html. Accessed 1 Nov 2022. At the same time, a "standard" is defined in a bit different fashion than in the TBT Agreement, the main difference being that a standard shall be established "by consensus".

openness with regard to the membership in international standardizing bodies to all relevant bodies of all WTO Members, including openness at every stage of standards development.[98]

Taking on those legal clues, the Appellate Body in *US – Tuna* provided a detailed explanation on how a "relevant international standard" should be understood:

> [A] required element of the definition of an 'international' standard for the purposes of the TBT Agreement is the approval of the standard by an 'international standardizing body', that is, a body that has recognized activities in standardization and whose membership is open to the relevant bodies of at least all Members.[99]

It appears that "openness" stands prominently as a criteria for a standardizing body, and subsequently is crucial for the determinations of a "relevant international standard". Another criterion identified by the Appellate Body is "recognized activities in standardization": at a minimum, the "WTO Members [shall be] aware, or have reason to expect, that the international body. . .is engaged in standardization activities".[100]

In *US – Tuna*, the Appellate Body rejected the qualification of AIDCP's standards as "relevant international standards" specifically for a lack of "openness" of AIDCP's membership. It noted that "the invitation to accede to the AIDCP was not issued automatically to a WTO Member interested in joining but required instead a decision by consensus of the parties to the AIDCP", meaning that AIDCP did not qualify as an international body that adopts "international standards" for the purposes of the TBT Agreement.[101]

To sum up, it appears that the criterion of openness of standard developing body's membership is crucial. Despite that an international organization might have recognised activities in standardization and have its standards widely recognized and accepted, it still has to have an open membership for that its standards could be recognized as "relevant" under the TBT Agreement.

---

[98] See WTO, Committee on Technical Barriers to Trade (2000) Second Triennial Review of the Operation and Implementation of the Agreement on Technical Barriers to Trade, Annex 4: Decision of the Committee on Principles for the Development of International Standards, Guides and Recommendations with Relation to art. 2, 5 and annex 3 of the Agreement," G/TBT/9, 13. 11. 2000.

[99] Appellate Body Report, *US – Tuna II (Mexico)*, paras. 357–359.

[100] Appellate Body Report, *US – Tuna II (Mexico)*, paras. 361–362. It is also worthwhile noting that the Appellate Body in *US-Tuna* followed its previous practice in *EC – Sardines* by rejecting a view that the "relevant international standard" has to be necessarily adopted by consensus of the international body's membership, despite that the "consensus" is a part of a "standard" definition in the ISO/IEC Guide. It pinpointed that the "standard" definition in Annex 1.2 of the TBT Agreement (explanatory note) deliberately rejects that consensus is necessary (Appellate Body Report, *EC – Sardines*, paras. 222–223.

[101] Appellate Body Report, *US – Tuna II (Mexico)*, paras. 398–399.

2.3.2.5.2 International Standards as a Basis for Domestic Technical Regulations

When it comes to the positive obligation to use international standards, Article 2.4 prescribes the following:

> Where technical regulations are required and relevant international standards exist or their completion is imminent, Members shall use them, or the relevant parts of them, as a basis for their technical regulations except when such international standards or relevant parts would be an ineffective or inappropriate means for the fulfilment of the legitimate objectives pursued, for instance because of fundamental climatic or geographical factors or fundamental technological problems.

There are few important inferences to be made here. First, the obligation denoted by the word "shall" goes beyond a simple encouragement.[102] Second, it is the extent to which the Members are required to use international standards, which comes down to the question on how to interpret the words "as a basis". Here, a certain guidance has been provided by the panel and the Appellate Body in *EC – Sardines*, where the issue was whether the EU based its technical regulation on a relevant international standard—Codex Stan 94. It is crucial that in *EC – Sardines*, the Appellate Body rejected the EU's position that it was sufficient for a technical regulation to have a "rational relationship" with an international standard to satisfy the requirements of Article 2.4 and pointed out that it requires more than simple relation. It agreed with the panel that a standard is used "as a basis" "when it is used as the principal constituent or fundamental principle for the purpose of enacting the technical regulation".[103] In particular, it noted the following:

> From these various definitions, we would highlight the similar terms 'principal constituent', 'fundamental principle', 'main constituent', and 'determining principle' – all of which lend credence to the conclusion that there must be a very strong and very close relationship between two things in order to be able to say that one is 'the basis for' the other.[104]

It remains to be seen how this "strong and very close relationship" is to be analyzed. In *EC – Sardines,* the case was relatively simple for adjudicators: it was found that the EU technical regulation "contradicted" Codex Stan 94, thereby contravening the minimum requirement of being used as a basis—at least not to be contradictory.[105] It could be imagined that there might be more complicated cases, which would require certain technical expertise to assess whether a technical regulation used an international standard as a "principal constituent". In this case, the panels would be required to examine the relevant international standards and how much flexibility, judging from design, object and purpose, they provide, as well as domestic technical regulations, i.e., on the subject of their consistency with international standards.[106]

---

[102] See Panel Report, *EC – Sardines*, para. 7.11.

[103] Appellate Body Report, EC – Sardines, para. 240–245.

[104] Appellate Body Report, EC – Sardines, para. 245.

[105] Appellate Body Report, *EC – Sardines*, para. 248.

[106] Zuniga Schroder (2011), p. 49.

Another important point to clarify in the provision of Article 2.4 is the case of deviation from international standards for a legitimate objective. Article 2.4 provides that such possibility exists in case a relevant international standard is "ineffective" or "inappropriate" to fulfil the said objective. The panel in *EC – Sardines* explained that "ineffective" means that it "does not have the function of accomplishing the legitimate objective pursued", while "inappropriate" refers to means that is "not specially suitable for the fulfilment of the legitimate objective".[107] This analysis to a certain extent reminds of an analysis of "alternative measures" in Article 2.2, as it also requires to demonstrate that the proposed measure (in this case the use of international standard) would be sufficient to address a legitimate objective at stake. Therefore, the main issue is to understand the features of an international standard and how they are prepared to attain a given legitimate objective.

It is also worthwhile to note that it does not appear that the panels and the Appellate Body demonstrated any bias either towards international standards, or domestic policy space. Depending on a case at stake, the jurisprudence demonstrated various results how the issue of deviation from a relevant international standard had to be tackled. For instance, in *EC – Sardines*, the panel (and later the Appellate Body) confirmed that Codex Stan 94 was an effective and appropriate international standard to fulfil a legitimate objective of the EU technical regulation of market transparency, consumer protection, and fair competition.[108] At the same time, in *US – COOL*, an international standard dealing with marking and labelling CODEX STAN 1-19851002 was an ineffective and inappropriate means for the fulfilment of the US objective, because this standard did not foresee to convey exact information to consumers on where the animals were born and slaughtered as was foreseen in the US objective.[109]

2.3.2.6 Recognition of Equivalence and Mutual Recognition

Apart from such a method of positive integration as harmonization with international standards, which is at the core of the TBT Agreement's disciplines, it is also important to note that the TBT Agreement contains provisions on other methods of positive integration—recognition of equivalence of other Member's regulation and conformity assessment and mutual recognition of conformity assessment. Moreover, certain features of these methods could be also inferred from the GATT disciplines.

---

[107] Panel Report, *EC – Sardines*, para. 7.116.

[108] Panel Report, *EC – Sardines*, para. 7.138; Appellate Body Report, *EC – Sardines*, paras. 290–291.

[109] Panel Report, *US – COOL*, paras. 7.734–7.735.

2.3.2.6.1 TBT Agreement

It is important to pinpoint that the TBT Agreement does not contain a binding obligation to recognize other Member's regulations or conformity assessment procedures. The main legal provisions of the TBT Agreement—Article 2.7 (on technical regulations) and Article 6.1 (on conformity assessment) have a rather soft language ("shall give positive consideration", "shall ensure, whenever possible"):

> 2.7 Members shall give positive consideration to accepting as equivalent technical regulations of other Members, even if these regulations differ from their own, provided they are satisfied that these regulations adequately fulfil the objectives of their own regulations.
>
> 6.1 … Members shall ensure, whenever possible, that results of conformity assessment procedures in other Members are accepted, even when those procedures differ from their own, provided they are satisfied that those procedures offer an assurance of conformity with applicable technical regulations or standards equivalent to their own procedures…

Based on this wording, one might conclude that these provisions are simply aspirational.[110] However, it is worthwhile to add that it clearly follows from the respective disciplines of the TBT Agreement that the intention behind these instruments was to open possibilities to liberalize trade and not to create exclusionary agreements that would favour only some of the WTO Members. The above provisions encourage Members to open up opportunities for other Members' technical regulations and conformity assessment procedures to be recognized in an open manner, i.e., without creating exclusionary arrangements, but based on the fact whether the respective technical regulations and conformity assessment procedures "adequately fulfil the objectives" of a recognizing Member's regulation or "offer an assurance of conformity" "equivalent" to procedures of a recognizing Member.

The TBT Agreement does provide certain rules regarding mutual recognition agreements with other Members too. It is especially relevant to look into Articles 6.3 and 10.7 of the TBT Agreement. Article 6.3 encourages Members to enter into negotiations for the conclusion of mutual recognition agreements with another Member upon request and Article 10.7 encourages Members, in case they concluded a mutual agreement with another Member, to enter into consultations with other Members to conclude similar agreements. Article 6.4 also encourages the Members to allow participation of conformity assessment bodies of other Members in their conformity assessment procedures "under conditions no less favourable than those accorded to bodies located in their territories or the territory of any other country".

2.3.2.6.2 GATT

At the outset, it is important to note that the GATT certainly does not contain explicit requirements on equivalence or mutual recognition. However, at the same time, it could be inferred from the Appellate Body's practice on Article XX of the GATT

[110] Churchman (2013), p. 287.

that the ideas similar to equivalence and mutual recognition had also gained some traction under the framework of the GATT, in particular, through the interpretation of the chapeau of Article XX, which provides that the Members' measures shall not be applied in a manner constituting "a means of arbitrary or unjustifiable discrimination between countries where the same conditions prevail or a disguised restriction on international trade".

In this respect, it is relevant to recall how this provision was interpreted by the Appellate Body in *US – Shrimp*. In this case, the US banned importation of shrimp harvested with commercial fishing technology that may adversely affect sea turtles, unless the exporting country is certified by the US Department of State, which essentially implied the adoption of the US program for the protection of sea turtles. This measure was considered discriminatory. In evaluating whether the measure satisfied the requirements of the chapeau of Article XX, the Appellate Body pointed out that the US made no effort to engage into negotiations with other countries to come to into an agreement regarding protection of sea turtles.[111] The Appellate Body faulted the US measure for its rigidity and inflexibility in that it required to adopt "essentially the same" programs.[112] At the same time, the Appellate Body confirmed that requiring programs "comparable in effectiveness" as opposed to "essentially the same" ones would satisfy the requirements of the chapeau.[113] This could be interpreted as an "embryonic" mutual recognition (equivalence) requirement.[114]

In addition, it is also relevant to pinpoint that it appears that this requirement is not favourable to a case of mutual recognition with exclusionary membership. In the *US – Shrimp* case, the US did negotiate a turtle protection agreement with a certain number of countries in the framework of the Inter-American Agreement, which was not available to other countries. This fact only served as a demonstration that a negotiated solution was possible, instead of the rigid requirement to accept the US program. The Appellate Body faulted the US for not making efforts to negotiate similar agreements with other countries or groups of countries.[115] Therefore, it is fair to conclude that the GATT approach also favours open recognition arrangements.

2.3.2.7 Applicability of the Exceptions

Another issue that is specifically important in the context of regional trade agreements is whether any departure from the GATT and TBT Agreement's disciplines could be justified by the exceptions contained in the GATT: the general exceptions of Article XX, as well as a specific exception for regional trade agreements of Article XXIV.

---

[111] Appellate Body Report, *US – Shrimp*, para. 172.

[112] Appellate Body Report, *US – Shrimp (21.5)*, para. 140.

[113] Appellate Body Report, *US – Shrimp (21.5)*, para. 144.

[114] Trachtman (2007b), pp. 641–642.

[115] Appellate Body Report, *US – Shrimp*, paras. 171–172.

First, with regard to the general exceptions of Article XX, the analysis on justification of a breach of the GATT agreement would be similar to the analysis of a "legitimate regulatory distinction" under Article 2.1 of the TBT Agreement (4.2.2.1), as has been mentioned above. When it comes to the question of availability of Article XX to justify the violation of the TBT Agreement, the Appellate Body's practice is clear on denying such a possibility. In *US – Clove Cigarettes*, the Appellate Body denied the application of Article XX for the TBT violation based on the fact that Article 2.1 of the TBT Agreement itself along with the sixth recital of the Preamble to the TBT Agreement contained a balance between trade liberalization and the members' right to regulate akin to Article XX GATT.[116] A similar understanding was expressed by the Appellate Body in *China – Rare Earths*, which pinpointed that the TBT Agreement does not contain a general exceptions clause, but it contains a similar balance between trade liberalization and a right to regulate which resides in its other provisions.[117]

When it comes to the regional exception clause—Article XXIV GATT—the issue of its applicability is a more complicated one and depends on the context. Therefore, it is analyzed in greater detail further in the next Chapter in a section dealing specifically with regional harmonization and mutual recognition.

2.3.2.8 Regulatory Cooperation and Good Regulatory Practices

Apart from the abovementioned disciplines, the TBT Agreement also contains a number of provisions that target specific technical issues, help facilitate trade and to maintain a regulatory dialogue. In this research, these provisions are framed as the provisions on regulatory cooperation and good regulatory practices.

It is worth noting at the outset that there is no unified definition of the terms "regulatory cooperation" and "good regulatory practices". The definitions given at the WTO TBT Committee and the OECD of "regulatory cooperation" are quite broad. The former states that "regulatory cooperation" is about regulators from different governments engaging with one another on rules and principles for regulating markets in the pursuit of more compatible, transparent and simple regulations, and the lowering of trade barriers".[118]The latter suggests that regulatory cooperation shall be understood as "any agreement or organizational arrangement, formal or informal, between countries to promote some form of cooperation in the design, monitoring, enforcement or ex-post management of regulation".[119] Some scholars differentiate internal and external dimensions of this cooperation. For instance,

[116] Appellate Body Report, *US – Clove Cigarettes,* para. 109.

[117] Appellate Body Report, *China – Rare Earths*, para. 5.56.

[118] WTO (2012) Summary Report of the TBT Workshop on Regulatory Cooperation between Members, G/TBT/W348, 14.02.2012.

[119] OECD (2013) International Regulatory Cooperation: Addressing Global Challenges. OECD Publishing, Paris.

Petros Mavroidis, referring to the approach used by the US Chamber of Commerce within the TTIP negotiations, distinguishes between the notion of "regulatory cooperation" and "regulatory coherence" (mentioned here as "good regulatory practices") by suggesting that the former "denotes the presence of an international element", while the latter "describes the quality of domestic regulatory process".[120] This research adopts the definitional approach mentioned by Mavroidis, by distinguishing between regulatory cooperation and good regulatory practices, although it also acknowledges that the two categories are interrelated. Essentially, good regulatory practices could be also viewed as elements of regulatory cooperation, as they contribute to understanding and trust between the parties' regulatory authorities "over the quality and efficiency of the regulatory policy frameworks", which is a "foundational element of successfully advancing into [international regulatory cooperation] approaches".[121]

The WTO work in terms of regulatory cooperation have been widely discussed as having a high potential. The committee work increases knowledge exchange and experience sharing between Members. Such bureaucracy is "key to formulating practical approaches to new rules".[122] In recent years, there have been multiple calls to strengthen this deliberative function.[123]

When it comes to the respective provisions of the TBT Agreement, the elements of good regulatory practices and regulatory cooperation can hardly be distinguished. The following elements are transparency disciplines, which could be viewed as good regulatory practices, but their purpose is also to provide necessary information about a Member's regulation so that other Members could act accordingly and raise concerns if necessary:

- publication of the new measures that may have a significant effect on trade or diverge from international standards[124] and their notification to the WTO Secretariat,[125]
- opening enquiry points[126]
- allowing a reasonable period of time between publication and entry into force of new regulations[127]

Other disciplines relate more to regulatory cooperation:

---

[120] Mavroidis (2016).

[121] Kauffmann and Saffirio (2021), p. 17.

[122] Marceau (2020), p. 1057.

[123] See, e.g., Gari (2020), p. 52.

[124] See Articles 2.9.1, 5.6.1 of the TBT Agreement.

[125] Articles 2.9.2, 5.6.2 of the TBT Agreement. The obligation of notification was confirmed to be a separate obligation from the publication requirement (Panel Report, *US-Clove Cigarettes*, para. 7.541).

[126] Article 10.1 of the TBT Agreement.

[127] Articles 2.12, 5.9 of the TBT Agreement.

- reasonable period of time for other Members to make written comments to the new regulations' drafts (a tool for the regulatory dialogue).[128] According to the TBT Committee's recommendations, such reasonable period should be at least 60 days;[129]
- the mechanism of "specific trade concerns" (STC), which is not directly mentioned in the TBT Agreement, but is codified in practice based on Article 13.1 and further adopted by the TBT Committee's decision.[130] This is a unique transparency and dialogue tool, which establishes a possibility for WTO Members to raise and discuss issues of concern with regard to TBT measures—anything from seeking information and clarification to violations of the TBT Agreement.[131]

It is worth noting that the TBT Committee provides an institutional underpinning for the Members' interactions. This is where the Members' delegates have the opportunity to consult with each other, exchange views, provide notifications and submit STCs.[132]

To stimulate the regulatory agenda, in 2012, the TBT Committee identified an open list of mechanism of good regulatory practices such as public consultations, impact assessment, review of existing technical regulations and conformity assessment procedures, etc.[133] However, this list is simply a recommendation and does not have a binding character. This issue has been brought up numerous occasions at the TBT Committee meetings.[134]

In recent years, there have been multiple calls to strengthen the deliberative function of the WTO.[135] The main argument is that the WTO is an exceptional multi-party forum, which presents a possibility to discuss and find solutions to tackle global challenges in an inclusive manner.

---

[128] Articles 2.9.4, 5.6.4 of the TBT Agreement.

[129] WTO TBT Committee (2017) Decisions and Recommendation Adopted by the WTO Committee on Technical Barriers to Trade since 1 January 1995, G/TBT/1/Rev.13, 8.03.2017, Section 5.3.1.8, p. 27.

[130] WTO, Committee on Technical Barriers to Trade (2009). Fifth Triennial Review, G/TBT/26, 13.11.2009.

[131] Holzer (2018), p. 4; Karttunen (2020), p. 94.

[132] More on TBT Committee, see, e.g., Macrory et al. (2005), p. 407.

[133] WTO, Committee on Technical Barriers to Trade (2015) Decisions and Recommendations, G/TBT/1/Rev.12, 21.01.2015, p. 6.

[134] Lin and Liu (2018), p. 157.

[135] See, e.g., Gari (2020), p. 52.

2.3.3 *Constraints to Furthering Liberalization of TBT at the WTO*

Further development of WTO rules faces multiple constraints. They could be depicted in reference to the failure of the Doha Round. The latter could be explained by a variety of reasons. Firstly, it has been noted above, WTO Members were adhering to contrasting values and priorities. Especially the disparities have been conspicuous between developed and developing countries. While developed countries were putting efforts to push through additional obligations with regard to a deep trade agenda, for example, the "Singapore issues" (brought about at the Singapore Ministerial Conference in 1996) including investment, competition, government procurement and trade facilitation,[136] developing countries, on the other hand, were still struggling to get a better market access in agriculture and textiles. At the Cancun Ministerial Conference (2003) that was supposed to consider the Singapore issues, the negotiations on agriculture and cotton subsidies proved to be futile, hence the developing countries' position was that the suggested ministerial declaration did not reflect their interests.[137]

The disparities between developed and developing countries have become especially relevant because of the shifting power balances in the global economy. The world has been transforming from the Cold War era bipolar power dynamics to the multipolar dynamics. This could be explained by a variety of factors among which the end of colonialism resulting in emergence of many independent states, the dissolution of the Soviet Union giving rise to movement towards a market-oriented economy in many countries of the former socialist block and the rise of emerging economies—Brazil, Russia, India and China (BRIC). As a result, the propensity of developed countries to advance the multilateral agenda was weakened.[138] Developing countries started to take a more proactive stance and to push for their own interests individually and through group collaboration. The diffusion of power oftentimes led to impossibility to reach consensus, which is explicitly demonstrated with the example of the Doha deadlock.

Against this backdrop, the negotiations were also very much complicated by the WTO existing legal structure based on reciprocity and a single-undertaking approach exercised through the negotiating rounds that bundle many diverse topics into a package deal ("all or nothing") creating a situation when particular issues would complicate the overall negotiation process.[139]

Another substantive constraint is related to the binding nature of negotiated outcomes and the application of dispute settlement. Issues of regulatory nature are closely related with public policy concern, and, therefore, adopting strict binding

[136] See more on the "Singapore issues" at the dedicated page of the WTO website, https://www.wto.org/english/thewto_e/whatis_e/tif_e/bey3_e.htm. Accessed 1 Nov 2022.

[137] Evenett (2007), p. 398; See also Elsig and Dupont (2012), pp. 587–606.

[138] Allee (2012), p. 249.

[139] Melo Araujo (2016), p. 22.

obligations enforced by dispute settlement might be associated with the fear of countries to lose their domestic policy space.

While one could argue that tariffs concessions also in a way limit national sovereignty, the NTMs brought about an additional level of complexity to this discussion as they oftentimes deal directly with issues of public policy such as human health, consumer protection and environmental regulation.[140] Melo Araujo explained that it was one of the reasons of the Doha Round's lack of success: "The unwillingness of WTO Members to pursue a "deep" trade agenda at the multilateral level was a reflection of a "deep-seated unease concerning the intrusion of international trade politics into areas that have hitherto been the preserve of national sovereignty".[141] Putting these areas on the negotiation table with a large number of parties having different levels of developments tends to be an even more complicated affair.

There is also a problem of legitimacy that might arise when addressing regulatory policies at the global level at the WTO.[142] It is important to recognize that country' preferences for regulatory policies might differ and, unlike as it is with tariffs, it might not be an easy task to negotiate a common denominator among a large number of participants, especially with different levels of development and different values and priorities. Another question—is it even desirable to have all regulatory policies being harmonized? Similar views have been expressed by Robert Lawrence praising the multilateral forum as a first best solution in case of tariff reduction, while when we look at deeper integration, it might not be the case due to a diversity of consumer choice. In case of deeper integration, there is always a tension between realizing economies of scale and a more precise matching of consumers' tastes and choices. Lawrence argues that some rules are better provided locally.[143] The choice to address regulatory issues at the regional level, primarily between countries that have homogeneous interests is substantiated by the discussions on fiscal federalism concerned with the "assignment of function to the levels of government' and argues that decentralized provisions might be welfare increasing by responding to local preferences".[144] The theory of fiscal federalism when applied in the context of regulatory cooperation between countries would suggest benefits for countries that have quite similar preferences. In case of cooperation between heterogeneous countries, there is a risk that local preferences would be left unaccounted.

To sum up, it is problematic to pursue further multilateral negotiations with regard to the issues pertaining to the "deep" trade agenda, because of the way the WTO system is built: Agreements have to be adopted as a "single undertaking", they have to be binding and enforceable by dispute settlement. While such an ambitious approach could work in the past in relation to tariff liberalization, now, with a large

[140] Ibid., p. 17.

[141] Ibid., p. 16.

[142] Gari (2020), p. 51.

[143] Lawrence (1996b), p. 13.

[144] Oates (1999), pp. 1121–1122.

number of countries with different priorities and different levels of development, it is particularly challenging and is not always desirable. Nevertheless, there is still a regulatory gap with regard to NTMs. By recognizing a trend of decreasing relevance of tariffs and a growing importance of NTMs, the WTO issued an annual report entirely dedicated to non-tariff measure where it stresses out their growing relevance in the globalized world and a need to incorporate them in future trade liberalization efforts.[145] It is clear, however, that the instruments and approaches to deal with NTMs at the WTO have to develop.

Regardless of the critique, the WTO remains a crucial forum for engagement between a large number of countries and customs territories on issues regarding trade, which hardly could be fully replicated in bilateral and regional fora. While its function with respect to negotiations for the conclusion of multilateral trade agreements is stalled, it still plays a major role in navigating trade relations between its Members. It represents a platform for political and technical discourse on trade matters. In particular, it is relevant to mention that when it comes to cooperation on regulatory matters, learning and socialization play one of major roles.[146] In the area of regulations and trade, there is a broad range of issues of multilateral dimension, such as environmental protection and economic development, which could be tackled in a multi-party setting.[147]

2.4 Towards a "Deep" Trade Agenda in RTAs

The gap between the limits of the WTO toolbox to address the challenges of the globalised commerce and the countries' ever-increasing need to move forward with further trade liberalisation prompts the WTO Members to conclude RTAs between each other. The WTO World Trade Report emphasized that countries increasingly put more attention on "behind-the-border" measures in their free trade agreements.[148] An empirical study of the OECD also underlined this trend concluding that countries are addressing a "deep" trade agenda in a broad range of policy areas—investment, IP, public procurement, the environment, and also TBT measures.[149] In fact, a "deep" trade agenda within RTAs started to develop long time ago with the European project and US regionalism in 1980s–1990s. It is also relevant to mention that these developments went in parallel to the Uruguay Round of

---

[145] WTO (2012) World Trade Report.

[146] WTO and OECD (2019) Facilitating Trade through Regulatory Cooperation The Case of the WTO's TBT/SPS Agreements and Committees, OECD Publishing, Paris, p. 5. https://www.wto.org/english/res_e/booksp_e/tbtsps19_e.pdf. Accessed 1 Nov 2022.

[147] See a similar line of reasoning in: Stoll (2020), p. 275.

[148] See WTO (2011) World Trade Report, p. 10.

[149] Lejárraga (2014), p. 15.

multilateral trade negotiations, which resulted in the creation of the advanced system of international rules.

Addressing regulatory issues within free trade agreements is an ever-increasing trend.[150] For instance, according to one study, of 238 analyzed FTAs, around 72 per cent included TBT provisions.[151] Disregarding the prevailing provisions that simply replicate the existing WTO rules, another study identified that TBT WTO plus provisions were found in more than 60 per cent of free trade agreements.[152]

The most ambitious agenda including harmonization and mutual recognition, according to the mapping of regional rules on TBT performed by Roberta Piermartini and Michele Budetta, is, unsurprisingly, driven by the United States and the European Union.[153] This is also confirmed by a more recent study, which concludes that the US and the EU "go systematically beyond the commitments of the WTO Agreement on TBT".[154]

TBT liberalization in RTAs could be represented by a variety of instruments with different levels of integration that may affect countries outside the preferential area in an utterly different fashion. The empirical study by Piermartini and Budetta identified the following ones:

- Harmonisation
- Equivalence and mutual recognition of rules
- Mutual recognition of conformity assessment
- Transparency and notifications
- Enforcement and dispute settlement
- Institutional and administrative provisions
- Further cooperation.[155]

A relevant question to be asked within this context would be how these WTO plus TBT provisions in RTAs converge towards the multilateral rules. Richard Baldwin calls these developments in linking trade and regulation a "21st century regionalism" and underlines a need to rethink how we assess RTAs.[156] In this respect, referring to these trends, the WTO World Trade Report also cautioned against fragmentation of global trade governance: "the process of deep regional integration must be a complement to rather than a substitute for the process of global integration".[157]

---

[150] OECD (2017) International Regulatory Co-operation and Trade. Understanding the Trade Costs of Regulatory Divergence and the Remedies, p. 4.

[151] Molina and Khoroshavina (2015).

[152] Lejárraga (2014), p. 15.

[153] Piermartini and Budetta (2009), p. 278.

[154] Alshareef (2019), p. 438.

[155] Piermartini and Budetta (2009), p. 256.

[156] Baldwin (2014).

[157] WTO (2011) World Trade Report, p. 114.

2.5 Global Trade Governance Structure: An Integrated Approach

When it comes to the "deep" trade agenda, as it has been described above, the governance issue is very complex. According to Richard Baldwin, the most efficient approach, considering the practical constraints, would be to organize the deeper disciplines at different levels: some left for national discretion, some—at the regional level (RTAs), and some could be multilateralized.[158] It remains to be an open question for trade practitioners and scholars, which disciplines could fall under which category.

Regarding the interaction between RTAs and the WTO, there are few considerations to bear in mind. Firstly, it appears that the universe of RTAs fills the gaps in global trade governance when it comes to the "deep" trade agenda, thereby sidelining to a certain extent the centricity of the WTO. Consistently with a view that some of the "deep" trade issues should probably be addressed at the regional rather than multilateral level, it might be reasonable to clarify the gap-filling role of RTAs in relation to the multilateral system in a way that does not go against the main WTO principles. Secondly, considering the benefits of the WTO as a multilateral forum, it might also be considered whether some of the RTA provisions could be addressed within the WTO framework.

2.6 Conclusion

This Chapter described the background of this research. It depicted a reality of global commerce where tariffs and other border measures are no longer the main focus of the international trade and that trade agenda is being merged with other issues, including those related to technical barriers to trade. It explained the meaning of technical barriers to trade and briefly addressed the issue how they are addressed at the WTO, as well as RTAs. It pinpointed that while the GATT/WTO system was initially mostly focused on tariffs and other border measures, along the way it demonstrated a possibility to adapt to new realities by including a progressive agenda on other trade-related issues, including on TBT. The WTO TBT Agreement's rules have become an advancement in terms of disciplining technical regulations, standards, and conformity assessment procedures. However, at the time being there are substantive constraints to moving forward the "deep" trade agenda at the WTO. Meanwhile, the regulatory gap is filled by RTAs, which raises the question of fragmentation of the global trade governance structure. It might be reasonable to reassess the interrelation between WTO and RTAs fora and to study the possibilities

[158] Baldwin (2014), p. 40.

where the TBT matters could be better addressed within RTAs, or incorporated into the modernized WTO framework.

References

Books and Book Chapters

Allee T (2012) The role of the United States: a multilevel explanation for decreased support over time. In: Daunton M, Narlikar A, Stern R (eds) The Oxford handbook on the World Trade Organization. Oxford University Press, Oxford, pp 235–251

Appleton A (2005) The agreement on technical barriers to trade. In: Macrory P, Appleton A et al (eds) The World Trade Organization: legal, economic and political analysis. Springer, Boston, pp 371–409

Appleton A (2013) Conformity assessment procedures. In: Epps T, Trebilcock M (eds) Research handbook on the WTO and technical barriers to trade. Edward Elgar Publishing, Cheltenham, pp 81–119

Appleton A (2017) Regulatory barriers to trade: regulations and standards. In: Cottier T, Nadakavukaren Schefer K (eds) Elgar Encyclopedia of international economic law. Edward Elgar Publishing, Cheltenham, pp 411–412

Baldwin R (2016) The great convergence: information technology and the new globalization. Harvard University Press, Cambridge

Churchman H (2013) Mutual recognition agreements and equivalence agreements. In: Epps T, Trebilcock M (eds) Research handbook on the WTO and technical barriers to trade. Edward Elgar Publishing, Cheltenham, pp 280–314

Elsig M, Dupont C (2012) Persistent deadlock in multilateral trade negotiations: the case of Doha. In: Daunton M, Narlikar A, Stern R (eds) The Oxford handbook on the World Trade Organization. Oxford University Press, Oxford, pp 587–606

Gari G (2020) Narrowed Down Utopia: adjusting the WTO to a changing trade environment. In: Kolski Lewis M et al (eds) A post-WTO international legal order. Utopian, Dystopian and other scenarios. Springer, Cham, pp 37–55

Hobbs J (2007) Technical barriers to trade. In: Kerr W, Gaisford J (eds) Handbook on international trade policy. Edward Elgar Publishing, Cheltenham, pp 394–403

Howse R (2013) Introduction. In: Epps T, Trebilcock M (eds) Research handbook on the WTO and technical barriers to trade. Edward Elgar Publishing, Cheltenham, pp 1–16

Karttunen M (2020) Transparency as a core principle under the SPS and TBT Agreements – the Real Jewel in the Crown. In: Karttunen M (ed) Transparency in the WTO SPS and TBT Agreements. Cambridge University Press, Cambridge, pp 46–99

Kudryavtsev A (2013) The TBT agreement in context. In: Epps T, Trebilcock M (eds) Research handbook on the WTO and technical barriers to trade. Edward Elgar Publishing, Cheltenham, pp 17–80

Lawrence R (1996) Regionalism, multilateralism and deeper integration. Brookings Institutions Press, Washington DC

Lester S et al (2018) World Trade Law. Texts, materials and commentary, 3rd edn. Hart Publishing, Oxford

Macrory P, Appleton A et al (eds) (2005) The World Trade Organization: legal, economic and political analysis. Springer, New York

Melo Araujo B (2016) The EU Deep Trade Agenda: law and policy. Oxford University Press, Oxford

Piermartini R, Budetta M (2009) A mapping of regional rules on technical barriers to trade. In: Estevadeordal A et al (eds) Regional rules in the global trading system. Cambridge University Press, Cambridge, pp 250–315

Stoll P-T (2020) Saving the World Trade Organization from the bottom up: a role for preferential trade agreements. In: Kolski Lewis M et al (eds) A Post-WTO international legal order. Utopian, Dystopian and other scenarios. Springer, Cham, pp 259–276

Tamiotti L (2007) Article 2 TBT. In: Wolfrum R et al (eds) Technical barriers and SPS measures. Martinus Nijhoff Publishers, Leiden, pp 210–234

Tinbergen J (1954) International economic integration. Macmillan, London

Wagner M (2013) International standards. In: Epps T, Trebilcock M (eds) Research handbook on the WTO and technical barriers to trade. Edward Elgar Publishing, Cheltenham, pp 238–279

Zuniga Schroder H (2011) Harmonization, equivalence, and mutual recognition of standards in WTO law. Kluwer Law International, Alphen aan den Rijn

Journal Articles

Alshareef S (2019) Technical standards liberalization in FTAs of the United States, the European Union and China. J World Trade 53(3):433–454

Ankersmit L, Lawrence J (2012) The future of environmental labelling: *US – Tuna II* and the scope of the TBT agreement. Legal Iss Econ Integr 39(1):127–147

Blind K, Jungmittag A (2008) The impact of patents and standards on macro-economic growth: a panel approach covering four countries and 12 sectors. J Prod Anal 29(1):51–60

Bull R, Mahboubi N et al (2015) New approaches to international regulatory cooperation: the challenge of TTIP, TPP, and mega-regional trade agreements. Law Contemp Probl 78(1):1–29

Conca K (2000) The WTO and the undermining of global environmental governance. Rev Int Polit Econ 7(3):484–494

Evenett S (2007) Five hypotheses concerning the fate of the Singapore issues at the Doha round. Oxf Rev Econ Policy 23(3):392–414

Gereffi G et al (2005) The governance of global value chains. Rev Int Polit Econ 12(78):78–104

Lin C-F, Liu H-W (2018) Regulatory rationalization clauses in FTAs: a complete survey of the US, EU and China. Melbourne J Int Law 19(1):149–177

Marceau G (2020) Book review "Trade and Environmental Governance at the World Trade Organization Committee on Trade and Environment by Manuel Teehankee". J Int Econ Law 23(4):1055–1058

Marceau G, Trachtman J (2014) A Map of the World Trade Organization Law of domestic regulation of goods: the technical barriers to trade agreement, the sanitary and phytosanitary measures agreement, and the general agreement on tariffs and trade. J World Trade 48(2): 351–432

Neumann J, Turk E (2003) Necessity revisited: proportionality in the World Trade Organization Law after *Korea-Beef*, *EC-Asbestos* and *EC-Sardines*. J World Trade 37(1):199–233

Oates W (1999) An essay on fiscal federalism. J Econ Lit XXXVII:1120–1149

Sykes A (1999) Regulatory protectionism and the law of international trade. Univ Chic Law Rev 66(1):1–45

Trachtman J (2007b) Regulatory Jurisdiction and the WTO law. J Int Econ Law 10(3):631–651

Other Articles

Lawrence R (1996b) Preferential Trade Agreements: the traditional and the New. Egyptian Center for Economic Studies, Working Paper, p. 13. https://searchworks.stanford.edu/view/5485161. Accessed 2 Nov 2022

Romanchyshyna I (2019) Standards as Transatlantic Trade Barriers: Is there a Future for the EU-US Regulatory Cooperation? Geneva Jean Monnet Working Papers. https://papers.ssrn.com/sol3/papers.cfm?abstract_id=3490517. Accessed 1 Nov 2022

Swann P (2000) The Economics of Standardization. Final Report for Standards and Technical Regulations Directorate, Department of Trade and Industry. Manchester Business School, p. 17. http://www.assalweb.org/assal_nueva/documentos/Estandares/file11312.pdf. Accessed 1 Nov 2022

Wouters J, Marx A, Hachez N (2008) Private Standards, Global Governance and Transatlantic Cooperation. The Case for Global Food Safety Standard. Leuven Centre for Global Governance Studies. https://ghum.kuleuven.be/ggs/research/biosafety_biodiversity/publications/wouters-marx-hachez_final.pdf. Accessed 1 Nov 2022

Research Papers of International Organizations and Research Institutions

Baldwin R (2014) Multilateralising 21st century regionalism, global forum on trade: reconciling regionalism and multilateralism in a Post-Bali World. OECD Publishing, Paris

Correia de Brito A et al. (2016) The Contribution of Mutual Recognition to International Regulatory Co-operation. OECD Regulatory Policy Working Papers. OECD Publishing, Paris, p 22. https://doi.org/10.1787/5jm56fqsfxmx-en. Accessed 1 Nov 2022

Holzer K (2018) Addressing Tensions and Avoiding Disputes: Specific Trade Concerns in the TBT Committee. WTO Staff Working Paper, Economic Research and Statistics Division https://www.wto.org/english/res_e/booksp_e/tbtsps19_e.pdf. Accessed 1 Nov 2022

Lejárraga I (2014) Deep provisions in regional trade agreements: how multilateral-friendly. An overview of OECD findings. OECD Publishing, Paris

Kauffmann C, Saffirio C (2021) Good regulatory practices and cooperation in Trade Agreements: a historical perspective. OECD Regulatory Policy Working Papers. OECD Publishing, Paris

Mavroidis P (2016) Regulatory Cooperation: Lessons from the WTO and the World Trade Regime, E15 Task Force on Regulatory Systems Coherence – Policy Options Paper. International Center for Trade and Sustainable Development (ICTSD), and the World Economic Forum. http://www3.weforum.org/docs/E15/WEF_Regulatory_Cooperation_Lessons_WTO_WTR_report_2015_1401.pdf. Accessed 1 Nov 2022

Menon Economics (2018) The Influence of Standards on the Nordic Economies. https://www.menon.no/wp-content/uploads/2018-31-Nordic-market-study-influence-of-standards.pdf. Accessed 1 Nov 2022

Molina AC, Khoroshavina V (2015). TBT Provisions in Regional Trade Agreements: To What Extent Do They Go Beyond the WTO TBT Agreement? WTO Staff Working Paper. https://www.econstor.eu/bitstream/10419/125799/1/845006401.pdf. Accessed 1 Nov 2022

OECD (2013) International regulatory cooperation: addressing global challenges. OECD Publishing, Paris. https://read.oecd-ilibrary.org/governance/international-regulatory-co-operation_9789264200463-en#page25. Accessed 1 Nov 2022

OECD (2016) Participation in Global Value Chains in Latin America. Implications for Trade and Trade-Related Policy. OECD Publishing, Paris. https://www.oecd-ilibrary.org/trade/participation-in-global-value-chains-in-latin-america_5jlpq80ts8f2-en. Accessed 2 Nov 2022

OECD (2017) International Regulatory Co-operation and Trade. Understanding the Trade Costs of Regulatory Divergence and the Remedies. OECD Publishing, Paris. https://www.oecd.org/gov/international-regulatory-co-operation-and-trade-9789264275942-en.htm. Accessed 1 Nov 2022

UNCTAD and World Bank (2017) The Unseen Impact of Non-Tariff Measures: Insights from a New Database, p iv. http://unctad.org/meetings/en/SessionalDocuments/ditc-tab-MC11-UNCTAD-NTMs.pdf. Accessed 1 Nov 2022

WTO (2005) World Trade Report: Exploring the Links between Trade, Standards, and the WTO

WTO (2011) World Trade Report: The WTO and Preferential Trade Agreements – From Co-existence to Coherence

WTO (2012a) World Trade Report: Trade and Public Policies: A Closer Look at Non-Tariff Measures in 21st Century

WTO and OECD (2019) Facilitating Trade through Regulatory Cooperation The Case of the WTO's TBT/SPS Agreements and Committees, OECD Publishing, Paris

Chapter 3
Regionalism and Multilateralism: The WTO Perspective

This Chapter examines the WTO perspective on regionalism and its relation with the multilateral system. The purpose of this Chapter is to understand how TBT cooperation could fit into the debate on regionalism and multilateralism. It explores the question how some of the TBT liberalization methods are viewed from the perspective of the WTO rules, including on regional integration, as well as how WTO approach could adapt to address TBT in a more comprehensive fashion.

Section 3.1 of this Chapter reviews the historical account of regional integration and the multilateral trading system to clarify which idea the negotiators put into the regional exception clause of the GATT and how it corresponds to the modern day regionalism. Sections 3.2 and 3.3 review the classic theory behind regionalism and how the TBT in RTAs could fit into its paradigm. Section 3.4 reflects on RTAs' limitations in securing "outcome multilateralism". Section 3.5 provides a legal analysis of existing provisions in the WTO Agreements. It clarifies the cases where RTAs could arguably run afoul of the WTO disciplines. Section 3.6 discusses cases where TBT rules in RTAs might be further multilateralized.

3.1 Historical Background on Regionalism

This subsection summarises the history of RTAs to clarify the underlying vision behind regionalism and its interrelation with the multilateral system. The purpose is to get a better understanding of how the concept of regionalism is placed within the idea of multilateralism and how the today's realities changed the interrelation between the two.

I. Romanchyshyna, *Technical Barriers to Trade in "New Generation" RTAs and in the WTO Agreements*, EYIEL Monographs - Studies in European and International Economic Law 29, https://doi.org/10.1007/978-3-031-25791-9_3

3.1.1 Origins

To begin with, it is worthwhile going back to the pre-GATT era when regional integration politics had been more about gains on account of exclusion of non-parties than actual trade liberalisation (e.g., the system of Imperial Preferences between Britain and its former colonies). In 1934, the US implemented the Reciprocal Trade Agreements Act (RTAA), which permitted the US President to negotiate reciprocal tariff reductions with individual countries and to extend the negotiated concessions to other countries that signed similar arrangements (MFN within the "club" of signatories). However, it did not lead to a significant reduction of the average tariffs and failed to address trade restrictions globally.[1] In this climate, as the existing preferences were to do little with protectionism leading to the global economic stagnation if not perpetuating it, the idea of a new multilateral economic order based on the broad application of the MFN principle has started to gain traction. Its often-cited advocate Cordell Hull (US Secretary of State in 1933–1944) also saw the principle of MFN in economic relations as a way to gain a much awaited lasting peace and security as "one country would not be deadly jealous of another" and thus "living standards of all countries might rise, thereby eliminating the economic dissatisfaction that breeds war".[2] He highly criticized protectionism as harming both the global and the US economy.[3] Reflecting this position in a post-World War II era, the United States were an ardent proponent of non-discrimination and rallied behind MFN as a way to tackle harmful protectionist practises.

Given a special prominence of MFN as a basis for architecting the new economic order and the underlying support from the United States which orchestrated trade negotiations at the time, a question arises as to how the provisions on regionalism after all sneaked into the text of the early GATT (Article XXIV) permitting customs unions (CUs) and free trade agreements (FTAs). There is a constellation of factors that explained it.

To begin with, it is crucial to draw a line between CUs and FTAs—only the former requires a common external tariff. Initially, CUs were viewed as more acceptable to depart from MFN. Firstly, it had a strategic underpinning: Regional exception for CUs was to accommodate the process of European integration—a strategically important goal that was aimed to reconstruct the war-torn Europe. This was supported by the United States in its belief that economic integration would create a secure space and stability in the European continent and materialised into the US proposals for the International Trade Organisation (ITO) (1946) envisaging a possibility to have a customs union.[4] Secondly, Clair Wilcox also draws attention to the economic factors: Despite being discriminatory against outsiders, a customs union, by creating a wider trading area and removing obstacles to competition,

[1] See the critics of the RTAA in: Bidwell (1943), p. 297; See also Winters (2015), p. 2.

[2] Winters (2015), p. 2.

[3] Ibid., p. 4.

[4] Wilcox (1949), p. 71.

contributes to a more efficient resources allocation and thus is "conducive to the expansion of trade on the basis of multilateralism and non-discrimination".[5] Could the same logic be applied with regard to FTAs? Wilcox argues that a preferential system that retains internal barriers "obstructs economy and production and restraints the growth of income and demand".[6] Chase also finds it puzzling that FTAs were included into the MFN exception on a par with CUs, while at the time international law did not find it as an acceptable departure from non-discrimination.[7] The idea to add FTAs to the MFN exception came about later with the development concerns coming into play. The proposal thereon was raised by Syria and Lebanon arguing that such model, which does not require harmonisation of trade policies is necessary to create a much needed leeway for developing countries' regional integration.[8] Chase, however, based on documentary evidence, argues that the inclusion of FTAs was lobbied by the US in pursuit of its secret political agenda—to negotiate a preferential arrangement with Canada (failed at a time), which created a change of heart in its initially strict pro-MFN stance.[9] The US, as Chase argues, in fact stage-managed the Lebanese and Syrian proposal to craft the MFN exception to its liking.[10] The provisions for FTAs first appeared at the Havana Conference in 1948, while earlier drafts dealt only with CUs.[11] Although the inclusion of FTAs was already questionable in terms of compatibility with multilateralism based on MFN, there was no apprehension at the time that FTAs would proliferate at such a great speed in later years that would endanger MFN. Alan Winters concludes that there was hardly a long-term economic estimation behind sanctioning of FTAs and the decision was more based on geopolitics.[12] What is crucial is that countries were also unsure about the costs (economic, as well as political) of their commitment to unconditional MFN and preferred to have more leeway in pursuing trade policies.[13] On the other hand, allowing for preferences came from a conviction that FTAs, as well as CUs would not largely compromise the multilateral ideas, but rather complement its goals. For instance, in one of its communication documents (in relation to the 1956 EEC negotiations) the US Secretary of State noted that the US changed its unfavourable position towards preferential agreements in a belief that by covering

[5] Ibid., pp. 70–71.

[6] Ibid.

[7] Chase (2005), p. 20.

[8] Ibid., See also Tevini (2006), pp. 215–216.

[9] Chase (2005), p. 3.

[10] Ibid., pp. 14–15.

[11] See US Department of State (1946–1947) Preliminary Proposals for an ITO, In: US Department of State, American Trade Proposals – A Series of Articles Looking Toward a World Conference on Trade, US Government Printing Office, Washington D.C., p. 10. In later drafts of the US Suggested Charter for the ITO, a provision allowing for preferential arrangements other than a CU appeared, however it was allowed in "exceptional circumstances" and subject to two-thirds majority vote of the ITO membership.

[12] Winters (2015), p. 7.

[13] Chase (2005), p. 27.

substantially all the trade between the parties, these agreements (both CUs and FTAs) could lead to an "overall expansion of international trade".[14]

The key point in crafting the exception for preferential arrangements was to restrict the scope of potential abuse. From the very inception of the idea incorporating preferentialism within the multilateral context, there was an understanding that it has to be subject to certain rules and conditions in order not to undermine the multilateral system. Already in works of Bidwell and Mead in the early 1940s, a concept of multilateral oversight of bilateral deals began to crystalize.[15] Bidwell wrote at the time that allowing for preferential agreements holds a "grave danger that the clause [MFN] may become so weakened . . . that it will lose all real significance", although at the same time these agreements may be very useful for the trade liberalization process meaning that a proper balance shall be maintained.[16]

Within the negotiations, the idea of disciplining regionalism was realized in a set of conditions that have to be stipulated at the multilateral level. The text of the Geneva Draft (1947) for the future ITO included specific conditions for CUs, so that any agreement short of that would not enjoy the exception: first, harmonization of external tariffs with regard to third countries and other restrictions in all constituent territories (constitutive element of a CU), and second, tariffs and other preferences shall not be on a whole more restrictive than the average applied in the constituent territories before the CU formation. These provisions were expected to balance multilateralism based on non-discrimination with the right to pursue CUs. The negotiators did not follow a route where the newly established organization for trade would be effectively authorized to mandate preferential arrangements. The Geneva Draft (1947) simply stated that the members had to consult the ITO upon the CU's formation, but did not provide a definitive authority for the ITO to approve or disapprove the union.[17]

The following major milestone in disciplining regionalism came along with the adoption of the Havana Charter, whose provisions were later transferred into Article XXIV of the GATT. Most prominently, it incorporated FTAs along with CUs.[18] It also instituted the final test for FTAs and CUs—a set of internal and external requirements that would balance trade liberalization with the right to pursue preferential deals.

Few substantive points are to be made here. Firstly, it is important to note that this balancing in its core is not an economic assessment, but is rather of legal nature, as a purely economic assessment comparing positive effects for the RTAs parties with

[14] Slany et al. (1956), p. 450. See Circular Airgram from the Secretary of State to Certain Diplomatic Missions, CA-454 Common Market Negotiations, 13 July 1956.

[15] This account is taken from Winters (2015), p. 4.

[16] Bidwell (1943), p. 306.

[17] United States Tariff Commission (1947) Analysis – Geneva Draft of Charter for an International Trade Organization, Washington D.C., p. 59.

[18] Article 44 of the Havana Charter. See at: United Nations Conference on Trade and Employment (1947–1948) Havana Final Act and Related Documents. https://www.wto.org/english/docs_e/legal_e/havana_e.pdf. Accessed 1 Nov 2022.

negative effects for non-parties would not provide enough clarity. As Peter Hilpold wrote, "it is not clear to discover the underlying settled economic theory on which the evaluation process [on whether trade creating effects prevail over the trade diverting ones] should be based".[19] Thus, it was important to have a straight legal test irrespective of economic welfare implications.[20]

Secondly, the test is meant to play an important role, as a failure to satisfy its conditions would result in a situation where a regional exception would not serve as a defence for violation of other WTO obligations. It is worthwhile noting that the Appellate Body in the *Turkey – Textiles* case rejected Turkey's argument that the right under Article XXIV GATT is an "autonomous right" in relation to other WTO obligations of members as opposed to "exceptions" under Articles XX and XXI of the GATT and confirmed that the role of GATT Article XXIV is to provide a possible "defence" for RTAs members that is subject to conditions.[21] Later on, in *Peru – Agricultural Products* the Appellate Body emphasized the key role of the Article XXIV legal test:

> …[P]roper routes to assess whether a provision in an FTA that may depart from certain WTO rules is nevertheless consistent with the covered agreements are the WTO provisions that permit the formation of regional trade agreements.[22]

As noticed by Robert Howse and Joanna Langille,

> [t]his arguably goes beyond the obvious purpose of ensuring that PTAs do not lead to more restrictive trade with third countries, or to ensuring that they in general result in freer trade, to assuring the unity and integrity of the WTO as a legal system.[23]

Certain major provisions of the Article XXIV GATT test are worth mentioning in this historical account as they embody the vision of parties on balancing between multilateralism and regionalism.

Firstly, it is the requirement for RTAs to eliminate duties and "other restrictive regulations of commerce" on "substantially all the trade" between its parties. It is not entirely clear what was the motivation behind the "substantially all the trade" formulation, as it has long been argued that the more comprehensive the trade deal is, the more distortions it brings as regards trade with non-parties.[24] It was arguably created to deal to minimize selective preferences, as there are reasons to suggest that selective preferences could in fact be more distortive for global welfare, as they would inevitably cater for interests of those industries who have a preference for diverting trade from third countries for their political gain.[25] However, this provision left too many blind spots. The exact measurement of the "substantially all trade"

[19] Hilpold (2003), p. 234.

[20] See also Mathis (2011), p. 39.

[21] Appellate Body Report, *Turkey –Textiles*, paras. 9, 45.

[22] Appellate Body Report, *Peru – Agricultural Products*, paras. 5.112, 5.113.

[23] Howse and Langille (2018), p. 678.

[24] Viner (1950) and Dam (1960).

[25] See, e.g., Hudec (1993), p. 155; Bhagwati (1992), p. 537.

condition remained unclear, in particular, what would be included into the category of "other restrictive regulations of commerce" that, on a par with tariffs, have to be eliminated on substantially all the trade between the parties. The latter question would become especially pertinent with the extension of the scope of RTAs to other areas of deep integration: Could they also be covered by Article XXIV?

Secondly, the negotiators agreed to the external requirements for the RTAs' formations to further preclude a situation of undermining trade with third countries. The general standard negotiated at Havana and further transposed to GATT Article XXIV is that in relation to third countries, "duties and other regulations of commerce shall not be higher or more restrictive than prior to the formation of an RTA."[26] It follows that the negotiators' intention was to limit preferential arrangements in a way that they would not negatively impact third parties, however, it is not quite clear how this goal could be attained, as many preferential arrangements necessarily include certain convergence of trade policies that could inevitably effectively impact the outsiders. Therefore, the legal test in Article XXIV posed more questions than it provided solutions for disciplining regionalism in a way consistent with the multilateral system.

Within time, the rules on regional integration have been expanding and reached several important milestones. In 1979, the GATT parties adopted the so-called "Enabling Clause", which allowed for a possibility to conclude preferential deals between developing countries without extending preferences to others.[27] In 1994, the Uruguay Round of negotiations brought few developments: it included a regional exception into the agreement on services (GATS Article V) and, in relation to goods, added the Understanding on Article XXIV that clarified some technical aspects of the provision (primarily on customs unions), as well as established a special body within a newly created WTO—the Committee on Regional Trade Agreements (CRTA), which was aimed to review preferential deals contributing to the overall transparency.[28] Transparency, however, largely remained a weak spot of the regional integration rules and existing rules still do not provide enough clarity as regards treating preferential agreements. In 2001, the urgency of clarification and improving the disciplines on RTAs prompted WTO Members to include it into the negotiating agenda of the Doha Round (para. 29 of the 2001 Doha Ministerial Declaration). As a result, in 2006, the WTO Members adopted the so-called Transparency Mechanism

---

[26] Article 44, para. 2 of the Havana Charter. See at: United Nations Conference on Trade and Employment (1947–1948) Havana Final Act and Related Documents, https://www.wto.org/english/docs_e/legal_e/havana_e.pdf. Accessed 1 Nov 2022.

[27] WTO (1979) Decision on Differential and More Favourable Treatment, Reciprocity and Fuller Participation of Developing Countries, 28.11.1979. https://www.wto.org/english/docs_e/legal_e/enabling1979_e.htm. Accessed 1 Nov 2022.

[28] See Understanding on Interpretation of Article XXIV of the General Agreement on Tariffs and Trade, para. 2. This Understanding is a part of GATT 1994. https://www.wto.org/english/tratop_e/region_e/region_art24_e.htm#understanding. Accessed 1 Nov 2022. See also information on the Committee on Regional Trade Agreements at: https://www.wto.org/english/tratop_e/region_e/regcom_e.htm.

for RTAs aimed at improving early notification and review of preferential deals by the CRTA.[29]

The sufficiency of the existing regulatory structure becomes, however, questionable, especially with the proliferation of RTAs that was not expected at the time when negotiators crafted the rules.[30] The changing trade policy landscape presents a challenge for these rules. The following paragraphs analyze the evolution of regional integration in different time periods in an attempt to demonstrate a trend of the changing landscape of preferentialism and the urgency of this matter for global governance.

3.1.2 Evolution

The practical interconnection between regionalism and multilateralism has been changing over time, with the latter becoming essentially a major driver of global trade governance. To better illustrate the underlying trends, it is worthwhile looking back into how the role of regional trade agreements evolved. The following analysis divides the pursuit of regionalism into three "waves".[31]

3.1.2.1 First Wave

What Bhagwati calls the "first regionalism" primarily denotes a major event in the aftermath of the GATT being negotiated, which was the establishment of the European Economic Community in 1958. Given that it occurred against the backdrop of the post-World War II crisis and a need to rebuild Europe, as well as the Cold War with its increasing adversaries between the major power blocks, the strategic premises of this regional integration project played an especially significant role. Following the European integration, a number of FTA proposals quickly mushroomed over the 1960s, the most successful of which were the East African Community and the Central American common market.[32] They were driven by economic motivation—to stimulate industrialisation by reducing the costs of trade and exploiting economies of scale. However, these attempts eventually failed because of inefficient allocation of industries, driven by bureaucratic negotiations

---

[29]This mechanism has been adopted at the General Council of the WTO and is agreed to be provisionally applied until Members replace it with the permanent mechanism. See at: https://www.wto.org/english/tratop_e/region_e/trans_mecha_e.htm.

[30]Winters (2015), p. 7.

[31]For previous works of scholars, which attempt to classify the phases of regionalism, see, for example, Bhagwati (1992), or Forere (2015), p. 59. The identification of the "waves" is approximate and draws from major events in regional integration.

[32]WTO (2011) World Trade Report, p. 52.

rather than trade liberalisation process.[33] The first wave of regionalism thus appeared to be largely non-threatening for the envisaged development of the multilateral project. Primarily, it could be explained by the fact that other major powers at the time, US and Japan, were rather disinterested in pursuing preferentialism, despite several proposals being made following the European integration project (e.g., proposals for the North Atlantic Free Trade Agreement centred around the US, or Japan's probe to make an arrangement with the United States in the 1960s).[34] At this point, the US remain a key defender of the multilateral route. Throughout 1960s and 1970s there was a limited track record of regional integration, as the efforts of major power blocks were focused on the GATT negotiations with major breakthroughs being achieved at the Kennedy (1964–1967) and Tokyo Rounds (1973–1979).[35]

3.1.2.2 Second Wave

The comeback of regionalism in the 1980s was different primarily due to a change of heart in the US towards exploring the route of preferential deals in addition to multilateral negotiations. It started with the FTA with Canada, which later was superseded by the North American Free Trade Agreement (NAFTA)—a larger deal including Canada and Mexico.[36] This shift, according to Bhagwati, signified that "regionalism is likely to endure this time" and he was right—a number of preferential deals started to increase ever since. There could be a variety of reasons explaining the US' conversion. Looking at it from the geopolitical perspective, the end of the Cold War marked a major breakdown of the former power structure. Although for some time the US remain a unilateral power, it soon became apparent that, as Mario Telo calls it, "US hegemonic multilateralism" begins to shatter. Tendencies continue to advance towards "heterogeneous and transitional globalised system".[37] In this context, the US starts to seek for alternatives routes that would secure its position as a world super power. It materialised into a policy of "competitive liberalisation"—active pursuance of FTAs to "place the US at the centre of the world trading system".[38] Moreover, at the time the European integration was quickly accelerating culminating in creation of the single market in 1993 and further enlargement into the Eastern Europe. Bhagwati also mentions this factor among the triggers of the US "competitive liberalisation" stance (out of a need to create a "countervailing block").[39]

[33] Ibid., Bhagwati (1992), p. 539.

[34] Bhagwati (1992), pp. 538–539; See also Grilli (1997), p. 197.

[35] See some thoughts on this period in Söderbaum (2016), p. 22.

[36] It is also relevant to mention the FTA with Israel, negotiated before the US-Canada agreement, however, it was mostly of strategic value, reflecting a special relationship with the US.

[37] Telo (2014), p. 60.

[38] Evenett and Meier (2007). See also Melo Araujo (2016), p. 33.

[39] Bhagwati (1992), p. 541.

What is crucial is that US competitive liberalisation and European integration created a sense that "regionalism is an order of a day", prompting other countries to follow suit.[40] This is when the question on the interrelation between regionalism and multilateralism became especially relevant and started to trigger extensive debates among scholars and policymakers.[41]

Nevertheless, during this "second wave" of regionalism, a comprehensive multilateralism was revived with a successful conclusion of the Uruguay Round leading to the creation of the WTO and a substantial expansion of global trade rules. The Uruguay Round still remains to date the highest point of multilateralism. There is an argument that regionalism has contributed to this success, which is predicated on the idea that regional integration strengthens domestic pro-trade (in comparison to anti-trade) interests paving way to more ambitious liberalisation projects.[42] Soongjoon Cho argues that it is especially relevant for new areas where RTAs could create a "knowledge base" ("laboratory effect" argument) and brings up the example of NAFTA and the EU integration, the agenda of which (e.g., on services and intellectual property) informed the Uruguay Round.[43] It follows (although not without controversy[44]) that regionalism of a "second wave" leading to the Uruguay Round fed the multilateral agenda. This view on RTAs as mostly complementary to the multilateral system was also supported in the WTO Secretariat's report at the time.[45]

Nevertheless, after the Uruguay Round, furthering of the multilateral negotiations stalled, while RTAs continued to proliferate. The new round of multilateral trade negotiations at Doha failed to deliver on its ambitious promises bringing up to light diverging preferences of an ever-increasing and diverse WTO membership.

3.1.2.3 Third Wave

Within the "third wave" of regionalism RTAs come to the forefront of global trade governance. When it became apparent that the Doha Round was going to be extremely difficult to conclude, a further surge of RTAs followed, which now causes greater concerns among experts than before.[46] William Davey illustrates it with the statistics as of 2008 when a number of RTAs grew by more than 100 per cent in

---

[40] Ibid., p. 542.

[41] Ibid; Bhagwati and Panagaria (1996), Freund (2000b), Grossman and Helpman (1995), etc.

[42] See, e.g., Baldwin (2006), p. 22.

[43] Cho (2001), p. 433. See also Davey (2011), p. 248.

[44] See, e.g., Picker (2005), p. 314, footnote 188; See also Bhagwati (1992), p. 548.

[45] WTO Secretariat (1995) Regionalism and The World Trading System, World Trade Organization, Geneva, p. 62.

[46] The major WTO-related expert reports at the time (notably, the 2003 WTO World Trade Report, the 2004 Sutherland Report and the 2007 Warwick Commission Report) were much less optimistic with regard to RTAs in comparison to the mentioned 1995 WTO Secretariat's study and rather expressed a critical position (This account is largely taken from Davey (2011, p. 243)).

comparison to 1995.[47] The statistics as of the 1 September 2019 show 302 RTAs in force.[48]

One of the reasons for this is the Doha's failure prompting RTAs to take the lead in guiding the global trade negotiations. Another related reason was the changing realities of the global commerce creating demand for trade governance that the multilateral negotiations cannot deliver. It slowly becomes apparent that tariffs, while being significantly reduced within the last couple of decades, do not play such a strong role as before and the growing complexity of world trade demands deeper disciplines—this is what is leading to, as Baldwin calls it, "the 21st century regionalism"—far more focused on regulations.[49] RTAs are now endowed with a task for disciplining "behind-the-border" measures, which are becoming more and more relevant for global trade, such as development of digital technologies and the urgency of addressing environmental threats.[50]

The "third wave" of regionalism could also be associated with the changing structure of RTAs in terms of membership. What becomes prominent already in the 1990s is the rise of global value chains,[51] in response to which RTAs have become more cross-continental including countries with different levels of development.

Another key feature of this period is the negotiation of mega-regionals (RTAs involving a large number of parties and/or covering a large proportion of world trade), which are believed to be this new type of trade governance that would shape the architecture of global rules substituting the existing structures.[52] The initial trade agreements of this type were the Trans-Pacific Partnership (TPP) and the Transatlantic Trade and Investment Partnership (TTIP), which were not finalized, *inter alia*, due to the US detraction from its previous multiple-party RTAs strategy. However, the provisions of the TPP found way into the United States-Mexico-Canada Agreement (USMCA), a renegotiated North-American Free Trade Agreement (NAFTA). Also, the TPP became the template for the Comprehensive and Progressive Agreement for Trans-Pacific Partnership (CPTPP), which is one of the largest free trade agreements in the world including eleven countries of the Asia-Pacific region—both developed and developing. Another example of mega-regional trade agreement is the recently negotiated Regional Comprehensive Economic Partnership (RCEP) between 15 countries of the Asia-Pacific region, including mostly developing countries, among which China, South Korea, and Japan.

---

[47] Davey (2011), p. 233, footnote 2.

[48] WTO, Regional Trade Agreements, Facts and Figures. https://www.wto.org/english/tratop_e/region_e/region_e.htm. Accessed 1 Nov 2022.

[49] Baldwin (2014).

[50] The WTO World Trade Reports for 2018 and 2019 are specifically dedicated to this emerging and urgent issues, demonstrating the global governance gap.

[51] Gereffi and Lee (2012).

[52] On mega-regionals, see, e.g., Bown (2016).

Notably, the European Union has also been quite active in pursuing bilateral trade negotiations, transferring from a mostly strategically oriented towards a more economically oriented RTAs policy and deepening its trade agenda to address the new trends in global commerce.[53]

With further growth of RTAs networks, a question on their interrelation with the WTO becomes more relevant. With trade negotiations being mostly moved to the RTA level, it becomes apparent that RTAs are not viewed as an addition to the multilateral system anymore, but rather standing on a par with it. In this climate, and especially with the introduction of new issues into the trade agenda, it is important to determine whether this new network of governance promotes coherence rather than fragmentation of global trade governance, as in the latter case there is a risk of sliding back to times when trade agenda was simply set by few "great powers".[54] According to a more positive outlook of RTAs in relation to the multilateral system, they are the components of the same process of trade liberalization.[55] Jagdish Bhagwati, despite clearly favouring multilateralism and even calling them "termites in the trading system", also recognises that multilateralism could be differentiated into "process-multilateralism" and as "outcome-multilateralism"[56] The former would strictly follow the procedure of multilateral trade negotiations while the latter would represent an alternative route towards achieving the goals of multilateralism—possibly through RTAs. The idea of "outcome multilateralism" is conceptually interesting, especially considering the complex realities of the "third wave" of regionalism, the context and priorities of which differ from the early RTAs, which Bhagwati had in mind. The following sections advocate for the approach where RTAs could be seen as securing "outcome multilateralism", where they go in line with main WTO principles and where they could favour a large number of actors.

3.2 Classic Theory of Regionalism

This section reviews the classic theory of regionalism, which serves as a background for the ensuing section. The purpose of this section is to point out what is the traditional analysis of regionalism, while the next section will re-evaluate this traditional analysis in the context of TBT.

Economists and policymakers have long been divided on the issue regarding the impact of RTAs for the multilateral trading system, especially when the "second wave" of regionalism marked a shift from mostly strategically based to economically reasoned deals. RTAs started to proliferate at a great pace ever since, which alarmed

---

[53] See Sects. 4.1.1 and 4.2.1 of Chap. 4.

[54] Baldwin (2011).

[55] See., e.g., Cottier et al. (2015).

[56] Bhagwati (1992), p. 536; Bhagwati (2008).

the international community worried that such trend could negatively impact the multilateral system.

The following paragraphs seek to introduce some key concepts, which underpin the analysis of RTAs in relation to the multilateral system following the approach, introduced by Jagdish Bhagwati, which includes the consideration of their static and dynamic effects. The former refers to the RTAs' immediate effects, while the latter looks into more far-reaching impact, i.e., whether RTAs could contribute to the goals of multilateralism by broadly expanding free trade.[57]

3.2.1 The Static Time-Path Question: Trade Creation, Trade Diversion, "Spaghetti Bowl"

The theory on welfare effects of regional trade agreements was firstly introduced by Jacob Viner, who argued that the overall welfare impact of trade agreements would depend on which of the two effects is stronger—trade creation or trade diversion.[58] Trade creation results in overall welfare gains: It occurs when removal of trade barriers leads to replacement of less efficient domestic production by more efficient imports coming from an RTA member. Trade diversion, on the other hand, occurs when more efficient imports from a third country are replaced by less efficient imports from an RTA member, thus leading in decrease in efficiency and overall welfare losses. Another salient concept added by Bhagwati is the "spaghetti bowl" phenomenon, according to which RTAs could overcomplicate the trade regime, necessitating the application of varying tariff rates to products coming from different countries. Different rules of origin (RoO) in RTAs make the application of preferential tariffs a burdensome task and could also diminish the trade creating effects of RTAs.[59]

For a long time, a prevailing opinion regarding the RTAs' static effects in academic literature has been mainly supporting the theory of preponderance of trade diversion and "spaghetti bowl" effects. Gene Grossman and Elhanan Helpman, for instance, argued that trade-diverting agreements might be more politically viable, as domestic interests groups are more prone to lobby to such effect rather than for trade creation that immediately leads to increased import competition.[60] Jagdish Bhagwati and Arvind Panagriya also argued that RTAs are fundamentally incompatible with principles of reciprocity and non-discrimination, thereby posing a threat to the multilateral system built on these principles.[61] More modern studies challenge such position arguing, for instance, that the extent of trade diversion would depend

---

[57] Bhagwati (1992), pp. 542–543.

[58] Viner (1950).

[59] See the summary of Bhagwati's findings in Bhagwati and Panagaria (1996).

[60] Grossman and Helpman (1995).

[61] Bhagwati and Panagaria (1996), p. 241.

on many factors including distance between the countries and the composition of trade, although they do not deny the fact that RTAs would still discriminate in favour of its partners, which in any case would put the partners to a certain degree in a more competitive position.

3.2.2 The Dynamic Time-Path Question: "Building" or "Stumbling" Block

Additional perspective in assessing the impact of RTAs is represented by the question whether they are conducive to multilateral trade opening, in other words, whether they constitute "building" or "stumbling" blocks to global economic integration, as Bhagwati famously put it.[62] Bhagwati was skeptical about any positive effects from regionalism for the multilateral system claiming that it would rather reduce the incentive to engage in the multilateral process: "if regionalism is available as a realistic option, it will encourage exit rather than the seeking of voice and even the manifestation of loyalty to multilateralism".[63]

However, other studies suggest that the dynamic time-path question is in fact more nuanced. Here, it is important to differentiate between the effects for the negotiation process at the WTO (what Bhagwati calls "process-multilateralism") from a broader category of global trade liberalization effects ("outcome-multilateralism"), which is not necessarily achieved through the WTO negotiations. The effects of RTAs on both these processes could be mixed. When pondering the effects on the WTO negotiations, on the one hand, as Bhagwati argues, RTAs could draw resources from the parties to engage in WTO trade talks. However, on the other hand, RTAs provisions could also feed the multilateral agenda, as it happened, for instance, with the North-American Free Trade Agreement (NAFTA) and European integration projects that inspired the Uruguay Round of the GATT negotiations.[64] The latter is called "laboratory effect", which has already been briefly mentioned in Sect. 3.1. The political economy argumentation of this phenomenon is that regionalism strengthens the pro-free trade forces in partner countries creating a launchpad for more ambitious deals in the future. Now, the role of RTAs has become more central given the existing climate of multilateral trade negotiations with substantial differences between WTO Members and the failure of the Doha Round to deliver on its promises. In fact, RTAs have become alternative vehicles to drive global trade opening to deliver "outcome multilateralism". Following this logic, Caroline Freund in her empirical analysis demonstrated that drawing from the experience from the European Union, regionalism presents a path to freer trade.[65] Moreover, according to

[62] Bhagwati (1991).

[63] Bhagwati (1992), p. 551.

[64] WTO (2011) World Trade Report, p. 52; Cho (2001), p. 433. See also Davey (2011), p. 248.

[65] Freund (2000a), p. 1317.

Richard Baldwin's "domino effect" theory, one RTA creates incentives for outsiders to conclude new RTAs as a means to limit trade diversion and presents an alternative form of active trade liberalization.[66]

However, a multiplicity of RTAs does not amount to the same effects as the WTO level trade negotiations—it still could produce trade diversion and spaghetti bowl effects. In classic theory, RTAs are viewed as a "second best" to WTO negotiations (the "first best"). This motivation is described by Kyle Bagwell and Robert Staiger when using the "terms-of-trade theory" of international trade cooperation. This theory suggests that the main motivation behind the countries' cooperative behaviour is the need to eliminate negative externalities of each country's trade policies aimed at improving the terms of trade, so as to make exports relatively more expensive than imports. Since individually countries strive to maximize their terms of trade by lowering imports and increasing exports, in a non-cooperative scenario they rest in the "terms-of-trade-driven Prisoners' Dilemma", where race to improve individual terms of trade leads to a lose-lose situation when trade volumes are low overall and thus no country actually succeeds.[67] In order to escape the Prisoners' Dilemma, countries resort to international cooperation and coordinate their policies. The empirical study by Bagwell and Staiger showed that under the terms-of-trade theory, the multilateral forum with its principles of reciprocity and non-discrimination would be the first best option to achieve global efficiency and to neutralize the negative terms of trade externalities, since it bounds a large number of countries to ensure that no one cheats. When it comes to RTAs, they could be considered only as a second best option to in cases where the multilateral system cannot deliver.[68]

It is important that the traditional theory on regional integration is still very much centered on tariff reduction. Its premises are not always applicable to the "deep" trade agenda especially when it comes to domestic regulation.

3.3 Rethinking the Classic Theory of Regionalism in View of TBT Complexity

This section takes the traditional frameworks of analysis as a starting point in examining TBT in RTAs in their interrelation with the multilateral system. The assessment of both the static and dynamic effects of RTAs is complicated by the dual character of TBT: firstly, as possible trade barriers, and, secondly, as measures to tackle public policy objectives. In short, there are numerous studies suggesting a less exclusionary effect of reducing TBT at the level of RTAs, however, there are certain conditions regarding the design of respective provisions.

---

[66] Baldwin (1995), pp. 25–48.

[67] Bagwell and Staiger (2011), p. 1241; Bagwell and Staiger (2003), p. 2.

[68] Bagwell and Staiger (1991), p. 241.

3.3.1 The Static Time-Path Question

In general, the distortive effects of TBT liberalization methods could hardly be compared to the effects of tariff liberalization. Richard Baldwin, for instance, suggested that almost all of the trade agreements under the analysis that had "deep" integration provisions led to the so-called "reverse trade diversion": in addition to trade between the parties, they intensified trade with non-parties. Therefore, their "beneficial effects tend to be less exclusive".[69] A similar finding was made by Aaditya Mattoo and others in the World Bank paper, although in relation to a broader category of measures, where they state that the "Vinerial logic may provide an incomplete guide to the effects of deep agreements".[70] In the same vein, the WTO World Trade Report recognized that "[b]y their very nature, some deep integration provisions are *de facto* extended to non-members because they are embedded in broader regulatory frameworks that apply to all trading partners".[71]

It is worth reminding that welfare effects of TBT liberalization would depend on the choice of specific instruments, such as harmonization, equivalence and mutual recognition, enhanced transparency, institutional cooperation, that may affect countries outside the preferential area in an utterly different fashion.[72]

It is fair to assume that transparency and institutional provisions aim to improve the regulatory environment, which eventually benefits the outsiders of trade agreements as well.

On the other hand, harmonization, equivalence (mutual recognition of rules) and conformity assessment assume a greater level of integration exclusively between the parties, which might lead to trade distortion. In this regard, the paper written by Maggie Chen and Aaditya Matoo is informative, as it evaluates the distortive effects of harmonization and mutual recognition for the outsiders and finds that such methods of trade liberalization may increase trade between the contacting parties, while the outsiders, especially developing countries, may feel the negative effects.[73] In the same vein, Alberto Pacheko in his empirical study on mutual recognition agreements (MRAs) found that excluded countries might face "a lower probability of exporting the products covered by the MRA" and their export might decrease being substituted by export from the MRA parties. Most importantly, such effects disproportionately impact developing countries.[74]

At the same time, it has to be noted that the effects of harmonization and mutual recognition could in fact vary depending on circumstances. As for the harmonization, it follows from the Chen and Matoo's paper quoted above that its trade divertive effect depends on the resulting stringency of the harmonized standard

[69] Baldwin (2014), p. 26.

[70] Mattoo et al. (2019), p. 34.

[71] WTO (2011) World Trade Report, p. 168.

[72] Piermartini and Budetta (2009), p. 256. See also Romanchyshyna (2020), p. 44.

[73] Chen and Matoo (2008).

[74] Amurgo-Pacheko (2007), p. 21.

and the extent to which a country's initial standard resembles this harmonized standard.[75] Therefore, outsiders' compliance costs might not be higher than the costs of that RTA party, whose standards differed from the harmonized standard. Following this logic, using widely accepted international standards as a basis for harmonization effects presumably would produce less trade distortive effects overall.[76] As for mutual recognition, its results tend to be far less exclusive if it is not subject to restrictive rules of origin.[77] The latter would limit the possibilities for outsiders to benefit from mutual recognition by, for example, obtaining certification at a mutually recognized facility of one party for further export to another party.[78]

3.3.2 *The Dynamic Time-Path Question and the "Laboratory Effect"*

There is no certainty regarding the possible impact of regional TBT liberalization for the global level. However, it could be suggested that the "laboratory effect" could also come into play.

In the context of regulations, the "laboratory effect" means that RTAs could present smaller scale experimentation projects to introduce new rules, which being successful on the small scale further could be transposed on a wider scale. Thus, as the argument goes, RTAs could create a "knowledge base" to provide guidance for adoption of new trade disciplines globally. It is essentially what happened with the provisions of the plurilateral Standards Code, which was initially a plurilateral agreement only between some of the GATT contracting parties and further moved to the multilateral level having transformed into the WTO TBT Agreement.

The argument from the classic theory of regionalism suggesting that regional trade agreements undertake the role of active trade liberalization and could serve to deliver on "outcome multilateralism" could probably sound even more convincing with respect to TBT than tariffs, as, according to what has been described above, the welfare effects of some of the TBT liberalization methods could be more widely shared.

To sum up, due to their specific nature, TBT measures in RTAs appear to be more difficult to address in the framework of the classic theory on regionalism vs. multilateralism. The welfare effects would depend on the type of TBT measures and the way they are designed. If mutual recognition, for instance, is based on rules of origin and specifically excludes products originating in third countries, such measures might be more trade diverting than measures without such exclusion. However, at the same time, it appears that overall, in comparison

---

[75] Chen and Matoo (2008), p. 840.

[76] Romanchyshyna (2020), pp. 46–47.

[77] Chen and Matoo (2008), p. 840.

[78] Romanchyshyna (2020), p. 47.

to tariffs, the TBT measures in RTAs could have positive static and dynamic effects for global welfare, as their benefits might be less exclusive due to the very nature of the measures in question. Moreover, they might also deliver with regard to certain public policy objectives. Hence, although the exact effects of TBT in RTAs could only be established on a case-by-case basis depending on a particular type and design of the measures at issue, it might be suggested that RTAs could become a driving force for moving global trade governance forward.

3.4 RTAs' Limitations in Securing "Outcome Multilateralism"

Keeping in mind the idea of "outcome multilateralism", which has been mentioned at the end of Sect. 3.1.2.3 of this Chapter, and which represents a vision where regional integration is a complement to the multilateral system and helps to achieve its goals, this section also reflects on the limitations of RTAs in terms of advancing the goals of multilateralism.

As it was pointed out by Gabriel Gari, the key task for the WTO is combating trade protectionism, which could be found in the Preamble to the Marrakesh Agreement, i.e. in the following language:

> entering into reciprocal and mutually advantageous arrangements directed to the substantial reduction of tariffs and other barriers to trade and to the elimination of discriminatory treatment in international trade relations.[79]

As long as RTAs could deliver on this core mandate, it is fair to state that they might secure what Jagdish Bhagwati called an "outcome multilateralism". As it has been pointed out above, when designed in a certain manner (e.g., without restrictive rules of origin), TBT liberalization in RTAs might have positive spillover effects for third countries.

Nevertheless, there are limitations for the "outcome multilateralism" function of RTAs. It might be difficult to efficiently tackle a broad range of issues of multilateral dimension, such as the environmental protection and economic development, especially in a manner that would be inclusive with regard to a multitude of interests at the international arena.[80] It has been mentioned before that regardless of its critique, the WTO remains a crucial forum for the engagement between a large number of countries and customs territories on issues of trade. In contrast, RTAs may lock in certain regulatory solutions that do not reflect a broad consensus between WTO Members. The current advantage of the multilateral system is that it aims to protect the interests of all its Members, including those less powerful.[81] As a result of RTAs

[79] See Gari (2020), p. 50.

[80] See a similar line of reasoning in: Stoll (2020), p. 275.

[81] Dieter (2014).

that provide for harmonization based on the approaches of the participating members (mainly from the developed world, as those issues are more likely to appear on their agenda), other countries, in particular the developing and least developed ones, could find themselves in a disadvantage.[82] The latter could become "standards takers" rather than "standards makers" as they might be pressured to adopt laws and regulations that do not fit well with their existing practices and business environment, as well as the development needs.[83]

In this respect, it could be argued again that it is more desirable to use international standards, which are more likely to be based on the more universally shared approaches.[84] Complying with the basic WTO provisions on technical regulations that ensure openness of regional agreements for the outsiders could also serve to address this concern.[85]

A brief conclusion regarding TBT in RTAs in relation to the multilateral system would be the following: Firstly, in terms of welfare affects, TBT in RTAs cannot be addressed within the classic Vinerian theory, as technical barriers to trade are too complex. It has to be taken into consideration that TBT in RTAs might have positive spillover effects for third countries and deliver on public policy issues. This function of RTAs should be recognized and taken into account when looking into the interrelation of RTAs with the WTO legal system. However, at the same time, the design of methods chosen to deal with technical barriers could reflect the preferences of the exclusive group of countries making it difficult to effectively deliver on issues of multilateral relevance.

3.5 Legal Analysis on the Interconnection Between Existing WTO TBT Rules and RTAs

It has been mentioned before that trade agreements can include a variety of disciplines on technical barriers to trade with different levels of integration, such as harmonization, mutual recognition, transparency and notifications, enforcement and dispute settlement, institutional and administrative provisions, or agreements on further cooperation.[86]

The provisions on technical barriers to trade in RTAs that have built on the existing WTO transparency, dialogue and development disciplines are generally

[82] See, e.g., Stoll (2020), p. 272.

[83] Mayeda (2013), p. 365.

[84] This argument, of course, not without reservations, as the developing countries businesses are less likely to meaningfully participate in international standard development due to lack of resources and expertise. See in International Trade Centre (2003) Influencing and Meeting International Standards: Challenges for Developing Countries. Commonwealth Secretariat, Geneva, p. 11.

[85] See more on this issue in the next section.

[86] Section 2.4 of Chap. 2. Also, see Piermartini and Budetta (2009), p. 256.

viewed as advancing the common goals with the multilateral system and "illuminate [ing] evolving practice within the WTO", thereby hardly creating any conflict, but rather improving the regulatory environment. They are generally described as net positive not only for the parties, but also for the outsiders.[87]

This section is focused on harmonization and mutual recognition, as these methods achieve a greater level of integration exclusively between the parties and therefore might cause some concerns with regard to the outsiders of such agreements or arrangements.

This section looks into the question whether harmonization and mutual recognition might run afoul of the WTO disciplines described in the previous section and whether potential violations could be justified under the regional integration exception of the GATT.

3.5.1 Harmonization and Mutual Recognition: Definitions

At the outset, the meaning of harmonization and mutual recognition requires clarification. Harmonisation represents the deepest form of integration and generally could be broadly defined as the adoption in multiple jurisdictions of similar domestic laws, regulations, principles and government policies.[88]

In essence, harmonization would be the optimal way to deal with regulatory divergences. However, in practice, it is not always feasible for countries to change their well-entrenched domestic rules and to agree on a common approach that would most likely lead to adjustment costs for producers at least on the side of one negotiating partner. To avoid a choice between freedom to develop domestic regulation and trade liberalization countries sometimes drift towards the idea of mutual recognition as, in contrast to harmonization, it is not directly aimed at creating a set of common rules.

As regards mutual recognition, first of all, it has to be pointed out that what is labelled in various sources as mutual recognition may represent somewhat different forms of engagement.[89] Some sources suggest that depending on whether the substance of rules is recognized (technical regulations or standards), or the conformity assessment procedures, it is important to distinguish mutual recognition of rules (otherwise called as "equivalence") and mutual recognition of conformity assessment.

More specifically, mutual recognition of rules means that the parties agree to recognize each other's regulations as equivalent in satisfying the regulatory objectives in question (health, safety, environmental protection). Thus, as soon as the

---

[87] Karttunen (2020), p. 47.

[88] Mayeda (2004), p. 740.

[89] See a comprehensive study on the spectrum of mutual recognition modalities in goods sectors in Correia de Brito et al. (2016).

objective is not undermined, parties are free to diverge in a way to accomplish it. Mutual recognition of rules, however, is an ambitious undertaking. It necessitates "a very high level of confidence in partners' regulatory, conformity and enforcement systems"[90] to make sure that none of the participating jurisdictions would lower the standards of protection for the important social values at stake. This may also require strong institutional cooperation.[91]

On the other hand, mutual recognition of conformity assessment refers to the parties' recognition of each other's authorities as competent to assess whether products satisfy the requirements of a relevant regulation. It is based on confidence that the designated bodies of an exporting country are capable of performing an assessment that is of no less quality than that of authorities in the importing country.[92]

It has been already mentioned before, in Sect. 3.3 that regional harmonization and mutual recognition might contribute to trade liberalization. After all, both the multilateral system, as well as regional trade agreements have a common enemy—national technical barriers that excessively burden international trade.[93] However, it is not excluded that the latter may also become an avenue of RTA protectionism.

In this respect, it is worthwhile noting that the multilateral rules (primarily the TBT Agreement, but also the GATT) essentially favour harmonization and mutual recognition as methods to deal with regulatory divergence, as long as they are not violating the respective disciplines. Moreover, it appears that multilateral rules, as evidenced specifically in rules on positive integration—international standards and mutual recognition—favour forms of integration, which are open and inclusive.

3.5.2 RTAs' Harmonization

RTAs' harmonization itself does not have a formal capacity to disproportionally favour certain imports. It is the result of harmonization—technical regulations, standards or conformity assessment procedures of Members—which could cause concern in case they are discriminatory, or unnecessarily burden certain imports, or fail to follow relevant international standards that could have been effective and appropriate to attain a legitimate objective at stake.[94] It could be imagined that regional harmonization could cause a "race to the top"—a more stringent set of

[90] OECD (2017) International Regulatory Co-operation and Trade. Understanding the Trade Costs of Regulatory Divergence and the Remedies, p. 42. The examples of such recognition could include EU and Trans-Tasman MRA between Australia and New Zealand. Both imply a high level of integration and trust in each other's systems.

[91] Ibid., p. 18.

[92] Ibid., p. 17.

[93] Trachtman (2013), p. 318.

[94] See a similar idea in Trachtman (2013), p. 319.

regulations in one of the RTA parties, which could disadvantage the imports from outside of an RTA. Whether or not it could be found inconsistent with the respective WTO disciplines, would depend on the design and application of these regulations. In case, one of the Members adopts a set of more stringent rules to correspond to an increased level of protection of a certain value (legitimate policy objective), as it follows from Sect. 2.3.2 of Chap. 2, this Member cannot be faulted for its new legitimate objective, but only for the manner in which the objective is pursued, which is to be determined depending on the circumstances of a given case.

Additionally, it has to be mentioned that in case an RTA has an institutional capacity to produce new regulations and standards, similarly to domestic regulatory frameworks, such regulations and standards also have to follow relevant TBT Agreement's disciplines, including being based on relevant international standards. Therefore, if RTA parties establish standards between each other, which would not comply with the TBT Agreement, for instance, by being unnecessarily trade restrictive or discriminatory, they would be accountable for the possible violations.

3.5.3 Mutual Recognition

With regard to mutual recognition of rules or conformity assessment, it appears that the fact of recognition itself resulting in favouring certain imports from certain Member(s), might cause a legal challenge under respective WTO disciplines.[95] These could primarily concern rules on non-discrimination, as well as "necessity".

3.5.3.1 Mutual Recognition and Non-discrimination

Mutual recognition regimes could run afoul of the non-discrimination (MFN) disciplines of Article 2.1 and 5.1.1. of the TBT Agreement, as well as Article I of the GATT. The latter would be especially relevant for technical barriers that might not be covered by the TBT Agreement: non-product related PPMs that are not reflected in marking and labelling of a product and might include environmental requirements in the production process, the prescription not to use child labour, etc.[96]

First of all, for the purposes of Article 2.1 of the TBT Agreement and Article I of the GATT, it could be determined that depending on a type of mutual recognition, there are two ways in which products from other countries could be treated in a less favourable manner.[97] First, products coming from countries that have concluded a mutual recognition agreement of rules (equivalence) would be automatically

[95] See Bartels (2005), Trachtman (2007b) and Mathis (1998).

[96] For more details, see Sect. 2.3.2.2 of Chap. 2.

[97] For more details of this analysis, see Bartels (2005), p. 696.

exempted from the application of national technical regulations, while products coming from outside the preferential area would still need to comply with all the national technical regulations. Second, products from countries that concluded agreements on recognition of conformity assessment would not need to pass through additional procedures except those held at their place of origin.[98] Also, for the same reasons, in reference to Article 5.1.1 of the TBT Agreement, it could be argued that suppliers of products coming from outside the preferential area are granted access under less favorable conditions than the suppliers from the preferential area.

It is worth pointing out that the above effects would be especially explicit in case the recognition regimes put restrictions on the origin of products (thereby *de jure* limiting the access for products from outside the preferential area).[99] If such restrictions are not in place, it could be argued that recognition regimes only apply to regulations and assessment procedures and that that they are origin-neutral, as products from outside the preferential area can also be tested in a similar fashion according to the recognized rules. However, in this case, one could claim a *de facto* discrimination as the products of certain origin would be indirectly affected.

The core issue here is to determine whether less favourable treatment within mutual recognition arrangements could be recognized as based on legitimate grounds, and thus not inconsistent with the respective provisions of the TBT Agreement and the GATT.

Following the analysis of "likeness" in Sect. 2.3.2.3.1, it is worth to note that there is a certain possibility to argue that the products at issue coming from the countries that enjoy the recognition preferences and other WTO Members are not "like". However, it would depend on specific circumstances of the case: whether there is a difference in products' physical characteristics that would, for example, as in *EC-Asbestos*, imply a different level of risk, or whether there is a strong consumer preference for a certain feature of given products or their production methods that underpins the products coming from the area of mutual recognition. One could imagine, for instance, certain environmental standards within such recognition arrangements. However, as has been mentioned in Sect. 2.3.2.3.1, the "likeness" test has never been used as an avenue of justification for less favourable treatment. Moreover, in case of mutual recognition agreements, where preferences are granted only based on membership and not on objective criteria, it might be even more difficult to argue that the products at issue are not "like", as the outsiders' products may perfectly satisfy the legitimate objective that is at stake.

With respect to the issue of legitimate policy considerations, as argued in Sect. 2. 3.2.3.2, they are more likely to be addressed through the prism of specific legal provisions.

Firstly, this is the "legitimate regulatory distinction" part of the non-discrimination test in Articles 2.1 (technical regulations) and paragraph D of Annex 3 "Code of Good Practice" (standards), which in addition to the identification

[98] Ibid., pp. 698–699.

[99] See a similar argument in Romanchyshyna (2020), p. 53.

of a legitimate objective at stake also include a requirement that a measure at issue should not be "applied in a manner which would constitute a means of arbitrary or unjustifiable discrimination" or a "disguised restriction on international trade"—a criterion of "even-handedness".[100]

When it comes to mutual recognition, while it might be accepted that a differentiation between products based on whether they are coming from a preferential area pursues a legitimate goal (which, depending on a design of the mutual recognition arrangement, might include environmental protection, safety, consumer protection, etc.), the way mutual recognition is applied can be problematic. In particular, in deciding whether the criteria of "even-handedness" has been observed, following the legal reasoning in *US – Clove Cigarettes* and *US – Tuna* (see Sect. 2.3.2.3.2), it must be evaluated whether there is a sufficient nexus between the legitimate goal and the way it is implemented through mutual recognition. It has to be noted in this regard that mutual recognition agreements with exclusionary membership could cause considerable doubt in terms of whether they pass this test, as they are hinged upon a country's membership in a mutual recognition deal and not on the objective criteria.

Secondly, a quite similar reasoning would apply for Article 5.1.1's "in a comparable situation" test which implies that Members may differentiate in terms of access to their conformity assessment procedures in a situation-appropriate manner. Similarly, as the Appellate Body clarified in *Russia – Railway Equipment*, such differentiation has to be based on objective evidence that the respective suppliers' situation is different, which constitutes a justification for a different treatment.[101] With regard to mutual recognition of conformity assessment, it could potentially be argued that the situation of suppliers' from one Member is not comparable to another Member based on a number of factors, such as the respective quality of the regulatory frameworks and supervisory systems. However, if a mutual recognition arrangement has an exclusionary membership rather than one based on certain objective criteria, it could be difficult to argue that the differentiation it provides is justified, as there might be other WTO Members whose regulatory framework could also satisfy high standards of quality.

Thirdly, for the similar reasons, the "even-handedness" in the application of a mutual recognition agreement could also be problematic in terms of justification under GATT Article XX. As has been mentioned in previous sections, this legal standard is similar to Article 2.1 of the GATT. Moreover, as it has been noted in Sect. 2.3.2.7, based on the Appellate Body's interpretation in *US – Shrimp* requiring flexibility of regulatory measures, it might be argued that mutual recognition agreements with exclusionary membership rather than objective criteria are not favoured by Article XX of the GATT.

In this context, it is also relevant to mention cases from the GATT era. In the case *EEC – Imports of Beef from Canada,* the panel ruled that the European Economic

---

[100] Chapeau of Article XX an the sixth recital of the TBT Agreement's Preamble.

[101] Appellate Body Report, *Russia – Railway Equipment*, para. 5.147. See more in Sect. 4.2.2.2.

Community's (EEC) regulation, which automatically granted the United States access to the tariff-rate quota for high quality beef, was inconsistent with the MFN principle (Article I:1 of the GATT). Canada, the complainant in that case, claimed that its beef was of similar quality and, therefore, the distinction that was made between then US and Canadian beef was origin-based. The panel agreed with Canada and ruled that while the EEC was permitted to set conditions for quota access, such conditions should not have included preferential access for products of a particular country.[102] Similarly, in the context of mutual recognition agreements, it could be argued that while Members are free to enter into such agreements, the relevant preferences cannot be based exclusively on the membership.

It is also important to add that some scholars argue that the TBT Agreement's provisions on equivalence and mutual recognition have a particular role in "supplementing" the understanding of MFN under the TBT Agreement in this specific context.[103] Lorand Bartels, for instance, makes an argument based on Articles 10.7 and 6.3 of the TBT Agreement. According to these articles, WTO Members are encouraged to enter into consultations/negotiations for the conclusion of recognition agreements in an open manner upon a WTO Member's request. Bartels suggests that these rules have to be read together with the MFN clause of the TBT Agreement, which would imply that there is a "conditionality" to MFN in the TBT Agreement.[104] The condition is that a Member must provide non-discriminative treatment to products of another Member if regulations/procedures of that Member are "adequate" to satisfy the regulatory objective in question. Thus, Members cannot just deny access to their recognition regime in case the products are of same quality. At least, they have to consider requests from other Members who wish to have their regulations/procedures recognized. According to such interpretation, "mutual recognition agreements (MRAs) and agreements on equivalence that have a closed membership would *per se* be of moot WTO legality".[105] A similar idea is advanced by Joel Trachtman arguing that "while it appears that [. . .] recognition arrangements may be legal under WTO law, there seems to be little support for 'closed' recognition. . .".[106]

3.5.3.2 Mutual Recognition and "Necessity"

Mutual recognition could also be assessed in terms of whether it creates an "unnecessary obstacle to international trade",[107] i.e., whether it complies with the

[102] Paras. 3.6., 4.3, 4.5.

[103] See Romanchyshyna (2020), p. 50.

[104] Bartels (2005), pp. 701, 709.

[105] See Romanchyshyna (2020), p. 50.

[106] Trachtman (2006), p. 16.

[107] See the articulation of such possibility in Bartels (2005), p. 703, footnote 51.

provisions of Article 2.2 (technical regulations), paragraph E of Annex 3 "Code of Good Practice" (standards) and Article 5.1.2 (conformity assessment).

There are few points to be made in terms of mutual recognition in this context.

The first point relates to the compliance with Article 2.2 of the TBT Agreement (similar to paragraph E of Annex 3 "Code of Good Practice") requiring technical regulations (and standards) not to be "more trade restrictive than necessary to fulfil a legitimate objective, taking account of the risks non-fulfilment would create". As has been pointed out in Sect. 2.3.2.4, although a Member's legislative choice to obtain a certain level of protection is not something that is questioned, the way this level is attained is exactly the subject of the "necessity" evaluation, i.e., whether a given level of protection is pursued in the least trade restrictive manner.

Firstly, in case of mutual recognition, it could be questioned whether it is "trade restrictive" at all, meaning, according to the Appellate Body's interpretations, that it creates a "limiting effect on international trade".[108] On the one hand, it might be argued that it does not have such an effect, as it is a trade-facilitative method, which additionally liberalizes trade with certain Members, while trade with other Members is not restricted. However, on the other hand, it could also be argued that it modifies the conditions of competition in favour of products from the preferential area. Such modification of competitive conditions, according to the Appellate Body's practice, could be sufficient to demonstrate trade restrictiveness.[109] At the same time, if mutual recognition is based on objective criteria rather than on exclusive membership, it is more likely that it might be defended as not trade restrictive. In this case mutual recognition would imply that any Member could qualify for recognition in case it satisfies certain conditions. Even though, some of the Members might find it more difficult to comply with these objective conditions, it has to be taken into account that the existence of initial compliance costs, according to the panel in *Australia – Tobacco Plain Packaging,* is not sufficient to demonstrate "limiting effects on international trade".[110]

Secondly, in case mutual recognition is recognized as trade restrictive, in order to find whether it "unnecessarily" burdens international trade in contravention of Article 2.2, it has to be assessed whether there could have been available less trade restrictive alternative measures that achieve the same level of protection of the legitimate objective at stake. As it has been analyzed in Sect. 2.3.2.4, it follows from the panels' and the Appellate Body's practice that to qualify as a possible alternative, a proposed measure has to satisfy a number of requirements: (i) it has to be less trade restrictive, (ii) it has to make at least an equivalent contribution to the objective being pursued through the challenged measure, and (iii) it has to be

[108] Appellate Body Report, *US – Tuna II (Mexico)*, para. 319; See also Panel Report, *Australia – Tobacco Plain Packaging*, para. 7.1166; Appellate Body Report, *Australia – Tobacco Plain Packaging,* para. 6.389.

[109] See, e.g., Appellate Body Report, *US – COOL (Article 21.5 – Canada and Mexico)*, para. 5.208.

[110] Panel Report, *Australia – Tobacco Plain Packaging*, para. 7.1235.

reasonably available.[111] In this regard, it could be pointed out that in case of mutual recognition with exclusive membership, a possible alternative measure that could arise is opening up the possibilities for other Members to qualify for mutual recognition under certain conditions.

However, it needs to be also pointed out that although this option could, at least theoretically, be less trade restrictive, it might be more difficult to demonstrate that it would achieve the same level of effectiveness in satisfying the pursued legitimate objective, as well as whether it would be reasonably available. The recognition arrangements are very much based on trust in other country's regulatory authorities. Even if the *de jure* regulatory framework of a Member applying for recognition is satisfactory, *de facto* inefficiencies in its administration may prevent trust, as well as a possibility of recognition. In this regards, it might be argued that the risks of non-fulfillment of the legitimate objective in this case would be higher, which should not be the case for a valid alternative measure according to the panel in *Australia – Tobacco Plain Packaging*.[112] This determination, however, would depend on the circumstances of a specific case. If a Member outside the recognition arrangement has a high quality of a regulatory framework, a lack of any possibility for its regulations and assessment systems to be recognized could be viewed as unreasonable. Thus, providing an opportunity for recognition subject to a number of conditions could be considered as an alternative measure.

It might also be argued that the proposed alternative could not be reasonably available as it would create an undue burden for the importing country that would be additionally tasked with evaluating and supervising other Members' regulatory frameworks and facilities. In this respect, one might recall that to be reasonably available the alternative measure shall not create an excessive burden,[113] such as substantial technical difficulties and prohibitive costs.[114] However, at the same time, it does not mean that the alternative measures are not supposed to generate any costs and burden.[115] Whether or not a burden associated with an alternative measure is excessive would be determined on a case-by-case basis.

[111] Panel Report, *Australia – Tobacco Plain Packaging*, para. 7.1364; Appellate Body Report, *Australia – Tobacco Plain Packaging*, para. 6.461.

[112] Panel Report, *Australia – Tobacco Plain Packaging*, para. 7.1528.

[113] Panel Report, *Australia – Tobacco Plain Packaging*, para. 7.1709. This interpretation also follows the Appellate Body's interpretation in *US – Gambling* in the context of the "necessity" analysis under Article XX of the GATT: "*An alternative measure may be found not to be 'reasonably available', however, where it is merely theoretical in nature, for instance, where the responding Member is not capable of taking it, or where the measure imposes an undue burden on that Member, such as prohibitive costs or substantial technical difficulties*." (para. 308).

[114] Appellate Body Reports, *US – Gambling*, para. 308, *Colombia – Textiles*, para. 5.74. See also Appellate Body Report, *EC – Seal Products*, where the Appellate Body agreed with the panel that the alternative measure would not be reasonably available, as it would be difficult to implement and enforce (para. 5.279).

[115] Appellate Body Report, *China – Publications and Audiovisual Products*, paras. 326–327.

A similar analysis of "necessity" could be made in the context of conformity assessment procedures under Article 5.1.2 requiring that the Members' conformity assessment procedures shall not be stricter than necessary to provide "an adequate confidence" to the importing Member that the products conform to the applicable technical regulations. Similarly, a key conceptual tool here would be to examine possible alternative measures that could have been less strict. In case of mutual recognition of conformity assessment, an alternative measure providing a possibility of access for other Members to the recognition arrangement could have similar reservations as described above. Therefore, mutual recognition agreements and arrangements with exclusionary membership risk being found as unnecessarily restricting trade.

3.5.3.3 SPS Agreement and the GATS: Openness of the Regional Agreements and Arrangements

A confirmation for the interpretation that mutual recognition agreements, in principle, have to provide a possibility for other WTO Members to enjoy a similar preferential treatment under certain conditions can be found in other WTO Agreements. These are the Agreement on Sanitary and Phytosanitary Measures (SPS Agreement) and the General Agreement on Trade in Services (GATS).[116]

The SPS Agreement provides a strong obligation of Members to accept the SPS measures of other Members as equivalent if the exporting Member objectively demonstrates that its measure achieves the importing Member's appropriate level of protection, despite that the measures themselves might differ. It further clarifies that

> Members shall, upon request, enter into consultations with the aim of achieving bilateral and multilateral agreements on recognition of the equivalence of specified sanitary or phytosanitary measures.[117]

Moreover, in 2001, the WTO SPS Committee explained the mechanism of this rule: The importing Member has to clearly identify the appropriate level of protection that the relevant measure is aimed to ensure, while the exporting Member has to provide a reasonable access to the importing Member to inspect its facilities in order to determine the equivalence between the two measures.[118] Therefore, the equivalence recognition is open and other Members might also be granted such recognition.

---

[116] See such interpretation in Bartels (2005), p. 705; Trachtman (2013), p. 354.

[117] Agreement on Sanitary and Phytosanitary Measures, Articles 4.1 and 4.2.

[118] WTO, Committee on Sanitary and Phytosanitary Measures (2001) Decision on the Implementation of Article 4 of the Agreement on the Application of Sanitary and Phytosanitary Measures, G/SPS/19, 2001. Reviewed in 2004; See the relevant interpretation of this provisions in Trachtman (2007a), p. 788.

Similarly, Article VII of the GATS, which allows for agreements or arrangements on recognition of standards, licensing and certification of services, also provides that members of such arrangements.

> shall afford adequate opportunity for other interested Members to negotiate their accession to such an agreement or arrangement or to negotiate comparable ones with it.[119]

Although the above provisions of the SPS Agreement and the GATS do not directly imply that a similar approach is taken in the TBT Agreement, but it might be considered as a "context" in the meaning of the Vienna Convention on the Law of Treaties[120] and as another argument of the drafters' preference for "open" mutual recognition. A possible argument that the drafters explicitly decided to exclude technical barriers to trade from the "open" type of recognition is not very convincing as it is difficult to imagine a reason why SPS measures (relating to risks to human, animal and plant life or health) would be subject to the equivalence consideration requirement, while TBT would not.

3.5.4 Is the Regional Exception Clause Available?

The present section analyses whether these regional provisions on mutual recognition are effectively captured by the specific regional integration disciplines in the GATT—Article XXIV—and thereby whether the latter can provide authorization for departure from substantive disciplines of the WTO agreements.

This research is focusing on mutual recognition and does not go further into the analysis whether regional harmonization disciplines could fall under Article XXIV. As was mentioned by Joel Trachtman, application of Article XXIV to regional harmonization would create an absurd situation where regular domestic rules would be subject to a stricter control than those measures adopted as a result of harmonization within an RTA.[121]

Because of a lack of clarity in Article XXIV on the issue of applicability to mutual recognition and considering the fact that Article XXIV was drafted decades ago when increasingly "deep" forms of integration could hardly be envisaged (Sect. 3.1), this question has been contentious and broadly discussed in academic literature, for example, in works of Joel Trachtman,[122] Lorand Bartels,[123] James Mathis,[124] Nicolas Lokhard and Andrew Mitchel,[125] notably without rendering consensus

---

[119] General Agreement on Trade in Services, Article VII:2.

[120] Vienna Convention on the Law of Treaties, Article 31, para. 2.

[121] Trachtman (2003), p. 463.

[122] Trachtman (2003).

[123] Bartels (2005).

[124] Mathis (1998).

[125] Lokhard and Mitchell (2005), p. 236.

among scholars. This section focuses particularly on FTAs, as they are subject of this research, although the analysis in respect of CUs would not essentially differ on this issue.

First, considering the legal test of Article XXIV and its relevant case law, this section provides arguments on whether harmonization and mutual recognition could fall under the scope of Article XXIV—in particular, whether technical regulations that they tackle could be considered as "other restrictive regulations of commerce" that have to be eliminated on "substantially all the trade" between the parties, and how, if it is the case, the requirement not to raise barriers for third parties could be satisfied. Second, it examines the relationship between Article XXIV GATT and the TBT Agreement to establish whether the provisions of Article XXIV could effectively be applied to cases of violation of the TBT Agreement.

3.5.4.1 Article XXIV GATT Legal Test

As was mentioned earlier, Article XXIV GATT exempts preferences negotiated within an FTA or a CU (or an interim agreement leading thereto) from their extension to all WTO Members as the MFN principle would require. This exemption is, however, subject to a set of conditions to minimize the adverse impact that preferential arrangements may have on the multilateral system. Before going into the analysis of the conditions, it is worthwhile to look into paragraph 4, which spells out the underlying aspiration of Article XXIV—to balance regional integration with multilateral liberalization:

> . . .They [the contracting parties] also recognize that the purpose of a customs union or of a free-trade area should be to facilitate trade between the constituent territories and not to raise barriers to the trade of other contracting parties with such territories.

A point should be made about the nature of paragraph 4 of GATT Article XXIV, as there have been discussions on its legal value: whether it provides a stand-alone obligation to balance the goals of regional integration and multilateralism.[126] It was made pretty clear by the Appellate Body in *Turkey – Textiles* that

> [p]aragraph 4 contains purposive, and not operative, language. It does not set forth a separate obligation itself but, rather, sets forth the overriding and pervasive purpose for Article XXIV which is manifested in operative language in the specific obligations that are found elsewhere in Article XXIV.[127]

Therefore, paragraph 4 does not require a separate balancing exercise. As was noted by the Appellate Body, its value is in providing a "context" to Article XXIV.[128] However, it is important to keep in mind that the context still might be very

[126] See., e.g., Davey (2011), p. 237.

[127] Appellate Body Report, *Turkey – Textiles*, para. 57.

[128] Ibid., para. 56.

important in interpreting the substantive obligations that are addressed in ensuing paragraphs.

3.5.4.1.1 Internal Requirement for FTAs Formation (Art. XXIV:8)

The internal requirement for the formation of RTAs is spelled out in paragraph 8 of Article XXIV, where an FTA is qualified as follows:

> . . .a group of two or more customs territories in which the duties and other restrictive regulations of commerce (except, where necessary, those permitted under Articles XI, XII, XIII, XIV, XV and XX) are eliminated on substantially all the trade between the constituent territories in products originating in such territories.[129]

Immediately it triggers the question which barriers have to be eliminated and to what extent. As regards the extent of trade liberalization, it is encoded in a phrase "substantially all the trade". It is not detailed how much trade between the parties it actually requires to liberalize and whether it is possible to shield certain sensitive sectors (for instance, agriculture) from the coverage. The Appellate Body's ruling in *Turkey – Textiles* also does not provide much guidance: "it is not the same as all the trade, and also. . . something considerably more than merely some of the trade."[130] The WTO Members' deliberations in the Committee on Regional Trade Agreements reflected a range of views on this issue as well.[131] What paragraph 8 clearly implies is that trade has to be liberalized in a comprehensive manner, which precludes sectoral deals. The example of the latter could be found in the *Canada – Autos* case, where Canada granted under its Auto Pact an import duty exemption to producers affiliated with Canadian producers, which were *de facto* American companies. The Auto Pact was found inconsistent with the MFN clause under the GATT[132] and although in this case the Article XXIV defense was rejected for different reasons, it could also be argued that the Auto Pact was not a sufficiently comprehensive deal, as paragraph 8 of Article XXIV requires.[133] There could be a case, however, where the result is less evident, as there is no prescription on the percentage of trade or the amount of tariff lines to be covered. Therefore, despite that conspicuously limited deals are prohibited, paragraph 8 allows the RTA's parties certain flexibility in designing their agreements.

Another troubling term contained in Article XXIV is "other restrictive regulations of commerce" (ORRC), which, along with tariffs have to be eliminated on

---

[129] Paragraph 8(b) of Article XXIV. A definition of a CU is essentially the same, except that it also requires that 'substantially the same duties and other regulations of commerce' to be applied to trade outside the union (para. 8(a)(i)(ii) of Article XXIV GATT).

[130] Appellate Body Report, *Turkey – Textiles*, para. 48.

[131] Davey (2011), p. 252.

[132] Appellate Body Report, *Canada – Autos,* para. 86.

[133] See this line of argumentation on *Canada-Autos* case in Lydgate and Winters (2019), p. 457; See on Article XXIV defense being denied, Panel Report, *Canada – Autos*, para. 10.56.

"substantially all the trade" between the RTA parties. Article XXIV leaves open the question on how broad this category is and what it should encompass.

However, along the term of ORRC there is also a term of "other regulations of commerce" (ORC), which, as paragraph 5 of Article XXIV states, should not be more restrictive after the formation of the FTA (or CU) than before its formation. This research considers ORRC and ORC as similar concepts. It agrees with Joel Trachtman's analysis that the text and context of paragraph 5 of Article XXIV suggests that "the only ORCs actually addressed are those that are 'restrictive'".[134]

The panel in *Turkey – Textiles* clarified the meaning of "other regulations of commerce" (ORC) (referred to in paragraph 5). In *Turkey – Textiles*, the panel ruled that ORC is an evolving concept (and thus the same is true for the ORRC) given the dynamic nature of RTAs and that it encompasses any regulation having an effect on trade:

> [T]he ordinary meaning of the terms "other regulations of commerce" could be understood to include any regulation having an impact (such as measures in the fields covered by WTO rules, e.g. sanitary and phytosanitary, customs valuation, anti-dumping, technical barriers to trade; as well as any other trade related domestic regulation, e.g. environmental standards, export credit schemes). Given the dynamic nature of regional trade agreements, we consider that this is an evolving concept.[135]

This broad reading raises however some doubts primarily for the fear that it could lead to an obligation for FTA parties to dismantle a broad range of restrictions, which might not always be feasible and desirable.[136] Paragraph 8 provides that measures permitted under Articles XI-XV and XX GATT are exempted from the requirement to eliminate duties and ORRC, but it poses more questions than it clarifies the situation. If the term ORRC is to be read broadly, would this mean that all other possible ORRC (except those covered by the exceptions) have to be necessarily eliminated for the RTA to be formed? This reading would lead to an absurd conclusion that RTA must include a "deep" trade agenda, which would obviously contradict years of WTO Members' practice when RTAs used to cover only tariffs.

On the other hand, if ORRC are read in a limited fashion (by only including tariffs and other border measures), it could mean that Article XXIV would not justify these measures and thus it could raise the question whether it is fit for today's realities of global commerce. It would also contradict the Appellate Body's interpretation of the ORRC as an "evolving concept", and it would not align with the purpose of the regional exception in the GATT "to facilitate trade between the constituent territories".

What we have to look into is the nature of the Article XXIV GATT legal obligation in paragraph 8. Would a qualification as ORRC necessarily imply that they have to be eliminated? Nicolas Lokhard and Andrew Mitchell pointed out in this regard that paragraph 8 "focuses on the level of restrictions, not the type", and

[134] Trachtman (2011), p. 139.

[135] Panel Report, *Turkey – Textiles*, para. 9.120.

[136] See., e.g., Howse and Langille (2018), p. 672.

therefore, the parties have a right to decide which restrictions to remove.[137] In the same vein, Joost Pauwelyn notes that Article XXIV requires to eliminate restrictions on "substantially all the trade" and not to eliminate all trade restrictions between the parties, except those necessary under the exceptions.[138] The list of exceptions, in Pauwelyn's view is misleading itself, as it creates an impression that all the other restrictions have to be eliminated, except those few. Even if the term ORRC is read in a limited fashion, it would be odd to assume that other possible GATT exceptions such as national security (Article XXI), or additional restrictions for developing countries (Article XVIII:B) would necessarily have to be eliminated between the RTA partners.[139] Therefore, the list of exceptions is not informative in interpreting a legal obligation in paragraph 8. Since paragraph 8 focuses primarily on the level of restrictions and not the type, as soon as the "substantially all the trade" requirement is met, an RTA has to be considered legal. This, however, does not mean that the parties cannot go further in liberalizing trade between them by dismantling a variety of ORRC that would be covered by the Article XXIV exception.

3.5.4.1.2 External Requirement for RTAs Formation (Art. XXIV:5)

The external requirement for the formation of an FTA embodies the WTO Members' intention to minimize the restrictive effects of preferential deals for the outsiders, which is in line with the very intent of Article XXIV: to liberalize trade while not raising barriers. Paragraph 5 of Article XXIV states as follows:

> . . .(b) with respect to a free-trade area, or an interim agreement leading to the formation of a free trade area, the duties and other regulations of commerce maintained in each of the constituent territories and applicable at the formation of such free trade area or the adoption of such interim agreement to the trade of contracting parties not included in such area or not parties to such agreement shall not be higher or more restrictive than the corresponding duties and other regulations of commerce existing in the same constituent territories prior to the formation of the free trade area, or interim agreement as the case may be. . .

Essentially, it envisages a comparison between "duties" and "other regulations of commerce" (ORC) before and after an FTA formation.[140] This comparison raises some difficult questions. The first one is how to demonstrate the deterioration of treatment vis-à-vis third countries. While to measure tariffs and quotas seems to be an easier task, the restrictive effects of "deep" trade provisions, as a rule, are more difficult to establish. The *Understanding on interpretation of Article XXIV* provides a certain guidance stating that for quantification of ORC, "the examination of individual measures, regulations, products covered and trade flows affected may

[137] Lokhard and Mitchell (2005), p. 227.
[138] Pauwelyn (2004), p. 127.
[139] Ibid.
[140] See Lokhard and Mitchell (2005), p. 251.

be required", essentially appealing to the economic test.[141] It is further interpreted by the panel in the *Turkey – Textiles* case:

> . . .the effects of the resulting trade measures and policies of the new regional agreement shall not be more restrictive, overall, than were the constituent countries' previous trade policies.[142]

Therefore, it begs the analysis of "trade restrictiveness" of the measures in question in relation to third countries before and after an FTA. However, certain negative external effects might inevitably stem from the fact of integration, which leads to a second major question—whether all the possible negative trade effects for third countries render the measure inconsistent with paragraph 5 of Article XXIV. This question was addressed by the Appellate Body in the *Turkey – Textiles* case, where it established the so-called "necessity test": the measure has to be indispensable for the RTA formation meaning that if it is not allowed, the RTA would be prevented.[143] The following sub-section explains this interpretation of the *Turkey – Textiles* "necessity test" in more details.

3.5.4.1.3 The Turkey – Textiles "Necessity" Test

The *Turkey – Textiles* case concerned the quantitative restrictions on textiles and clothing, which Turkey imposed as a result of negotiating a CU with the EU in 1996. India, the complainant, argued that these restrictions were inconsistent with Articles XI and XIII of the GATT, as well as Article 2.4 of the Agreement on Textiles and Clothing, while Turkey justified the alleged violations by resorting to an Article XXIV defense.

Importantly, when analyzing the legal test of Article XXIV, the Appellate Body drew particular attention to the chapeau of paragraph 5:

> Accordingly, the provisions of this Agreement shall not prevent, as between the territories of contracting parties, the formation of a customs union or of a free-trade area or the adoption of an interim agreement necessary for the formation of a customs union or of a free-trade area. . .

In examining the text of the chapeau, the Appellate Body emphasized the words "shall not prevent" and "the formation of a customs union" and came to the following conclusion:

> This wording indicates that Article XXIV can justify the adoption of a measure which is inconsistent with certain other GATT provisions only if the measure is introduced upon the

---

[141] Understanding on Interpretation of Article XXIV of the General Agreement on Tariffs and Trade, para. 2. This Understanding is a part of GATT 1994. https://www.wto.org/english/tratop_e/region_e/region_art24_e.htm#understanding. Accessed 1 Nov 2022.

[142] Panel Report, *Turkey – Textiles*, para. 9.121. The Appellate Body also agreed with this interpretation, see Appellate Body Report, *Turkey – Textiles*, para. 55.

[143] Appellate Body Report, *Turkey – Textiles*, paras. 46, 58.

formation of a customs union, and only to the extent that the formation of the customs union would be prevented if the introduction of the measure were not allowed.[144]

This analysis on whether a measure is necessary for the formation of an RTA ("necessity test") was introduced as a separate step of the Article XXIV consistency examination, in addition to internal and external requirements. The Appellate Body also pointed out that such interpretation would go in line with the purpose of Article XXIV contained in paragraph 4, which constitutes a context for the chapeau of paragraph 5—to balance trade liberalization within an RTA with trade restrictiveness for third parties. Further to this legal reasoning, the Appellate Body concluded that the quantitative restrictions imposed by Turkey were not "necessary" for the establishment of a CU with the EU as the parties could introduce rules of origin as a less trade restrictive alternative, and thus the measure did not pass the Article XXIV consistency test.[145]

Later on, validity and precise meaning of the "necessity test" have been subject to debate among legal scholars. Since the "deep" trade provisions go beyond the minimalistic scope of tariff reductions, on first reading, it follows that, based on the *Turkey – Textiles* "necessity test", they might not enjoy the Article XXIV exception (broad interpretation of "necessity test" where every measure upon RTA's formation has to be assessed). Lorand Bartels applies this understanding, when contending that mutual recognition is highly unlikely to fall under the Article XXIV exception as it could hardly be viewed as necessary to establish an RTA.[146]

A polar view was put forward by Joost Pauwelyn, who overall criticized the Appellate Body's determination of the "necessity test" claiming a lack of textual basis thereof, and also pointing out that such determination would unduly constraint the ability of WTO members to liberalize trade, which is at the core of Article XXIV GATT.[147] Similarly, Christoph Herrmann underlines that measures necessary for deeper economic integration go further than what is necessary for the establishment of a customs union. Therefore, a broad reading of the *Turkey – Textiles* test could render all deeper integration illegal from the WTO perspective.[148]

Also, Joel Trachtman, as well as Nicolas Lockhard and Andrew Mitchel, while not dismantling the Appellate Body's ruling on "necessity", suggest to interpret it in a more confined fashion as pertaining only to inconsistencies arising from external trade restrictions (narrow interpretation of "necessity test").[149] First, Lockhard and Mitchel notice that the Appellate Body did not formulate the test clearly by not distinguishing between inconsistencies arising from internal or external trade restrictions, but the case with Turkey certainly involved restrictions on the external trade of a CU, which could suggest that the "necessity test" was designed only for this

[144] Appellate Body Report, *Turkey – Textiles*, para. 46.

[145] Appellate Body Report, *Turkey – Textiles*, para. 62.

[146] Bartels (2005), p. 713.

[147] Pauwelyn (2004), pp. 134–135.

[148] Herrmann (2008), p. 278.

[149] Trachtman (2013), pp. 338–340; Lokhard and Mitchell (2005), pp. 226–227.

specific context.[150] This understanding was supported by the panel in the *US – Line Pipe* case where it denied the broad interpretation of "necessity" in *Turkey – Textiles*. The panel emphasized the value of Article XXIV:8 as being decisive in determining the scope of Article XXIV. It found that if the measure at issue constitutes "the elimination of 'duties and other restrictive regulations of commerce'", the question of necessity of such measure should not be raised anymore.[151] Such interpretation also goes in line with the principle of effectiveness in treaty interpretation, which requires adopting a reading that would give meaning to all the provisions in the agreement.[152] The broad interpretation of "necessity" would deprive paragraph 8 of its meaning specifically when it comes to a requirement to discipline ORRC, which, as the panel confirmed in *Turkey – Textiles*, is an evolving concept and could include a broad range of measures.[153] Thus, incorporation of ORRC would in most cases inevitably lead to more than a minimalistic scope of an RTA and would risk failing to pass the "necessity test". It would result in an odd situation, when one clause of Article XXIV would require a measure to be disciplined, while another would lead to it being found unnecessary. Moreover, the broad interpretation of "necessity" would hardly represent a fair balance between RTA's integration benefits and detriments to third party commerce—aspiration of Article XXIV contained in paragraph 4, to which the Appellate Body in *Turkey – Textiles* also refers in developing its "necessity test".[154] It would simply constrain the preferential agreements to a very basic scope.

A narrow reading of the "necessity test" is consistent with the panel's conclusion in *US – Line Pipe*, which juxtaposed the measure in *Turkey – Textiles* to the measure in *US – Line Pipe*. The measure in the latter case was the exclusion of FTA partners from safeguard measures. It found that while in the case of *Turkey – Textiles* it was entirely appropriate to require the parties to demonstrate necessity of the measure (as it directly deteriorates trade with third parties), the measure in the *US – Line Pipe* case should not face an identical approach as it arises from elimination of duties and ORRC, the very *raison d'être* of an FTA.[155]

Following this interpretation, it would be logical to consider the "necessity test" as an element of the "external requirement" for RTAs formation. It is also relevant that the provision, which gave rise thereto, is contained in paragraph 5 of Article

---

[150] Lokhard and Mitchell (2005), p. 226.

[151] Panel Report, *US – Line Pipe*, para. 7.148.

[152] See the *US – Gasoline* case, where the Appellate Body used the principle of effectiveness emphasizing that the "interpreter is not free to adopt a reading that would result in reducing whole clauses or paragraphs of a treaty to redundancy or inutility" (Appellate Body Report, *US – Gasoline*, para. 21).

[153] Panel Report, *Turkey – Textiles*, para. 9.120.

[154] See this argument also in Trachtman (2013), p. 340.

[155] Panel Report, *US – Line Pipe*, para 7.148. The Appellate Body did not review this argument. It denied the overall applicability of Article XXIV in the case because of the failure of the US to satisfy the requirement of "parallelism" between investigated imports and imports subject to a safeguard, Appellate Body Report, *US – Line Pipe*, paras. 198, 199.

XXIV. Therefore, despite that the Appellate Body in *Turkey – Textiles* considered the "necessity test" as a separate legal requirement, it appears more consistent to view it as a part of analysis under paragraph 5. Such an interpretation would also better reconcile with the fact that the Appellate Body is supposed to only interpret existing WTO Agreements and it is not supposed to create law in its own right.

3.5.4.2 Mutual Recognition in RTAs and Article XXIV of the GATT

As for the application of the Article XXIV legal test to mutual recognition in FTAs, several issues are to be explored. The main question is whether TBT measures could fall under the category of ORRC and thereby be subject to Article XXIV coverage according to the internal requirement for FTA formation (paragraph 8). Another question is whether Article XXIV would justify harmonization and mutual recognition, despite that it creates a more favorable regime for RTA partners. Here, consistency with the external requirements under paragraph 5 should be analyzed and whether the *Turkey – Textiles* "necessity test" is to be applied.

It is worth mentioning that there is no consensus regarding whether TBT measures could fall under the purview of Article XXIV of the GATT. It has already been stated above that Article XXIV was developed when tariffs were considered to be the most relevant trade barriers and thus it could be suggested that it fails to adequately address today's realities. Whether or not Article XXIV has to be interpreted in the evolutionary manner, it is up to further practice.

The below approach presents a mere possibility (based on the author's own interpretation) that TBT measures could in principle be addressed under Article XXIV of the GATT when it comes to the justification based on GATT, but Article XXIV of the GATT cannot justify the inconsistency arising from the TBT Agreement.

3.5.4.2.1 Internal Requirement for RTAs Formation: TBT Measures as ORRC

The difficulty in interpreting TBT measures as ORRC mostly stems from the fact that they have a dual character—on the one hand, they are targeted at legitimate public policy objectives, but on the other—they may as well restrict trade.

Some scholars argue that considering all TBT measures as ORRC would go against the countries' notion of sovereignty in establishing their regulatory framework, as it would imply that the parties would be required to eliminate TBT measures on "substantially all the trade", which would be highly intrusive into the WTO members' domestic regulatory policies, especially taking into account the legitimate character of TBT measures.[156] In this regard, a previously discussed broad reading of the *Turkey – Textiles* "necessity test" comes into play.

There are few arguments that have to be made in this regard. Firstly, as was mentioned earlier, paragraph 8 of Article XXIV does not necessarily imply that all ORRC have to be eliminated. It focuses on the level and not the type of restrictions: As soon as an RTA eliminates barriers on "substantially all the trade" between the parties, the requirement of paragraph 8 is satisfied.

Secondly, a qualification of TBT measures as ORRC would not mean that the parties necessarily have to negotiate mutual recognition as a method to address them. While the term "elimination" is clear in relation to duties or other quantifiable restrictions, it is far less clear when it comes to TBT measures, in particular, which level of integration it would imply. There is nothing suggesting that it would necessarily require the closest forms of integration. It appears that in any case the RTA parties have a flexibility when it comes to methods to address TBT measures. When criticizing the application of Article XXIV to TBT measures, Robert Howse by "elimination" means such close forms as harmonization and mutual recognition. However, there exist a multiplicity of other forms to tackle this type of measures. For instance, Joel Trachtman points to non-discrimination and necessity requirements.[157] Nothing in Article XXIV precludes the parties from choosing one type of TBT liberalization over another.

Thirdly, in case it is found that the elimination requirement under Article XXIV encompasses the closest form of integration and such elimination is necessary to achieve "substantially all the trade" level of concessions within an RTA, there is a possibility to exclude genuinely legitimate TBT measures from its scope by way of applying Article XX—an exception from the elimination requirement according to Article XXIV:8.

All in all, as it follows from this analysis, TBT measures could potentially fall under the category of ORRC under paragraph 8 of Article XXIV.

---

[156] Howse and Langille (2018), p. 672; See also Trachtman (2013), p. 346; It is also relevant to note that there appears to be no consensus among WTO members on this issue. In early 2000s, WTO members expressed diverging views on this issue at the Doha Round: Korea, for instance, argued that all non-tariff measured should fall under a broad category of regulations of commerce, while India denied this possibility for TBT and SPS measures and the EU argued for the neutrality test: a regulation of commerce can only be permissible if it is consistent with WTO Agreements. For reference, see the following WTO negotiation records: TN/RL/W/114, 2003, pp. 3–5; TN/RL/W/116, 2003, pp. 2–3; TN/RL/W/179, 2005, p. 4. (This account has largely been taken from Davey (2011)).

[157] Trachtman (2013), pp. 349–350. On a separate note, Trachtman also argues that these are the only forms of tackling TBT and SPS measures that could be required under Article XXIV, but further on he notes that this does not seem to have a particular significance, as the WTO Agreements already have similar provisions.

3.5.4.2.2 External Requirement for RTAs Formation: Trade Restrictiveness of Mutual Recognition for Third Countries

The applicability of Article XXIV to mutual recognition would also depend on how it is balanced against trade restrictiveness for third countries. Following the clarifications of the *Understanding on interpretation of Article XXIV,* this would require the examination of trade restrictiveness of a new RTA in comparison to the constituent territories' previous trade policies. Therefore, the main question should be whether and to which extent mutual recognition could negatively affect trade from third countries. If such negative effect is established, then, further to the above clarifications on the *Turkey – Textiles* "necessity test", it should be examined whether it was necessary for RTA establishment.

As it was described in Sect. 3.3 of this Chapter, mutual recognition might be a trade facilitative tool, which could also benefit the outsiders. The adverse trade divertive effects would depend on a design of mutual recognition. In particular, if mutual recognition is subject to rules of origin, the positive implications for outsiders are diminished and, similarly to the effects of tariffs, "the intra-regional trade can be expected to increase at the expense of imports from third countries".[158] In this case, the "necessity" of such measure may be questioned under the *Turkey – Textiles* "necessity test". According to the standard established by the Appellate Body, the analysis has to take into account less trade restrictive alternative measures that could achieve a similar level of integration, in which case a model without rules of origin might be suggested. Application of rules of origin would be difficult to justify as "necessary", as it would treat differently products coming from outside the preferential area even when that they are fully compliant with the recognized regulations and could pass all the necessary assessment procedures.

Therefore, it could be suggested that mutual recognition falls under the purview of Article XXIV of the GATT. However, this answers only a part of the question of their possible justifiability under the regional exception clause, as the main question would be whether Article XXIV could justify potential inconsistencies under the TBT Agreement.

3.5.4.2.3 Is Article XXIV GATT Applicable to Violations of the TBT Agreement?

A finding that mutual recognition could fall under the Article XXIV GATT legal claim establishes a possibility to use Article XXIV as a defence in case a substantive obligation under the GATT is being violated by these measures. However, what is more important whether Article XXIV could be used as a defence in case of violations of the TBT Agreement.

---

[158] Chen and Matoo (2008), p. 840.

Article XXIV and Other Multilateral Agreements

Notably, Article XXIV GATT clearly states that its provisions refer to "this Agreement" (GATT), and, although it could be argued that this text is simply an inheritance from the old GATT era, when GATT 1947 was the only multilateral agreement, while after the Uruguay Round and the adoption of a set of other multilateral agreements on goods, this wording should not be understood in such a limited fashion, it still remains unclear what exactly the relationship is between GATT Article XXIV and other Uruguay Round agreements on goods—in this context, the TBT Agreement.

To begin exploring this question, an important stipulation has to be made regarding the relationship between the multilateral agreements. The fact is that they have been adopted as "integral parts" of a single treaty—the Marrakesh Agreement establishing the WTO. Article II:2 of the Marrakesh Agreement clearly states this status. Here is how the Appellate Body in *China – Rare Earths* interprets this relationship:

> …[T]he Marrakesh Agreement is the umbrella under which all of the annexed Multilateral Trade Agreements are united in a single package of rights and obligations.[159]

A number of clarifications in case law also mostly refer to the "cumulative" application of obligations under the WTO agreements. For example, this has been established in relation between GATT and GATS in *EC – Bananas III*[160] and *Canada – Periodicals*,[161] or between GATT and the Agreement on Safeguards in *Korea – Dairy*[162] and *Argentina – Footware*.[163] However, while the general "cumulative" application test seems to be well established, what remains less clear is how individual provisions of the WTO agreements relate to each other, especially in cases when they discipline the same subject matter but approach it differently. In this context, would the "cumulative" application of WTO agreements allow for a possibility of a cross-application of exceptions from one agreement to another?

There is a variety of views on this matter. Lorand Bartels, on the one hand, denies this possibility when looking into the relationship between the GATT exceptions and the TBT Agreement. His argument is premised on the analysis of the General Interpretative Note to Annex IA of the Marrakesh Agreement, which clarifies the relationship between various WTO agreements on goods by stating the following:

> In the event of conflict between a provision of the General Agreement on Tariffs and Trade 1994 and a provision of another agreement in Annex 1A to the Agreement Establishing the World Trade Organization (referred to in the agreements in Annex 1A as the "WTO

[159] Appellate Body Report, *China – Rare Earths,* para 5.47.

[160] Appellate Body Report, *EC – Bananas III*, p. 591.

[161] Appellate Body Report, *Canada – Periodicals*, p. 449.

[162] Appellate Body Report, *Korea – Dairy*, para. 77.

[163] Appellate Body Report, *Argentina – Footwear*, para. 81.

Agreement"), the provision of the other agreement shall prevail to the extent of the conflict.[164]

In Lorand Bartel's view, following this provision, in case the GATT allows some measure by virtue of its exceptions but TBT prohibits it, that would create a "conflict" in which the TBT prohibition should prevail.[165]

A polar opinion was expressed by Trachtman, who argued that the two agreements should not be read in total isolation, but as a single package of rights and obligations. He promotes the idea of "effective interpretation" of WTO agreements, according to which more specific provisions on goods in the TBT and SPS agreements, as being parts of a "single undertaking", should be treated in the same manner as the general provisions on goods in the GATT agreement and hence should enjoy the same exceptions.[166] He contends that the General Interpretative Note does not provide much guidance when it comes to cross-application of exceptions, as, based on available case law, a "conflict" between agreements should be understood as when one agreement requires (and not when it authorizes) what another agreement forbids. This is not the case when it comes to the exceptions provided in the GATT. According to Trachtman, a situation where there is a prohibition under a more specific agreement on goods and a right to use an exception under the GATT would not amount to a conflict.[167] The problem with Trachtman's reading is that the substantive obligations under the two agreements could differ bringing about a question whether it is going to be appropriate to transpose an exception, which was foreseen for a different set of obligations. If there is no link to the GATT exceptions in the TBT Agreement, how is it possible than to identify that the negotiators indeed intended to have it for measures covered by the TBT Agreement?

When we turn to case law, we see that the panels and the Appellate Body did not deny the cross-application of exceptions, but the only fact that all the multilateral agreements constitute a "single undertaking" was found insufficient for such application. The Appellate Body looked into the question whether there was a direct reference or a close link between the provisions in the GATT and the other multilateral agreements on goods. Nicolas Lokhard and Andrew Mitchell illustrate it with the examples from the *Turkey – Textiles* and *US – Line Pipe* cases, where the Appellate Body in the former case and the panel in the latter applied Article XXIV to agreements other than the GATT.[168] In *Turkey – Textiles*, the Appellate Body's conclusion is explained by the fact that the allegedly violated Agreement on Textiles

---

[164] General Interpretative Note to Annex IA of the Marrakesh Agreement, Annex IA of the Marrakesh Agreement establishing the World Trade Organization, 1994.

[165] Bartels (2005), p. 714.

[166] Trachtman (2003), p. 473.

[167] Ibid., p. 472 (Trachtman cites Appellate Body reports on *Guatemala – Cement* (1998), para. 65; *Indonesia – Automobiles* (1998), paras. 14.29–14.36; *US – Hot-Rolled Steel* (2001), paras. 55, 62, etc.).

[168] Appellate Body Report, *Argentina-Footwear,* footnote 13; Panel Report, *US – Line Pipe*, para. 7.150. This account is largely taken from Lokhard and Mitchell (2005), pp. 228–229.

and Clothing makes a direct reference to restrictions allowed under the GATT. In *US – Line Pipe,* there was no such direct reference, but the panel's finding is based on the close link between Article XIX of the GATT and the Agreement on Safeguards, as the latter is a development of the former. The Appellate Body in *US – Line Pipe* did not review the applicability of Article XXIV leaving this question subject to speculation, however, there is a number of cases which also interpreted the Agreement on Safeguards as a direct elaboration of Article XIX GATT, although for other purposes—e.g., *Argentina – Footwear (EC)*[169] and *US – Steel Safeguards.*[170] In *Argentina – Footwear*, the Appellate Body held that the requirements of the GATT and the Agreement on Safeguards should apply cumulatively.[171] Joost Pauwelyn contends that this close link is a channel through which Article XXIV GATT should be applied. He underscores that Article XIX of the GATT links the Agreement on Safeguards back to the GATT, which should then allow for the application of the GATT exceptions, including Article XXIV.[172]

It is instructive to look into recent WTO jurisprudence on a cross-application of exceptions, where the determinative elements also included either a direct reference or a close link. These cases examined the relationship between the provisions in China's Accession Protocol and the GATT general exceptions (Article XX). China's Accession Protocol is an integral part of the WTO package by virtue of Article XII of the Marrakesh Agreement (which defines the status of the accession protocols) and, therefore, its relationship with the GATT would equally (on the par with other multilateral agreements) be relevant in the present discussion. To date, there have been three major disputes addressing this relationship—*China – Audiovisual Products*, *China – Raw Materials* and *China – Rare Earths*, but only in one—*China – Audiovisual Products*—the Appellate Body found that Article XX was applicable to the provisions in China's Accession Protocol.[173] It has merit to look closer into the reasoning of the Appellate Body in these cases to identify why it adopted different findings in disputes involving the same agreements (GATT and the China's Accession Protocol) and eventually to better understand its approach for cross-application of exceptions.

In *China – Audiovisual Products*, China claimed its measures restricting market access and discriminating against imports of audiovisual products in violation of Article 5.1 of its Accession Protocol was justified under Article XX (a) GATT (protection of public morals). Reviewing admissibility of the GATT Article XX claim, the Appellate Body drew special attention to the wording of Article 5.1. This article generally provides for China's obligation to progressively liberalize trade to ensure that within three years as of its accession all its enterprises can have the right

---

[169] Appellate Body Report, *Argentina – Footwear*, para. 79.

[170] Appellate Body Report, *US – Steel Safeguards*, para. 275.

[171] Appellate Body Report, *Argentina – Footwear*, para. 89.

[172] Pauwelyn (2004), p. 129.

[173] Appellate Body Report, *China – Audiovisual Products*; Appellate Body Report, *China – Rare Earths*.

to import and export all goods, but also makes an important qualification in its first sentence: "[w]ithout prejudice to China's right to regulate trade in a manner consistent with the WTO Agreement...".[174] A reference to the WTO Agreement (the Marrakesh Agreement along with all multilateral agreements that are annexed thereto) was picked up by the Appellate Body as a link to the GATT exceptions. The Appellate Body found that the term "consistent with the WTO agreement" would include both the substantive obligations under the WTO agreements, as well as rights to derogate in line with the relevant exceptions.[175] Accordingly, this textual basis, which tied the provision of China's Accession Protocol with the exceptions under the WTO agreements, led to the Appellate Body's finding on the availability of Article XX GATT for the Accession Protocol violation.

The later disputes, in particular, *China – Raw Materials* and *China – Rare Earths* involved a different provision of China's Accession Protocol: Article 11.3 (prohibition of export restrictions), which in both cases China sought to justify pursuant to Article XX (g) of the GATT (protection of natural resources). The panels' and Appellate Body's decisions to deny the recourse to the GATT exception in these cases were based on several considerations. The first one followed the *China – Audiovisual Products'* reasoning. It examined whether there was direct textual basis in the allegedly violated provision that would permit its application, which rendered a negative answer. The panel in *China – Raw Materials* emphasized that what made the present situation distinct from *China – Audiovisual Products* is that in contrast to Article 5.1, Article 11.3 "does not include any express reference to Article XX of the GATT 1994, or to provisions of the GATT more generally".[176] Instead, Article 11.3 includes a "specific set of exceptions: those covered by Annex 6 [of the Accession Protocol] and those in conformity with GATT Article VIII" (based on the text of Article 11.3), hence the panel noted that it was not intended to incorporate any other exceptions for a given context.[177] In the appellate review, China claimed that Article XX should be applied via the Article VIII reference in Article 11.3; however, the Appellate Body denied this claim as Article VIII explicitly excluded the type of measures at issue—export duties—from its scope.[178]

What is also interesting in the Appellate Body's findings in both disputes is that they were not limited to the textual interpretation of the Protocol's provision alone. In *China – Raw Materials* the finding also relied onto other elements, such as China's Accession Working Party Report, the overall structure of Article 11 and a thorough analysis of its exceptions, to understand the context of the provision at issue and the intent of the negotiators.[179] This permitted the Appellate Body to conclude that

[174]WTO, Protocol of Accession of the People's Republic of China, WT/L/432, 23.11.2001.

[175]Appellate Body Report, *China – Audiovisual Products*, paras. 223, 228.

[176]Panel Report, *China – Raw Materials*, para. 7.124.

[177]Panel Report, *China – Raw Materials*, paras. 7.126–7.129.

[178]Appellate Body Report, *China – Raw Materials*, para. 290.

[179]This fact is specifically pinpointed in Appellate Body Report, *China – Rare Earths*, para. 284.

> . . .had there been a common intention to provide access to Article XX of the GATT 1994 in this respect, language to that effect would have been included in Paragraph 11.3 or elsewhere in China's Accession Protocol.[180]

In *China – Rare Earths*, the Appellate Body reached a similar conclusion, but its reasoning deserves particular attention, as it systematized the legal test for the cross-application of exceptions. Firstly, it confirmed a holistic interpretation of rights and obligations under the WTO agreements, but at the same time, clarified that

> [n]either obligations nor rights may be automatically transposed from one part of the legal framework into another.[181]

It also noted that

> . . .the mere fact that each of the Multilateral Trade Agreements is an integral part of the Marrakesh Agreement by virtue of Article II:2 of the Marrakesh Agreement does not, in and of itself, answer the question as to how specific rights and obligations contained in those Multilateral Trade Agreements relate to each other, particularly when they are contained in different instruments that nevertheless relate to the same subject matter.[182]

In order to establish this relationship between the specific provisions of the multilateral agreements and to identify whether there is an "objective link" between them, the Appellate Body took into account a number of factors and stated that the decision has to be made on a case-by-case basis.[183] The scrutiny of the text of the provision at issue should serve as a starting point, however, in many instances (here, the Appellate Body refers to the disputes involving the GATT and the Safeguards Agreement) the express language is not a sufficient indicator, in which case a "recourse to other interpretative elements will be necessary"[184] The interpretative elements are those which could help to identify the context of a provision: the text of the agreement at issue, other agreements of the WTO legal framework, or "any specific provisions that govern or shed light on the relationship between the provisions of different instruments".[185]

Additionally, it should be pointed out that one of the indicators of the context that could discern the intentions of the negotiators regarding this matter could be the fact that the issue of exception is resolved differently in the provision of the analyzed agreement. This was the case, for instance, in *China – Raw Materials*, where Article 11.3 specifically carved out two conditions where the parties could depart from the rule. Similarly, it is worthwhile taking a close look at the *US – Clove Cigarettes* case, where the Appellate Body denied the application of Article XX for the TBT violation based on the fact that Article 2.1 of the TBT Agreement itself along with the sixth

[180] Appellate Body Report, *China – Raw Materials*, para. 297.

[181] Appellate Body Report, *China – Rare Earths*, para 5.57.

[182] Appellate Body Report, *China – Rare Earths*, para. 5.53.

[183] Appellate Body Report, *China – Rare Earths*, para. 5.55.

[184] Appellate Body Report, *China – Rare Earths*, para. 5.56, see also para. 5.53.

[185] Appellate Body Report, *China – Rare Earths*, paras. 5.55, 5.62.

recital of the Preamble to the TBT Agreement contained a balance between trade liberalization and the members' right to regulate akin to Article XX GATT.[186]

The Case of Article XXIV and Mutual Recognition

Going back to the question of whether Article XXIV GATT could authorize the departure from the TBT Agreement, it is necessary, in line with the above case law, to analyze whether there is a reference in the text of the TBT Agreement or other contextual elements that would prove a link with the Article XXIV GATT exception.

The MFN obligation, which mutual recognition could potentially violate, is contained in the TBT Agreement, but is also disciplined by Article I:1 of the GATT. Could this, despite a lack of textual reference, point to an objective link between these provisions, where provisions of more specific agreements are the evolvement of a general one, similar to the case with the Agreement on Safeguards? Joost Pauwelyn disagrees with such interpretation noting that "[u]nlike in the Agreement on Safeguards, nothing in the SPS or TBT Agreement links the entire agreement back to a GATT provision."[187] The Agreement on Safeguards includes multiple references to the GATT,[188] while the TBT Agreement only briefly mentions in its preamble that it is concluded "desiring to further the objectives of the GATT".

However, based on the above cases involving China's Accession Protocol, the direct textual reference is not the only indicator of the close link between the multilateral agreements. It also requires a context to understand whether a lack of direct reference is an intentional omission.

For that, it could be instructive to analyze other parts of the TBT Agreement.[189] As discussed in Sect. 2.3.2.6 of Chap. 2, Articles 2.7 and 6.1 of the TBT Agreement already touch upon the issue of recognition of equivalence of other Members' technical regulations and conformity assessment procedures. In a non-binding manner they establish a possibility for recognition of equivalence of other Members regulations and conformity assessment procedures. These provisions, however, are not framed as exceptions from the TBT Agreement's obligations. They simply encourage Members to open up opportunities for other Members' technical regulations and conformity assessment procedures to be recognized. Moreover, as it was discussed in Sect. 2.3.2.6 of Chap. 2, they encourage to do it in an open manner, i.e., based on the fact whether the respective technical regulations and conformity assessment procedures "adequately fulfil the objectives" of a recognizing Member's regulation or "offer an assurance of conformity" "equivalent" to procedures of a recognizing Member. The equivalence has to be based on objective criteria, which

[186] Appellate Body Report, *US – Clove Cigarettes*, para. 109.

[187] Pauwelyn (2004), p. 129.

[188] E.g., the Preamble to the Agreement on Safeguards states that it serves to "clarify and reinforce the disciplines of the GATT 1994". Also, Article 1 states that the safeguard measures "shall be understood to mean those measures provided for in Article XIX of GATT 1994".

[189] Appellate Body Report, *China – Rare Earths*, paras. 5.55, 5.62.

other WTO Members (apart from the selected group) could potentially satisfy.[190] Moreover, Articles 6.3 and 10.7 specifically address the issue of mutual recognition agreements by encouraging their negotiation, but at the same time also require to enter into consultations with other Members to conclude similar agreements.

One could argue that it proves that the TBT Agreement's approach towards preferential deals is effectively different from Article XXIV GATT. As this issue is addressed in the TBT Agreement, the lack of similar disciplines as in Article XXIV might be intentional. This line of reasoning resonates with the *US – Clove Cigarettes* case where Article XX GATT was found inapplicable as the TBT Agreement itself contained a members' right to regulate based on legitimate objectives balanced against trade liberalization commitments.[191]

In sum, it appears that although Article XXIV could potentially be applicable to the inconsistencies arising from mutual recognition in RTAs (if to interpret Article XXIV in the evolutionary manner), there is little chance it could be used as a defence for TBT Agreement's violations.

3.5.5 *Proposal to Clarify Recognition Provisions of the TBT Agreement*

It has to be taken into account that mutual recognition agreements are the reality of today's world. They are concluded in various forms and modalities, within and outside the scope of RTAs. In view of the argument, that mutual recognition agreements have a trade facilitative function and deliver on the agenda of trade liberalization in the domains, where the WTO cannot offer an efficient instrument, it would not be the best strategy to discourage them. The argument that these agreements are not open enough to satisfy WTO requirements, does not seem to stop countries from entering into such agreements. Moreover, there has been no instance where any of mutual recognition agreements were challenged, although scholars have been repeatedly bringing to light their problematic legality under the WTO law: for example, mutual recognition under the EC – Turkey CU or MRA between the US and the EU.[192]

At the same time, in order to create a greater openness of the Members' regulatory regimes and to ensure that the motivation behind the Members' regulations are non-protectionist, but strictly based on legitimate considerations, it is worthwhile clarifying the mechanisms for recognition in the TBT Agreement. Although, as it was noted in Sect. 2.3.2.6 of Chap. 2, it appears that the respective WTO provisions have a preference for "open" recognition regimes, this "openness" is not enforceable.

---

[190] Bartels (2005), p. 705.

[191] Appellate Body Report, *US – Clove Cigarettes*, para. 109.

[192] For the former, see Bartels (2005), and, for the latter, Mathis (1998).

The equivalence provisions are contained in Articles 2.7 and 6.1 of the TBT Agreement. They are different from mutual recognition, as they do not have an element of reciprocity, but only unilateral equivalence based on the consideration that one Member's rules could satisfy the legitimate objective of another Member's regulation. They state the following:

> 2.7 Members shall give positive consideration to accepting as equivalent technical regulations of other Members, even if these regulations differ from their own, provided they are satisfied that these regulations adequately fulfil the objectives of their own regulations.
>
> 6.1 ... Members shall ensure, whenever possible, that results of conformity assessment procedures in other Members are accepted, even when those procedures differ from their own, provided they are satisfied that those procedures offer an assurance of conformity with applicable technical regulations or standards equivalent to their own procedures...

The language of these provisions could be rather considered as a "soft law" ("*shall give positive consideration*", "*shall ensure, whenever possible*"). As it was already mentioned in Sect. 3.5.3.3, similar equivalence and mutual recognition provisions that are found in other WTO Agreements, such as the SPS Agreement and the GATS, have stronger commitments. They are less ambiguous in requiring the Members to consider equivalence requests from other WTO Members. However, as it was already mentioned above, it might be odd for the TBT Agreement to have a starkly different approach to this matter. Moreover, in contrast to Articles 6.3 and 10.7, which only "*encourage*" Members to enter into such agreements, Articles 2.7 and 6.1 contain the verb "*shall*", which could indicate a stronger commitment. The commitment could refer not necessarily to "*accepting*" Members' regulations as equivalent, but "*considering*" to accept them.

What could be improved is to define more clearly the procedure for such equivalence considerations similarly as it was done by the SPS Committee in relation to the similar obligation. As was mentioned before, the SPS Committee provided that the importing Member has to clearly identify the appropriate level of protection that the relevant measure is aimed to ensure, while the exporting Member has to provide a reasonable access to the importing Member to inspect its facilities in order to determine the equivalence between the two measures.[193]

It could be imagined that a clearer mechanism of equivalence consideration could also benefit the Members in the context of the TBT Agreement.

[193] WTO, Committee on Sanitary and Phytosanitary Measures, *Decision on the Implementation of Article 4 of the Agreement on the Application of Sanitary and Phytosanitary Measures*, G/SPS/19, 2001, reviewed in 2004; See a relevant interpretation of this provisions in Trachtman (2007a), p. 788.

3.5.6 Interim Conclusion for Sect. 3.5

To conclude the analysis of Sect. 3.5 of this Chapter, the "black letter" WTO law does constraint the design of TBT in RTAs. In particular, there are basic WTO disciplines that have to be observed when designing disciplines on harmonization and mutual recognition. The harmonized rules, for instance, are subject to similar conditions as national legislation, i.e., they should not be discriminatory or unnecessarily restrictive, and they have to be based on international standards. When it comes to mutual recognition, it could also potentially run afoul of similar WTO disciplines. This research suggests to clarify the TBT Agreement's provisions dealing with recognition, which could ensure a greater openness of the WTO Members' regulatory regimes.

3.6 From Regional Towards Multilateral Agenda

So far, this Chapter has been focusing on the argument that RTAs, which include TBT, are the reality of global commerce. They set the direction of global trade governance on TBT, and they have to be approached differently within the regionalism vs. multilateralism discussion, as they could fill in the gaps within global trade governance and, when designed in an open manner, they might create positive effects that are more widely shared than preferential tariff liberalization. Accordingly, it was suggested to adjust some of the WTO rules on regional integration to recognize this reality.

At the same time, it was mentioned in Sect. 3.4 that RTAs have limitations. It might be difficult to efficiently tackle a broad range of issues of multilateral dimension, such as environmental protection and economic development. In some aspects, the specific features of the multilateral trading system could be beneficial in tackling these challenges. The global trading system might benefit from the multilateralization of some of the RTA disciplines. This process has been already mentioned before (the "laboratory effect"): when norms tested in the RTA context are further transposed to the multilateral level.

This section describes the reasons for and mechanisms of multilateralizing regionalism. It sets the scene for the following Chapter, which discusses in more detail the direction of global governance on TBT in RTAs (on the example of US and EU "new generation" RTAs) and their possible impact on the development of the multilateral rules.

3.6.1 Why There Is a Need to Multilateralize Regional Cooperation

First of all, it is worth reminding the idea from the paper by Richard Baldwin on the levels of governance with respect to regulatory issues: some rules should be left for national discretion, some should be negotiated at the regional level (RTAs), and some could be multilateralized.[194] There have to be sufficiently meaningful reasons for the parties to bring their cooperation to the multilateral level instead of giving preference to other means.[195] It could be suggested that there are two main contexts in which multilateral cooperation could have such reasons.[196]

First of all, multilateral cooperation is suited in areas involving the global public good.[197] A clear and a relevant example is the protection of the environment. The need to strengthen environmental protection, in particular, to mitigate harmful climate change effects, has been widely recognize worldwide. Since it is a global challenge, there is a need for efficient and effective global action. Trade law itself could be a vehicle to tackle environmental challenges if the respective rules provide preferences to more environmentally friendly products and technologies.[198] Similarly, cooperation at bilateral and plurilateral levels could also be useful in promoting this goal. However, since there is a high level of regulatory interdependence in this area, in order to have more impact, a more global action is needed. This is where the WTO could play a role.

It is worthwhile to note that the objectives of sustainable development and, in particular, the preservation of the environment are clearly mentioned in the Preamble to the WTO Agreement (Marrakesh Agreement) meaning that from the very beginning it was envisaged that the WTO should keep these objectives high on the agenda. Over the years, there have been multiple initiatives to advance these objectives, for instance, via the Environmental Goods Agreement, which aims to eliminate tariffs on a number of important environment-related products. It could be also imagined that a similar multilateral action could be designed for non-tariff measures.

Coming back to the subject of TBT, these barriers are often overlooked within the context of environmental discussion. Nevertheless, it is important to keep in mind that there is a close link between TBT and the environment. Firstly, TBT measures are oftentimes implemented to protect the environment. Secondly, some TBT measures might restrict trade in environmental goods and services. These effects need to be taken into consideration when liberalizing technical barriers. Designed in a way that takes environmental concerns into account, the regulatory cooperation between states could streamline environmental protection, for instance by creating

---

[194] Baldwin (2014), p. 40.

[195] Bollyky (2017), p. 4.

[196] Ibid.

[197] Ibid.

[198] Leas-Arcas (2019).

more efficient and targeted measures to protect certain environmental concerns without a "race to the bottom" in terms of regulatory protection, or by facilitating trade in environmental goods, which might stimulate more environmentally-friendly production.

Other areas where multilateral cooperation could be beneficial relate to sectors, dominated by global value chains, where production is affected by regulations in many jurisdictions and where the regulatory paradigms are less entrenched.[199] This could include cooperation with regard to issues arising from the use of new technologies. One crucial example in this regard is regulation of digital products. Digital products, intangible by nature, such as artificial intelligence, telecommunications, or internet technologies are a part of a modern life, they are often embedded into physical objects. There is a substantial gap in the international regulatory framework for such products. As it was pointed out by Canada in its proposal to the TBT Committee for the Ninth Triennial Review, "[j]ust as the emergence of new goods in the 1940s and 1950s necessitated the creation of relevant new standards, technical regulations, and conformity assessment procedures, so too the emergence of intangible digital products is spawing the development of applicable novel regulatory measures".[200] Canada also points out in its proposal that one of the options could be to consider "to clearly specify that intangible digital products are covered by the obligations in the TBT provisions", or "to replicate TBT provisions in digital agreements".[201] Here, it is worthwhile to note that the current WTO e-commerce negotiations touch upon those issues, for instance, by covering measures that the parties may apply to products that use cryptography, but the comprehensive approach is lacking.[202]

It has been mentioned before (Sect. 3.4) that the relevant provisions of RTAs may lock-in certain regulatory solutions that do not reflect a broad consensus between WTO Members. Countries, which dominate the global economy, might use their status to advance their strategic interests leaving countries with less influence to "dance to the tunes of more powerful".[203] In this respect, the advantage of the WTO system is that it aims to protect the interests of all of its membership, including less powerful Members. It would limit the need to create multiple parallel initiatives at the bilateral level between countries and their regulatory bodies involved in global

[199] Bollyky (2017), p. 4.

[200] WTO Committee on Technical Barriers to Trade (2021) Proposals on Conformity Assessment, Environment and Climate Change, Transparency, Digital Products, and Micro, Small, and Medium-Sized Enterprises (MSMEs), Ninth Triennial Review, Submission from Canada, G/TBT/W/745, 28.04.2021, para. 4.2.

[201] Ibid., para. 4.4.

[202] WTO Electronic Commerce Negotiations Consolidated Negotiating Text – December 2020 Revision, pp. 54–55. This account is taken from the World Trade Organization, Committee on Technical Barriers to Trade (2021) Proposals on Conformity Assessment, Environment and Climate Change, Transparency, Digital Products, and Micro, Small, and Medium-Sized Enterprises (MSMEs), Ninth Triennial Review, Submission from Canada, G/TBT/W/745, 28.04.2021.

[203] Steward (2016), p. 2.

value chains.[204] The WTO provides a forum where the interests of all of the Members could be taken into consideration.

3.6.2 Options for Multilateralizing RTA Cooperation

The options for multilateral cooperation, are limited given the diversity of WTO Members' preferences and their levels of development, which prevents the WTO from expanding its provisions with hard collective obligations.[205] A few possible mechanisms could be imagined at this level. First is the departure from a single undertaking approach and accepting agreements between a sub-set of WTO Members on specific issues of interest ("plurilateral agreements"). Another option could be to strengthen the overall deliberative function of the WTO focusing on identifying common goals and creating mechanisms to achieve those goals. In order to improve the efficiency of these options, the change in the governance of the WTO would be required.

3.6.2.1 Plurilateral Route

In view of the extended Doha Round halt, a number of proposals have appeared to consider the option of plurilateral agreements—agreements in the WTO framework only between some of the like-minded Members.[206] It is argued that such type of agreements could become an "escape route from the stalemate of the Doha Round"[207] and that "decisions taken between a sub-set of members could facilitate the adoption of a forward-moving agenda".[208]

The plurilateral agreements date back to the Tokyo Round of multilateral trade negotiations (1973–1979) predating the WTO, which resulted in the adoption of the "codes" (the Standards Code further evolved into the TBT Agreement), applied only for a sub-set of the GATT contracting parties. These codes appeared at the moment when regulation of non-tariff measures has become an extremely relevant issue, but the contracting parties could not come to a consensus how to tackle it. The same dynamics are present nowadays, and, therefore, it is perhaps worth reconsidering the option of resorting to plurilateral agreements when looking for the model of cooperation on regulatory issues at the WTO.[209]

---

[204] Bollyky and Mavroidis (2017), pp. 3, 22.

[205] Gari (2020), p. 52.

[206] See, e.g. Adlung and Mamdouh (2018); Bollyky and Mavroidis (2017); Low (2012), p. 309.

[207] Adlung and Mamdouh (2018), p. 85.

[208] Low (2012), p. 311.

[209] Bollyky and Mavroidis (2017), p. 26.

Essentially, there are two main models of plurilateral engagement: exclusive plurilateral agreements and open plurilateral agreements (the latter are sometimes called the "critical mass agreements"). The difference between the two is that the benefits negotiated in the framework of the latter are extended on an MFN basis to all WTO Members (e.g., the Information Technology Agreement), while exclusive plurilateral agreements do not extend their benefits to the outsiders, although there is a possibility of becoming a signatory for other WTO Members when a number of criteria is satisfied (e.g., the Government Procurement Agreement).[210] The procedural difference between the two is that the exclusive plurilateral agreements have to be agreed by consensus of all WTO members, while it is not required for the open plurilaterals.[211]

Both models of plurilateral engagement might be useful to move forward on the regulatory agenda depending on the issues at stake. Open plurilaterals could be useful in case the participating members would represent a large share of the global trade ("critical mass"), as the "free rider" problem arising from extending the benefits on the MFN basis could otherwise represent a significant risk factor.[212] It could also be imagined that they might be relevant for issues of global concern to promote a common understanding on certain issues among a large group of countries, such as treatment of environmental goods, or subjecting digital goods to the provisions of the TBT Agreement. With regard to the latter, it is worthwhile to note that the current WTO e-commerce negotiations are essentially pursued in this fashion.

In contrast, the exclusive plurilateral agreements do not pose a "free rider" problem, and, therefore, they might take more sophisticated forms tailor-made to specific concerns of certain WTO Members. Thomas Bollyky and Petros Mavroidis, for instance, suggest to have a set of baseline rules and goals for cooperation, pursuant to which the parties would be able to collaborate on topic-specific emerging issues, coupled together with mechanisms for monitoring and reporting.[213] The working groups created pursuant to these rules would be able to prepare and approve common standards, technical regulations, and conformity assessment procedures. The parties could also develop confidentiality arrangements, within which they would be able to share technical data and inspection reports in order to implement best possible solutions. The agenda of the working groups could cover a wide range of issues depending on the parties' priorities.[214] For instance, it could build on the various proposals at the Doha Round, such as harmonization of information

[210]Adlung and Mamdouh (2018), pp. 93–102.

[211]Ibid., p. 104.

[212]Basedow (2018), p. 417.

[213]Bollyky and Mavroidis (2017), p. 27.

[214]Ibid.

requirements on labeling of textiles and clothing products, conformity assessment of electronics, conformity assessment in the automotive sector, etc.[215]

One might wonder why exclusive plurilateral agreements are a better option than RTAs with similar provisions, as both models are exclusive for their members or signatories. There are few considerations that should be taken into account. Firstly, plurilateral agreements could provide greater transparency, as they exist within the WTO system of institutions and would be better connected with the organization's processes.[216] Secondly, plurilateral agreements would provide a possibility and a clearer procedure for future accession of non-party WTO Members.[217] Since they are in the WTO framework, other Members would be able to accede subject to a list of conditions.

The problem with exclusionary plurilateral agreements is that they could be very difficult to achieve because of the "consensus" rule, according to which all WTO Members have to agree to add them to the WTO legal architecture. This rule is very explicit in Article X:9 of the Marrakesh Agreement. Although the benefit of plurilateral agreements on regulatory issues might also extend to the outsiders, it might still be difficult to persuade all 164 WTO Members at the same time. Here, a suggestion could be made to amend the consensus requirement for plurilateral agreements. Bollyky and Mavroidis also suggest to provide clear binding principles, which would limit the use of plurilateral agreements and give assurances to the outsiders that they would not be forced to sign those agreements and that, in case, they would want to sign, they would face the same conditions, which applied to the original signatories.[218]

Another issue that could be problematic with respect to opting for the plurilateral agreements, is the application of the dispute settlement. The fear might be associated with losing policy independence and might discourage the parties to adopt ambitious provisions. Therefore, another suggestion with respect to adjusting the mechanism of plurilateral agreements to better serve the purpose of regulatory convergence, would be to not apply the dispute settlement provisions to those agreements, unless the parties explicitly decide otherwise.[219]

When considering how to improve the model of plurilateral agreements, it is also worthwhile to mention the development perspective. To target specifically the problems of least developed countries (LDCs), Bernard Hoekman and Petros Mavroidis suggest to include an aid-for-trade component into plurilateral agreements—"mechanisms to assist the LDCs improve their standards, regulations,

---

[215] There proposals have been briefly mentioned in Sect. 2.3.1 of Chap. 2: WTO EU Proposal TN/MA/W/93/Rev.1 and Add.1, 15.09.2009; WTO, EU Proposal TN/MA/W/118/Rev.1, 4.12.2009; WTO, EU Proposal TN/MA/W/129, 7.12.2009; WTO, US Proposal TN/MA/W/105/Rev.2, 15.09.2009; WTO, US Proposal TN/MA/W/120,15.09.2009, etc.

[216] Adlung and Mamdouh (2018), p. 104.

[217] Bollyky and Mavroidis (2017), p. 26.

[218] Ibid.

[219] Ibid., p. 28.

and so on to the level that is required to benefit from the [plurilateral agreement]".[220] It could be imagined that this could be realized via specific plurilateral agreement's platforms, which would be tasked with analysis of the status quo and identifying the action plan for needed reforms. Funding and assistance could be provided by high-income plurilateral agreements' signatories.[221]

3.6.2.2 Strengthening the Overall Deliberative Function of the WTO

Another mechanism for multilateral cooperation could take the form of strengthening the deliberative function of the WTO.[222] The role of the WTO as a forum for deliberations and consultations has been often overlooked, while most of the attention has always been placed on the other WTO functions—negotiations and dispute settlement.[223] Nowadays, in dealing with various challenges, including those arising from non-tariff measures, the deliberative function of the WTO might be particularly relevant, as it has a potential to contribute to greater transparency, monitoring, and cooperation between the interested actors. Strengthening the deliberative function could also facilitate the process of cooperation.

The WTO already has a structure of committees where trade officials from Members engage on variety of issues. As it was discussed in Sect. 2.3.2.8 of Chap. 2, there is a number of activities performed by the TBT Committee to facilitate regulatory cooperation and to advance transparency. Still, more could be done to advance the this institutional structure to help promote regulatory coherence.

First of all, changes could be implemented with regard to the governance of the committees. Gabriel Gari and Bernard Hoekman suggest that the committees could connect better with the stakeholders—Members' officials responsible for regulatory policy, in addition to trade officials, who usually take part in the committee deliberations.[224] Moreover, the WTO committees could also develop mechanisms to engage with industries and civil society groups to get a non-governmental perspective and to formulate best practices.[225] This process, as well as the responsibility for other technical issues could be assigned to the WTO Secretariat.[226]

Secondly, the committees could reinforce cooperation with international organizations and bodies that work on a non-tariff measures agenda, such as the OECD, APEC, international standard developing bodies, and international conformity

[220] Hoekman and Mavroidis (2015), p. 338.

[221] Ibid.

[222] See, e.g., in: Evenett (2009); Gari (2020), p. 52.

[223] Evenett (2009), pp. 359–360.

[224] Gari (2020), p. 53; Hoekman (2019), p. 387.

[225] Gari (2020), p. 53.

[226] Ibid, p. 54.

assessment quality networks.[227] This could contribute to a greater understanding of the link between trade and regulation and promote coherence of work in the WTO and those organizations and bodies. Additionally, cooperation with Multilateral Development Banks and other capacity building projects could help in terms of technical assistance to developing countries and LDCs in implementing the suggested regulatory initiatives.[228]

Thirdly, the WTO could implement a platform, which would closely analyze and discuss the initiatives adopted at the level of regional trade agreements. It has been done previously in WTO bodies on an ad-hoc basis. The suggestion would be to make it a regular item on the agenda of committees. As it was pinpointed by Bernard Hoekman, "[it] would not only improve transparency, but, more importantly, potentially inform a process of learning about what works and what does not and identify options that might eventually be multilateralized through initiative under the WTO umbrella".[229]

The next Chapter looks precisely into more concrete terms on how cooperation on regulatory matters is tackled in trade agreements, how it interrelates with the WTO provisions and what could be options for multilateralizing these types of cooperative efforts.

3.7 Conclusion

Although RTAs essentially contradict one of the fundamental WTO principles—MFN, it was accepted that they constitute a complementary way to liberalize trade. However, now, with the Doha agenda being stalled and little progress on the "deep" trade agenda at the WTO, they took the central role in liberalizing trade, which became especially prominent within the "third wave" of regionalism as soon as it became apparent that the Doha Round was going to be extremely difficult to conclude. The ensuing surge of RTAs now causes concerns among experts in terms of the interrelation with the multilateral trading system.

RTAs, which go further in terms of disciplining TBT measures are generally more difficult to address in the framework of the classic theory on regionalism vs. multilateralism, which focuses mostly on tariffs. The welfare effects would depend on the type of TBT measures and the way they are designed. It appears that overall, in comparison to tariffs, TBT measures in RTAs could have positive static and dynamic effects for global welfare, as their benefits might be less exclusive due to the very nature of the measures in question. However, in RTAs, the design of methods chosen to deal with technical barriers could reflect the preferences

[227] For the role of international organizations in advancing regulatory coherence, see, e.g., Lin and Liu (2018), p. 158.

[228] Gari (2020), p. 54.

[229] Hoekman (2019), p. 387.

of the exclusive group of countries making it difficult to effectively deliver on issues of multilateral relevance. This concern is mostly prominent with respect to harmonization and mutual recognition.

When analyzing respective legal disciplines of the WTO Agreements, one might conclude that RTAs' mutual recognition with exclusionary membership could run afoul of WTO disciplines. Moreover, it is quite unlikely that the regional exception clause (GATT Article XXIV) could be instrumental in justifying the violations under the TBT Agreement.

It does not mean, however, that mutual recognition should necessarily have an open membership. As mutual recognition arrangements are related to important public policy issues, this level of "openness" is practically impossible. However, what could be improved is the procedure for recognition of equivalence, similar to how it was done by the SPS Committee in relation to the equivalence obligation. It could be imagined that a clearer mechanism of equivalence consideration could also benefit Members in the context of the TBT Agreement. Potentially, such clarification could contribute to greater openness and transparency of WTO Members' regulatory regimes.

Cognizant of the RTAs limitations, this Chapter also suggested to consider, in parallel, to multilateralize some of the RTA disciplines on TBT that relate to the issues of multilateral dimension. It argued that multilateral cooperation would be especially relevant in areas involving global public goods, such as the protection of the environment, as well as in sectors dominated by GVCs and where the regulatory paradigms are less entrenched, such as sectors involving goods with new technologies. The options for multilateralizing cooperation are limited given a number of constraints for negotiations at the WTO described in Sect. 2.3.3 of Chap. 2. However, a few possible mechanisms could be imagined, such as the conclusion of plurilateral agreements, as well as strengthening the overall deliberative function of the WTO focusing on identifying common goals and creating mechanisms to achieve those goals. In order to improve the efficiency of those options, the change in the institutional governance of the WTO would be required.

References

Books and Book Chapters

Baldwin R (1995) A Domino theory of regionalism. In: Baldwin R et al (eds) Expanding membership in the European Union. Cambridge University Press, Cambridge, pp 25–48

Bhagwati J (1991) The world trading system at risk. Princeton University Press. Princeton (reprinted in 2016)

Bhagwati J (2008) Termites in the trading system – how preferential agreements undermine free trade. Oxford University Press, New Delhi

Bhagwati J, Panagaria A (1996) Preferential trading areas and multilateralism: strangers, friends or foes. In: Bhagwati J, Panagaria A (eds) The economics of preferential trade agreements. AIE Press, Washington DC

Cottier T, Sieber C et al (2015) The dialectical relationship of preferential and multilateral trade agreements. In: Dür A, Elsig M (eds) Trade cooperation: the purpose, design and the effects of preferential trade agreements. Cambridge University Press, Cambridge, pp 465–496

Davey W (2011) A Model Article XXIV: are there realistic possibilities to improve it? In: e Bagwell K, Mavroidis P (eds) Preferential trade agreements – a law and economics analysis. Cambridge University Press, New York, pp 233–261

Forere M (2015) The relationship of WTO law and regional trade agreements in dispute settlement – from fragmentation to coherence. Kluwer Law International, Alphen aan den Rijn

Gari G (2020) Narrowed Down Utopia: adjusting the WTO to a changing trade environment. In: Kolski Lewis M et al (eds) A post-WTO international legal order. Utopian, Dystopian and other scenarios. Springer, Cham, pp 37–55

Grilli E (1997) Multilateralism and regionalism: a still difficult coexistence. In: Faini R, Grilli E (eds) Multilateralism and regionalism after the Uruguay round. Palgrave Macmillan, London

Hilpold P (2003) Regional integration according to Article XXIV GATT — between law and politics. In: Bogdandy A et al (eds) Max Plank yearbook of United Nations Law Office, vol 7. Brill, Leiden, pp 219–260

Hudec R (1993) Discussion of the Chapter by M. Finger, "GATT's Influence on Regional Arrangements". In: De Melo J, Panagariya A (eds) New dimension in regional integration. Cambridge University Press, New York, pp 148–158

Karttunen M (2020) Transparency as a core principle under the SPS and TBT Agreements – the Real Jewel in the Crown. In: Karttunen M (ed) Transparency in the WTO SPS and TBT Agreements. Cambridge University Press, Cambridge, pp 46–99

Leas-Arcas R (2019) Using Trade Agreements to achieve sustainability: a counter-intuitive conundrum. In: Leas-Arcas R (ed) Solutions for sustainability. Springer, Cham, pp 109–182

Lokhard N and Mitchell A (2005) Regional Trade Agreements under GATT 1994: an exception and its limits. In: Mitchel A (ed) Challenges and prospects for the WTO. Cameron May, London, pp. 217-252

Low P (2012) The TPP in a multilateral world. In: Lim CL et al (eds) The trans-pacific partnership. Cambridge University Press, New York, pp 299–315

Mathis J (2011) The "Legalization" of GATT Article XXIV – can foes become friends. In: Bagwell K, Mavroidis P (eds) Preferential trade agreements – a law and economics analysis. Cambridge University Press, Cambridge, pp 31–39

Mayeda G (2013) The TBT agreement and developing countries. In: Epps T, Trebilcock M (eds) Research handbook on the WTO and technical barriers to trade. Edward Elgar Publishing, Cheltenham, pp 358–390

Melo Araujo B (2016) The EU Deep Trade Agenda: law and policy. Oxford University Press, Oxford

Piermartini R, Budetta M (2009) A mapping of regional rules on technical barriers to trade. In: Estevadeordal A et al (eds) Regional rules in the global trading system. Cambridge University Press, Cambridge, pp 250–315

Romanchyshyna I (2020) Tackling technical barriers to trade in EU "New Generation" FTAs – an example of open, competing or conflicting regionalism? In: Weiss W, Furculita C (eds) Global politics in EU Free Trade Policy. Springer, Cham

Söderbaum F (2016) Rethinking regionalism. Palgrave, London

Stoll P-T (2020) Saving the World Trade Organization from the bottom up: a role for preferential trade agreements. In: Kolski Lewis M et al (eds) A Post-WTO international legal order. Utopian, Dystopian and other scenarios. Springer, Cham, pp 259–276

Telo M (2014) The three historical epochs of multilateralism. In: Telo M (ed) Globalization, multilateralism, Europe – towards a better global governance. Ashgate Publishing Ltd., Farnham

Tevini A (2006) Article XXIV GATT 1994. In: Wolfrum R, Stoll P-T, Kaiser K (eds) WTO - institutions and dispute settlement. Martinus Nijgoff Publishers, Leiden

Trachtman J (2011) The limits of PTAs – WTO legal restrictions on the use of WTO-Plus standards regulation in PTAs. In: Bagwell K, Trachtman J (eds) Preferential trade agreements – a law and economic analysis. Cambridge University Press, New York, pp 115–149
Trachtman J (2013) The limits of PTAs. In: Epps T, Trebilcock M (eds) Research handbook on the WTO and technical barriers to trade. Edward Elgar Publishing, Cheltenham, pp 315–357
Viner J (1950) The Customs Union Issue. Carnegie Endowment for International Peace, New York
Wilcox C (1949) The charter for world trade. The Macmillan Company, New York

Journal Articles

Adlung R, Mamdouh H (2018) Plurilateral agreements: an escape route for the WTO. J World Trade 52(1):85–111
Bagwell K, Staiger R (1991) An economic theory of GATT. Am Econ Rev 89(1):215–248
Bagwell K, Staiger R (2003) Protection and the business cycle. Adv Econ Anal Policy 3(1):1–45
Bagwell K, Staiger R (2011) What do trade negotiators negotiate about? Empirical evidence from the World Trade Organization. Am Econ Rev 101(4):1238–1273
Bartels L (2005) The legality of the EC mutual recognition clause under the WTO law. J Int Econ Law 8(3):691–720
Basedow R (2018) The WTO and the rise of plurilateralism – what lessons can we learn from the European Union's experience with differentiated integration. J Int Econ Law 21(1):411–431
Bhagwati J (1992) Regionalism versus multilateralism. World Econ 15(5):535–556
Bidwell P (1943) Controlling Trade after the War. Foreign Aff 21(2):296–311
Bollyky T, Mavroidis P (2017) Trade, social preferences and regulatory cooperation. The new WTO-think. J Int Econ Law 20(1):1–30
Chase K (2005) Multilateralism compromised: the mysterious origins of GATT Article XXIV. World Trade Rev 5(1):1–30
Chen M, Matoo A (2008) Regionalism in standards: good or bad for trade. Can J Econ 41(3): 838–863
Cho S (2001) Breaking the barrier between regionalism and multilateralism: a new perspective on trade regionalism. Harv Int Law J 42(2):419–465
Dam K (1960) Regional economic arrangements and the GATT, the legacy of a misconception. Univ Chic Law Rev 30(4):615–665
Evenett S (2009) Aid for Trade and the "Missing Middle" of the World Trade Organization. Glob Gov 15(3):359–374
Freund C (2000a) Different paths to free trade: the gains from regionalism. Q J Econ 115(4): 1317–1341
Freund C (2000b) Multilateralism and endogenous formation of Free Trade Agreements. J Int Econ 52(2):359–376
Gereffi G, Lee J (2012) Why the world suddenly cares about global supply chains. J Supply Chain Manag 48(3):24–32
Grossman G, Helpman E (1995) The politics of Free Trade Agreements. Am Econ Rev 85(4): 667–690
Hoekman B (2019) Urgent and important: improving WTO performance by revisiting working practices. J World Trade 53(3):373–394
Hoekman B, Mavroidis P (2015) WTO "à la carte" or "menu du jour"? Assessing the case for more plurilateral agreements. Eur J Int Law 26(2):319–343
Howse R, Langille J (2018) Spheres of commerce: the WTO legal system and regional trading blocks – a reconsideration. Georgia J Int Comp Law 46(3):650–687
Lin C-F, Liu H-W (2018) Regulatory rationalization clauses in FTAs: a complete survey of the US, EU and China. Melbourne J Int Law 19(1):149–177

Lydgate E, Winters A (2019) Deep and not comprehensive? What the WTO rules permit for a UK-EU FTA? World Trade Rev 18(3):451–479
Mathis J (1998) Mutual recognition agreements. Transatlantic parties and the limits to non-tariff barrier regionalism in the WTO. J World Trade 32(6):5–31
Mayeda G (2004) Developing disharmony? The SPS and TBT agreements and the impact of harmonization on developing countries. J Int Econ Law 7(4):737–764
Pauwelyn J (2004) The Puzzle of WTO safeguards and Regional Trade Agreements. J Int Econ Law 7(1):109–142
Picker C (2005) Regional Trade Agreements vs. The WTO: a proposal for reform of Article XXIV to counter the institutional threat. University of Pennsylvania. J Int Econ Law 26(2):267–319
Trachtman J (2003) Towards open recognition? standardization and regional integration under Article XXIV of the GATT. J Int Econ Law 6(2):459–492
Trachtman J (2007a) Embedding mutual recognition at the WTO. J Eur Publ Policy 14(5):780–799
Trachtman J (2007b) Regulatory Jurisdiction and the WTO law. J Int Econ Law 10(3):631–651

Other Articles

Amurgo-Pacheko A (2007) Mutual Recognition and Trade Diversion: Consequences for Developing Nations. Graduate Institute of International Studies, Working Paper, p. 21. http://repec.graduateinstitute.ch/pdfs/Working_papers/HEIWP20-2006.pdf. Accessed 1 Nov 2022
Baldwin R (2006) Multilateralising Regionalism: Spaghetti Bowls as Building Blocks on the Path to Global Free Trade. Working Paper No. 12545, National Bureau of Economic Research Working Paper Series
Baldwin R (2011) WTO 2020: 21st Century Trade Governance. Workshop at Research Institute for Economy, Trade and Industry. https://www.rieti.go.jp/en/events/11020201/summary.html. Accessed 1 Nov 2022
Bown C (2016) Mega-Regional Trade Agreements and the Future of the WTO. Council on Foreign Relations, Part of Discussion Paper Series on Global and Regional Governance. https://www.piie.com/commentary/speeches-papers/mega-regional-trade-agreements-and-future-wto. Accessed 1 Nov 2022
Evenett S, Meier M (2007) An Interim Assessment of the US Trade Policy of "Competitive Liberalization". University of St. Gallen Discussion Paper No. 207-18. https://papers.ssrn.com/sol3/papers.cfm?abstract_id=985521. Accessed 1 Nov 2022
Herrmann C (2008) Bilateral and Regional Trade Agreements as a Challenge to the Multilateral Trading System. Aussenwirtschaft, University of St. Gallen, School of Economics and Political Science, Swiss Institute for International Economics and Applied Economics Research 63(03): 263–286
Steward R (2016) State Regulatory Capacity and Administrative Law and Governance under Globalization. Institute for International Law and Justice of the New York University School of Law, MegaReg Series, Working Paper 2016/1
Trachtman J (2006) Embedding Mutual Recognition at the WTO, p. 16. https://ssrn.com/abstract=923903 or https://doi.org/10.2139/ssrn.923903. Accessed 1 Nov 2022
Winters A (2015) The WTO and Regional Trading Agreements: Is It All over for Multilateralism? EUI Working Papers, p 2. https://www.ssrn.com/abstract=2707104. Accessed 1 Nov 2022

Research Papers of International Organizations and Research Institutions

Baldwin R (2014) Multilateralising 21st century regionalism, global forum on trade: reconciling regionalism and multilateralism in a Post-Bali World. OECD Publishing, Paris

Bollyky T (2017) The role of regulatory cooperation in the future of the WTO. RTAs Exchange. International Centre for Trade and Sustainable Development (ICTSD) and the Inter-American Development Bank (IDB)

Correia de Brito A et al. (2016) The Contribution of Mutual Recognition to International Regulatory Co-operation. OECD Regulatory Policy Working Papers. OECD Publishing, Paris, p 22. https://doi.org/10.1787/5jm56fqsfxmx-en. Accessed 1 Nov 2022

Dieter H (2014) The Return of Geopolitics, Trade Policy in the Era of TTIP and TPP. Friedrich Ebert Stiftung. https://library.fes.de/pdf-files/iez/global/11114.pdf. Accessed 1 Nov 2022

International Trade Centre (2003) Influencing and Meeting International Standards: Challenges for Developing Countries. Commonwealth Secretariat, Geneva

Mattoo A et al (2019) Trade Creation and Trade Diversion in Deep Agreements. World Bank Policy Research Working Paper, p. 34. Available at https://openknowledge.worldbank.org/handle/10986/28451?locale-attribute=en. Accessed 2 Nov 2022

OECD (2017) International Regulatory Co-operation and Trade. Understanding the Trade Costs of Regulatory Divergence and the Remedies. OECD Publishing, Paris. https://www.oecd.org/gov/international-regulatory-co-operation-and-trade-9789264275942-en.htm. Accessed 1 Nov 2022

WTO (2011) World Trade Report: The WTO and Preferential Trade Agreements – From Co-existence to Coherence

WTO Secretariat (1995) Regionalism and the World Trading System. World Trade Organization, Geneva

Chapter 4
Development of TBT Rules in EU and US RTAs

Continuing the discussion from the previous Chapter on the role of RTAs and their interrelation with the multilateral system, this Chapter focuses more specifically on TBT provisions in free trade agreements of the European Union and the United States as major rule makers in the area of TBT liberalization.

It has already been mentioned in Sect. 2.4 of Chap. 2 that the most ambitious agenda when it comes to regional rules on TBT is driven by the US and the EU. In this respect, to better understand the trend of TBT rules addressed within RTAs, the experience of the US and the EU with disciplining TBT in their RTAs is especially relevant.

The objective of this Chapter is twofold. Firstly, this Chapter articulates the most recent approaches to TBT to understand the direction of TBT liberalization, what instruments countries are using in this regard, and how they interrelate with the WTO disciplines. Secondly, taking into account RTAs limitations referred to in Chap. 2, and also, in view of the EU and US strong commitment to multilateralism, this Chapter speculates on which issues from the EU and US FTA agenda on TBT could be brought to the multilateral level.

The structure of this Chapter is the following: Sect. 4.1 focuses on the EU and US trade policy and how the proactive agenda is reconciled with the support for multilateralism. Sections 4.2 and 4.3 map the EU and US approaches to negotiating technical barriers in their RTAs. Section 4.4 reflects on how some of the aspects of TBT regulation in EU and US RTAs could be multilateralized.

4.1 EU and US "Deep" Trade Agenda and Multilateralism

This section clarifies the way in which the EU and the US pursue "deep" trade agendas in their free trade agreements. It demonstrates the evolvement of these agendas and their current direction to further provide a ground for a reflection on the

I. Romanchyshyna, *Technical Barriers to Trade in "New Generation" RTAs and in the WTO Agreements*, EYIEL Monographs - Studies in European and International Economic Law 29, https://doi.org/10.1007/978-3-031-25791-9_4

US and EU role in shaping globalisation, as well as the place they assign to the multilateral trading system within this process.

4.1.1 EU Trade Policy and a "Deep" Trade Agenda

This sub-section demonstrates the changing priorities within the EU free trade policy from multilateral to bilateral and regional fora to pursue a "deep" trade agenda in view of the WTO Doha Round failure. It discovers how this proactive trade policy correlates with the EU's enduring support for the multilateral trading system. It also positions the EU trade policy of "free and fair trade" into the context of external economic challenges and clarifies why it is important for the EU to maintain providing support for the rules-based multilateral system.

4.1.1.1 Bringing a "Deep" Trade Agenda into EU FTAs

The EU has been a supporter of the multilateral trading system since its very inception. It backed the creation of a common institutional framework for the GATT "to ensure the effective implementation of the results of the Uruguay Round"[1] and it had been one of the architects of the WTO legal framework. Notably, the EU doubled down on its trade policy activism at the multilateral forum during the Uruguay Round, which could be explained by a constellation of internal and external factors.[2] The external factor was a need to strengthen the multilateral system in view of then decreasing support on the side of the US, and the internal factor—the completion of the EU single market: A more integrated EU market led to strengthening of the external trade policy.[3] The Uruguay Round showed the EU's increasing preference for the rules-based multilateral system and along the way the EU responded positively to moving further with the "deep" trade agenda. It was advocating for the inclusion of the "Singapore issues" into a new round of negotiations. However, soon it became clear that it would be extremely difficult to pursue the "deep" trade agenda at the multilateral level, which pushed the EU to reconsider the forum for its trade policy.

[1] See GATT (1990) Communication from the European Community, No. MTN.GNG/NG14/W42, 9.07.1990, p. 2.

[2] Melo Araujo (2016), p. 16.

[3] Ibid.

4.1.1.1.1 Moving Away from the "All-Eggs-in-Multilateral-Basket" Approach

Favouring the multilateral forum over bilateral and regional negotiations was at the core of the EU trade agenda post-Uruguay. Relying on the progress at the newly established Doha Round and in order not to undercut its credibility and not to disperse the negotiating resources, the EU from 1999 had been pursuing a *de facto* moratorium on RTAs.[4] It hailed the launch of the new Doha round with an optimistic outlook it could bring for the future of world trade.[5] However, the new round had to incorporate new expectations. The key vision was, as the incumbent head of the Directorate General (DG) for Trade Pascal Lamy further explained in his assessment, the "managed globalization" (*globalisation maîtrisée*), which would respond to the needs of the people in the increasing pace of free trade. To reach it, classical market opening was no longer sufficient; the new round had to include some disciplines on internal policies as well.[6]

However, at the Cancun Ministerial Conference in 2003, the aspirations for the "deep" trade agenda to be included into the Doha Round were heavily criticized and it became pretty clear that the multilateral forum was not apt to deliver an ambitious agenda in the near future. Pascal Lamy himself, although being an ardent proponent of moving along the multilateral route, recognized after the Cancun Ministerial Conference that trade policy should be diversified through the mix of multilateral and bilateral agreements.[7] He wrote in his later assessment:

> [T]rade policy at the WTO has too often been the sole focus for efforts to strengthen international governance, which risks weakening its legitimacy both internally within the Union, and in the outside world. I don't believe the WTO can or should remain the sole island of governance in a sea of unregulated globalization.[8]

The Cancun Ministerial Conference thus proved to be the first step in the realization of failure of the EU's "all-eggs-in-multilateral-basket" approach. Although the Doha Round still remained a priority, EU trade policy was slowly drifting towards RTAs.

Apart from the ever-increasing realisation of the Doha Round's failure, a shift of EU trade policy could be explained by the changing patterns of the geo-economic and geo-political situation at the time. First and foremost, the EU had a fear to loose leverage in shaping global trade governance in view of the US "competitive liberalization" strategy, which is addressed in the next section. In brief, this strategy meant active pursuance of RTAs in order to "place the US at the centre of the world

---

[4] Woolcock (2007), p. 2.

[5] See Lamy (1999) Speech 99/132. https://europa.eu/rapid/press-release_SPEECH-99-132_en.htm. Accessed 2 Nov 2022.

[6] Lamy (2004) Trade Policy in the Prodi Commission 1999-2004: An Assessment, pp. 3,6. https://pascallamyeu.files.wordpress.com/2016/11/1999_2004_pl_legacy_e.pdf. Accessed 2 Nov 2022.

[7] See Lamy (2003) Speech 03/514. https://europa.eu/rapid/press-release_SPEECH-03-514_en.htm. Accessed 2 Nov 2022.

[8] Lamy (2004), p. 5.

trading system".[9] While earlier US agreements such as NAFTA and APEC were mostly a "bilateral means to the end of multilateral liberalization", from the beginning of the 2000s, the US have been viewing RTAs as alternative fora for achieving trade policy goals.[10] Another reason was an ever-increasing economic growth in Asia: ASEAN countries, India and South Korea had become especially important destinations for trade and investment. This situation made a case for seeking ways to strengthen the economic ties with these markets,[11] especially considering the fact that the US had already been targeting them.[12]

In 2006 a successful outcome of the Doha Round became increasingly unlikely, the negotiations were suspended indefinitely. Even though later on, several attempts secured few breakthroughs in the areas of agriculture, intellectual property and trade facilitation, they were limited in comparison to the Doha Round's global ambitions.[13] The year 2006 had become a turning point in the EU trade policy orientation, as with the final realisation of the Doha's halt, it had to rethink its strategy of "putting all eggs into the multilateral basket".

4.1.1.1.2 "Global Europe": from a "Shallow" to a "Deep" Trade Agenda in RTAs

The 2006 EU Commission's strategic document "Global Europe: Competing in the World" finally marked a shift in priorities from multilateral integration to RTAs.[14] It reasoned this new agenda by the need to engage with emerging economies whose growth has been a major feature of the international economic environment over the last decades and therefore demanded a new set of market access rules, as well as a need to move forward the "deep" trade agenda addressing non-tariff barriers—tasks not easily achievable via the failing Doha Round. Notably, the Global Europe strategy stressed that it would not mean a retreat from multilateralism, but that EU trade policy had to adapt to new challenges and FTAs could go "further and faster in promoting openness and integration".[15]

By bringing EU free trade agreements to the fore of the trade liberalisation agenda, Global Europe aimed to endow them with new features: firstly, economic factors had to play a primary role in the choice of future trade agreements, and, secondly, their focus had to transform to incorporate deeper and more ambitious

---

[9] Evenett and Meier (2007); See also Melo Araujo (2016), p. 33.

[10] Woolcock (2007), p. 5.

[11] Ibid.

[12] See e.g., *US-Korea* FTA signed in 2007.

[13] See WTO News, Talks Suspended. Today there are Only Losers, July 2006. https://www.wto.org/english/news_e/news06_e/mod06_summary_24july_e.htm. Accessed 2 Nov 2022.

[14] Melo Araujo (2016), p. 34.

[15] European Commission (2006) Global Europe: Competing in the World, https://eur-lex.europa.eu/legal-content/EN/TXT/?uri=celex:52006DC0567. Accessed 2 Nov 2022.

disciplines than before. Prior to the Global Europe strategy, throughout the 1990s and early 2000s the EU in fact had also been quite active in pursuing trade agreements. However, these agreements were targeted primarily at certain strategic and not economic objectives, as the latter were left for the multilateral venue.[16] For example, agreements with central and eastern European and Mediterranean countries had been pursued for the sake of economic and political stability, and with the African, Caribbean and Pacific (ACP) countries—to promote development of least-developed countries (LDCs). Even the commercially driven FTAs at the time with South American countries (Mexico and Chile) had a mainly strategic motivation behind them—they were for the most part aimed at neutralising the trade divertive effects emanating from FTAs between these countries and the United States.[17] Now, being at the centre of the trade liberalisation agenda, trade agreements have become more based on economic than purely strategic considerations. Those issues of economic character, which the EU was going to tackle through the multilateral forum, now were also addressed through RTAs.

In line with its earlier positions in the Doha Round, the EU makes an emphasis on a "sharper focus on barriers to trade behind the border". This focus is made very explicit in the Global Europe strategy, which notes in relevant parts:

> The openness is no longer simply about tariffs. Securing real market access in the 21st century will mean focusing on new issues and developing the tools of trade policy to achieve the types of opening that make a real difference.[18]

By resolving to address the "deep" trade agenda, RTAs were targeted at issues on which Doha failed to deliver.[19] Were, nevertheless, the goals in the Global Europe strategy any different than a range of issues brought up within the Doha Round? Reflecting on this question, Billy Melo Araujo, on the one hand, points out the similarity of objectives in the Doha Round and the EU Global Europe strategy and that the latter "does not represent a significant departure from the EU's attempts to bring reform at the level of the WTO". He adds that "the setting might be different, but the objectives are similar".[20] On the other hand, it does not mean that the Global Europe strategy simply replicated the EU's previous Doha positions. In fact, it goes further by covering a broader range of areas and the applicable instruments.[21] What is especially relevant for the regulatory agenda is that it also points to the concrete possible methods to deal with regulatory divergences:

> Instruments such as mutual recognition agreements, international standardisation and regulatory dialogues, as well as technical assistance to developing countries, will play an

[16] Melo Araujo (2016), p. 32.

[17] Woolcock (2007), p. 3; See also Melo Araujo (2016), pp. 32–33.

[18] European Commission (2006) Global Europe: Competing in the World, https://eur-lex.europa.eu/legal-content/EN/TXT/?uri=celex:52006DC0567. Accessed 2 Nov 2022.

[19] Woolcock (2007), p. 4.

[20] Melo Araujo (2016), p. 46.

[21] Ibid., p. 38.

> increasingly important role in promoting trade and preventing distorting rules and standards.[22]

The bolder approach in the Global Europe strategy could be assumed to reflect a change of venue as it is easier to pursue certain issues (especially, when it comes to regulation) with few like-minded partners than a variety of states having different perspectives (that was exactly one of the reasons of the Doha halt), but also a changing vision for global governance, a demand for more progress being made, which was suppressed by the Doha Round limitations.

4.1.1.2 Complementing the RTA Focus with the Support for Multilateralism

A shift towards RTAs in Global Europe begs a question regarding the place of the multilateral forum in the current EU trade policy orientation. One could infer that the EU trade agreements of a "new generation" were sought to substitute for multilateral negotiations, as the ambitious trade agenda was now moved to the RTAs venue.[23] However, at the very least at the strategic level it is clear that the WTO still remains among the key priorities of the EU trade policy.

First and foremost, the support for multilateralism is embedded in the very foundation of the EU. Article 3(5) of the Treaty on European Union (TEU) sets its objectives in relation to the wider world, including contribution to free and fair trade and strict observance of international law and universal values.[24] In more concrete terms, when setting general provisions on the external action, Article 21(1)(2) clarifies that the EU "shall promote multilateral solutions to common problems" and names a list of objectives that shall be pursued with a high degree of international cooperation, such as sustainable development or integration of all countries into the global economy.[25] The objective to "promote an international system based on stronger multilateral cooperation and global governance" is also underlined as a one of key undertakings.[26]

Post Global Europe, these tasks were also moved to the RTAs agenda, but with a clear view to ensure compatibility with the multilateral system,[27] evidenced by communication and reflection documents coming from the European Commission. Global Europe itself pinpoints that "there will be no European retreat from multilateralism" and cautions that a shift towards RTAs should serve as a stepping stone and not a stumbling block to multilateral liberalization. RTAs are seen as

[22] European Commission (2006) Global Europe: Competing in the World, p. 5. https://eur-lex.europa.eu/legal-content/EN/TXT/?uri=celex:52006DC0567. Accessed 2 Nov 2022.

[23] See, e.g., Garcia-Duran (2016), pp. 27–29.

[24] Treaty on European Union, OJ C326/13, 26.10.2012.

[25] Ibid., Art. 21, paras. 1, 2(d) and (e).

[26] Ibid., Art. 21, para. 2(h).

[27] See Heydon and Woolcock (2009), p. 167.

complementary—a means to tackle issues that "are not ready for multilateral discussion" and which also set "the ground for the next level of multilateral liberalisation". The emphasis on keeping the multilateral forum a priority has been repeatedly confirmed in later documents. The Trade for All communication also suggests that "the EU should do everything possible to restore the centrality of the WTO as a trade negotiation forum".[28] With a similar emphasis on complementarity of FTAs, it envisages them as a "laboratory for global trade liberalisation" and puts lots of attention on avoiding fragmentation, which FTAs may possibly entail. The Harnessing Globalisation reflection paper also confirms that multilateral cooperation remains a preferred option, although it recognises its limits (and thus a need for a reform).[29] The model of EU regionalism, as made clear from these strategic EU Commission documents, constitutes an open approach that goes beyond the scope and depth of WTO rules but takes due account of them and tries to avoid fragmentation. At the same time, in reality, whether or not EU RTAs provide fragmentation to the multilateral system is a complicated question and hence is subject to further discussion to which this research also aims to contribute.

4.1.1.3 In a World of External Economic Challenges, a Search for EU Priorities

With the changing paradigms of global commerce, the question of a possible direction and underlying priorities of EU trade policy becomes especially acute. What adds to these complexities is the growing tension between the major economies US and China and the affirmation of more power-based politics as a result. These two powers represent models, completely distinct from the EU and very much based on *realpolitik*. As argued by Stephen Woolcock, the US uses threat of denying market access to get concessions from its trading partners, while China pursues strategic trade policies to get an unfair competitive advantage. The EU cannot match any of these approaches.[30] As argued by Anu Bradford and Stephen Woolcock, the EU does not have a coercive power and its strength lies rather in a normative (regulatory) power underpinned by the international rules-based system of multilateral institutions.[31] The argument goes that the EU should focus on this strength when pursuing its trade policy.

[28] European Commission (2015), pp. 27, 29.

[29] European Commission (2017), p. 13.

[30] Woolcock (2019), p. 3.

[31] Bradford (2015), p. 165; Woolcock (2019), p. 8.

4.1.1.3.1 EU: A Regulatory Power

Throughout the process of its economic integration, the EU established itself as a major source of regulatory standards with global influence. Its standards have been prominent across a range of areas such as agricultural products, chemicals, environment, competition, data protection affecting industries and consumers around the globe.[32] Interestingly enough, in many areas the EU standards constitute a predominant regulatory regime, while other large markets like US and China lack this regulatory power.[33]

International legal scholarship developed many characterisations of a normative dimension of EU trade policy, among which two legal concepts crystalized over time and later became almost buzzwords when it comes to defining the EU influence around the globe. These are "normative power Europe" (NPE) and "market power Europe" (MPE).

The former, prominently advocated by Ian Manners, denotes the EU's power in exporting its norms through non-coercive ways, such as "contagion, informational diffusion, procedural diffusion, transference, overt diffusion and the cultural filter".[34] It is predicated, however, on quite an idealistic conceptualization of the EU normative power projecting certain values such as the rule of law, human rights, social solidarity, sustainable development, good governance and others, which builds up the very identity of the EU model other countries aspire to.[35] Other countries may emulate the EU regulatory regime being inspired by the progressive agenda in protection of these values.

A more pragmatic explanation behind the EU normative power is provided through a MPE concept. As argued by Chad Damro, it is the size of the EU market, which makes it an attractive destination for international trade and investment and creates incentives for external actors to converge towards EU internal preferences.[36] Thus, emulation of the EU regulatory model follows purely economic motivations to obtain market access. There are doubts, however, that the market is the only proxy for EU internal regulatory influence.[37] Otherwise, we would see more regulatory influence coming, for instance, from emerging economies. Within a theory of "Brussels effect", Anu Bradford contends that along with market power, the sources of EU normative influence also lie in its "regulatory capacity"—"institutional structures that are capable of producing and enforcing regulations effectively", as well as "regulatory propensity"—"prevailing domestic preferences for high standards in the EU internal market".[38] The latter is an emanation of the so-called

---

[32]Bradford (2015), p. 158.

[33]Ibid., p. 161.

[34]Manners (2002), pp. 244–245.

[35]Ibid.

[36]Damro (2012), pp. 686–687.

[37]Bradford (2015), p. 161.

[38]Ibid.

"California effect" when producers find it reasonable to adjust their production processes to the most strict existing standards—in this case being EU standards embedding high preferences of the EU consumers. The former—regulatory capacity—has also been a major argument in explaining the EU normative power in academic literature. Grainne de Burca, for instance, argues that EU external policy mirrors the governance model the EU has developed internally.[39] Billy Melo Araujo points out that the EU "deep" trade agenda in FTAs was coming from the ambitious regulatory agenda of the internal market and, in particular, the experience the EU acquired in the process of "coordinating the different interests of sovereign states with a view to addressing common problems".[40]

It could be suggested that the combination of the factors mentioned above—NPE (in a sense of the ability to set the agenda), MPE (the attractiveness of the EU market), as well as regulatory capacity and propensity reinforce the EU external regulatory power in a distinctive fashion.

Another issue worth looking into is the projection of this regulatory power and the role of international cooperation within this process. When reflecting on the theory of "Brussels effect", Bradford focuses mostly on market-driven unilateral adjustment towards EU standards that external actors are compelled to undertake either for economic or additionally for more altruistic purposes (this is what she calls a "Brussels effect").[41] Although, for the reasons described above, a mere existence of stringent EU standards might be a powerful force securing an EU role in international global governance, it is doubtful that the "Brussels effect" alone would be sufficient to project the EU regulatory power in a globalised and increasingly multipolar world. Bradford herself recognises that there might be reasons for the EU to seek specifically political harmonisation in order to lock-in certain EU standards—to reach markets unaffected by the Brussels effect, to promote non-economic objectives: e.g., to ensure a high level of environmental or consumer protection, or to avoid a harmful impact of more lenient standards existing in other countries.[42] Here is where international cooperation comes into play.

With current trends in technological development and a growing economic rise of emerging economies, international cooperation becomes even more important to ensure influence on future access to major markets. Heydon and Woolcock mention this among the EU's reasons to pursue a "deep" trade agenda in RTAs.[43] One can see this growing importance of international cooperation in the rhetoric of EU Commission's strategic documents on trade. The Global Europe strategy envisages for the EU a "leading role in sharing best practice and developing global rules and

[39] De Burca (2013a).

[40] Melo Araujo (2016), p. 36.

[41] Bradford (2015), p. 159.

[42] Ibid., p. 167.

[43] Heydon and Woolcock (2009), p. 166.

standards".[44] It is picked up by the Trade for All and Harnessing Globalization papers, which put a lot of attention on shaping the global rules in line with EU values.[45]

4.1.1.3.2 Support for Multilateralism

What is crucial in establishing and projecting EU regulatory power is its underlying support for the multilateral rules-based system. Some authors emphasize that reliance on multilateral institutions is in fact one of the core elements of this power and is key in achieving international progress.[46] Stephen Woolcock, for instance, suggests that it is a distinctive feature of the EU model deeply rooted in international cooperation. He contrasts it with other major powers—China and the US—whose interests are not as closely associated with the rules-based global order and in recent times even have been going against this order, while the EU continues to have a direct interest in maintaining the system.[47]

One part of the argument is that the support for the multilateral system is rooted in the very foundation of the EU. Woolcock, by referring to European integration, emphasizes that EU law developed from transforming international law into hard law and adapting it to the specifics of the European market—thus, there was the "synergic relationship between developments in the EU and international norms and standards."[48] This synergic relationship remains, which could be observed in EU's enduring support for the international rules and institutions. As an example, the EU stresses the use of international standards in the areas of technical barriers to trade, public procurement and intellectual property.[49] A similar argument is made by Joanne Scott claiming that the EU model of regulatory influence is characterized by international orientation: Rather than seeking to export its own norms, in most instances, it rather promotes the rules that have been internationally agreed upon.[50]

Another part of the argument is that the objectives of the EU external trade agenda clearly necessitate multilateral cooperation. As one can see in the provisions of the TEU, the EU objectives in relation to a wider world are depicted as being about much more than trade[51]—at very least politically, and are focusing on areas such as

---

[44] European Commission (2006) Global Europe: Competing in the World, p. 12. https://eur-lex.europa.eu/legal-content/EN/TXT/?uri=celex:52006DC0567. Accessed 2 Nov 2022.

[45] E.g., Trade for All mentions regulatory cooperation as a "way that will help consumers everywhere to benefit from the highest and more effective levels of protection" (European Commission (2015), p. 20), and Harnessing Globalization purports to "shape globalization in line with [EU] own values and interests" (European Commission (2017), p. 21).

[46] Manners (2002), p. 237; Twitchett (1976), pp. 1–2; Maull (1990), pp. 92–93.

[47] Woolcock (2019), pp. 6–9.

[48] Ibid., p. 2.

[49] Heydon and Woolcock (2009), p. 168.

[50] Scott (2014), p. 87.

[51] See Art. 3(5) and 21 of TEU; Also, see Larik (2011).

the protection of the environment, economic development, democracy and human rights. Grainne de Burca contends that this is what distinguishes the EU as a global actor and is a part of its "mission legitimacy"—not only to deliver peace and prosperity internally, but to "exercise international leadership on a range of crucial global challenges".[52] In the same vein, Bart Van Vooren argues that Art. 3(5) TEU implies that "the Union is not just morally but in fact legally obliged to pursue equality amongst wealthy and poorer nations, to support their development and ensure 'fairness' between them".[53] This is an important aspect of EU's "raison d'être" today.[54] To achieve these ambitious goals, multilateral cooperation is inevitable, as finding solutions to global issues demands a broad consensus. Even though bilateral cooperation, as well as unilateral actions may also contribute to these goals, only multilateral cooperation can bring about the most inclusive solutions (based on balance of interests of a large number of actors). Also, a respect for existing multilateral rules creates a platform for further build-ons in other fora.

To summarize, the EU is an active user of RTAs as a means to pursue a "deep" trade agenda with its trading partners. The crucial part of this approach is the continuing support for the multilateral forum and pursuing RTAs negotiations in an open manner to avoid fragmentation of the global trade governance in line with existing multilateral rules.

4.1.2 US Trade Policy and a "Deep" Trade Agenda

The structure of this sub-section is the following: Sect. 4.1.2.1 discusses the changing priorities of the US with regard to addressing global governance in trade. Section 4.1.2.2 reviews the place of multilateralism within this process.

4.1.2.1 Changing Priorities on Trade Governance

The US was at the roots of creating the multilateral institutions, including the WTO. However, its relationship with the multilateral trading system have not been entirely consistent due to internal factors, such as domestic politics and mistrust towards trade liberalization within domestic interest group, as well as external factors, such as the changing power reconfiguration, a move from a bipolar to multipolar power structure in the global economy (the end of the US economic hegemony), which prompted the US to seek different policy solutions to maintain its influence. Nevertheless, the multilateral agenda most of the time has been an important pillar of US trade policy.

---

[52] De Burca (2013b), pp. 36–37.

[53] Van Vooren (2013), p. 332.

[54] De Burca (2013b), pp. 36–37, footnote 52.

4.1.2.1.1 From the Multilateral Focus to the Policy of "Competitive Liberalization"

As mentioned before, the United States never pursued the "all-eggs-in-the-multilateral-basket" approach. It balanced its policy at the multilateral level with regional trade initiatives. However, multilateral trade liberalization was viewed as a major policy goal. In particular, the earlier US efforts in pursuing regionalism, such as the conclusion of the North American Free Trade Agreement (NAFTA), is generally recognized as a contributing factor to the development of the multilateral agenda, as many issues from NAFTA were further transferred into the Uruguay Round of multilateral negotiations.[55] The situation somewhat shifted after the Uruguay Round, when the Clinton administration lost the Trade Promotion Authority (TPA)—a "fast track authority" granted by the Congress, which strengthens the president's powers in negotiating trade agreements. According to the TPA, the US Congress may approve or reject a trade agreement as a whole, however it cannot make amendments to the negotiated document and delay the whole process. When the TPA expired, the momentum for liberalization was stalled.[56] When the new Bush administration regained the TPA, it became clear that the public felt very divided on the question of globalization. Also, multilateral trade negotiations are facing paramount challenges with diverging interests hardly being matched.

At this time, the US government introduced a new strategy on trade, which was later called "competitive liberalization", according to which trade negotiations were to be pursued at multiple levels: bilateral, regional and multilateral. A pursuit of bilateral and regional negotiations simultaneously with multilateral negotiations had to exert pressure on countries to cooperate not to be left behind. This strategy should have restored the momentum for trade liberalization, as well as to generate more domestic support with tangible results being seen much earlier as a result of the conclusion of bilateral and regional agreements.[57] This strategy had become dominant.

When it comes to the interrelation with the multilateral trading system, it is important to pinpoint that the strategic outlook of the "competitive liberalization" agenda did not exclude the need to pursue multilateral negotiations. On the contrary, it explicitly identified the multilateral trade negotiations as an avenue of trade liberalization.[58] However, an argument could be also made that the inclusion of bilateral and regional negotiations into the trade strategy shifted the focus away from the multilateral negotiations and that the US started to perceive RTAs as an alternative mode for achieving trade policy goals.[59] Jagdish Bhagwati called this policy "divide and rule" and noted that it undermined US opposition at the multilateral level

[55] Cooper (2003), p. 23; Cho (2001), p. 433.

[56] Bergsten (2002), pp. 88–90.

[57] Ibid., p. 94.

[58] Evenett and Meier (2007), p. 8.

[59] Woolcock (2007), p. 5.

of trade negotiations,[60] which does not appear to be in the spirit of multilateralism. Simon Evenett and Michael Meier also gave an unfavourable outlook of such policy concluding that "if multilateralism and leading regional trade initiatives remain stalled, then competitive liberalization may amount to little more that bilateral opportunism masquerading as high principle with apparently compelling narrative.[61] Nevertheless, it is important to emphasize that undermining multilateralism was never on the agenda of the "competitive liberalization" strategy.

An active pursuance of RTAs within the "competitive liberalization" strategy was also a response to the WTO's inability to move forward on the issues of new dimensions of globalization ("deep" trade agenda). Therefore, RTAs were to fill this gap.[62] These were the issues, such as international investments, trade vs. environment and labour, etc.

Since the recovery from the Great Recession (2007–2009), there has also been a shift towards so-called mega-regional trade agreements including a large number of parties outside the WTO.[63] The US was quite active in pursuing mega-regional trade deals by negotiating the Trans-Pacific Partnership (TPP) and the Transatlantic Trade and Investment Partnership (TTIP). The mega-regional trade agreements further expanded the "deep" trade agenda, by including areas such as e-commerce, regulatory cooperation and regulatory coherence.

4.1.2.1.2 Unilateralism and a Return to the Conservative US Trade Policy

Later on, the US trade policy became quite erratic and driven by a distrust towards globalization. With the Donald Trump administration (2016–2020), the US trade policy shifted significantly into the direction of unilateralism and disengagement from the multilateral trading system. As it was put by Ashley Tellis, the US commitment to free trade "was always subordinated to politics".[64] However, at all times, the US has always championed the free trade universalism, (both under the republicans, as well as democrats). Yet, with the arrival of the Trump administration, this strategy was called into question. The new paradigm along the lines of the Trump's presidential race promise "Make America Great Again" followed the pattern of "nostalgic nationalism". It essentially embodied the idea that if the global trading system was no longer working for the US, then it should be broken up.[65] The Trump administration withdrew from the TPP and disengaged from the TTIP negotiations, imposed unilaterally tariffs on a number of Chinese products, and

[60]Evenett and Meier (2007), p. 20.

[61]Ibid., p. 27.

[62]Ibid., p. 9.

[63]Bown (2017), p. 108.

[64]Tellis (2015), p. 114.

[65]Financial Times (2019) Trump's Angry Unilateralism Is a Cry of Pain. https://www.ft.com/content/7b9da60a-70b7-11e9-bf5c-6eeb837566c5. Accessed 2 Nov 2022.

stalled the process of WTO Appellate Body members appointment, thereby threatening the stability of the global trading system. At the same time, the international trade agenda was expanded to serve narrow interests: it was confined to renegotiating the existing trade agreements: Korea-US FTA (KORUS) and NAFTA, which was renamed as United States-Mexico-Canada Agreement (USMCA), as well as creating limited bilateral solutions with main trading partners, such as the EU and Japan. Most importantly, the analysists of this strategy brough out the worrying trend of undermining the stability of the trading order which has been carefully built over the years.[66]

The newly elected president Joe Biden undertook to roll back Trump's isolationist and protectionist trade agenda and made a course towards more engagement with allies and a restored commitment towards multilateralism:

> The Biden Administration will seek to repair partnerships and alliances and restore U.-S. leadership around the world. The Biden Administration will reengage and be a leader in international organizations, including the World Trade Organization (WTO). The United States will work with Director-General Ngozi Okonjo-Iweala and like-minded trading partners to implement necessary reforms to the WTO's substantive rules and procedures to address the challenges facing the global trading system, including growing inequality, digital transformation, and impediments to small business trade[67]

President Biden's idea is to get the US "back at the head of the table", re-establish its role as the "writer of rules":

> For 70 years the United States...played a leading role in writing the rules, forging the agreements, and animating the institutions that guide relations among nations and advance collective security and prosperity – until Trump. If we continue his abdication of this responsibility, then one of two things will happen: either someone else will take the United States' place, but not in a way that advances our interests and values, or no one will, and chaos will ensue.[68]

Nevertheless, it appears that US trade policy "will continue to be influenced by domestic opposition to free trade".[69] A lot of attention in Biden's trade policy is dedicated to shaping globalization in a way that would not be harmful for the domestic industries.[70] At the same time, there is also a place for bilateral and multilateral engagement:

> Through bilateral and multilateral engagement, the Biden Administration will seek to build consensus on how trade policies may address the climate crisis, bolster sustainable renewable energy supply chains, end unfair trade practices, discourage regulatory arbitrage, and foster innovation and creativity.

[66] See such criticism, e.g., in Brewster (2018).

[67] United States Trade Representative (2021), p. 4.

[68] Biden (2020), p. 71.

[69] Foulon (2021), p. 1.

[70] United States Trade Representative (2021) 2021 Trade Policy Agenda and 2020 Annual Report. See, e.g., an emphasis on putting workers at the centre of trade policy (p. 2), standing up for American farmers, ranchers, food manufacturers and fishers (p. 5), etc.

In sum, it is worth to note that US trade policy has been changing its focus over the years depending on the geopolitical situation and the changing perceptions of globalization. At the time being, it appears that the current administration is determined to reestablish its global leadership and to combine domestic actions with bilateral and multilateral engagement to achieve its far-reaching goals.

4.1.2.2 Reflecting on the Role of Multilateralism in the US System of Priorities

Despite that the US remains a major superpower and can allow to act unilaterally in some aspects, its engagement in multilateral institutions is crucially important as an element of this power. The importance of the rules-based international system was nicely pinpointed by the Financial Times: "The postwar decades saw an extraordinary alignment of the American national interests with a rules-based international system. In designing and building the institutions of a liberal global order, the US promoted its own prosperity and security…"[71] There are multiple issues of the multilateral dimension that have to be tackled collectively. Unilateral actions, or bilateral engagement might not be effective to deal with this task. Also, it is worth to mention that there have been multiple studies showing that the US greatly benefits from the rules-based system.[72]

Moreover, it has already been mentioned that the world is not the same as it was decades ago. The global power structure has changed, with the rising power of other developing countries, primarily China. The US, therefore, needs to seek different instruments to reinstate its influence, by engaging in various ways with its trading partners. It appears that the modes of engagement will be diversified, including both bilateral ways, as well as engaging at the multilateral level.

From the discussion above, we could draw the following conclusions. Firstly, both the EU and US have moved on with addressing a "deep" trade agenda at the level of RTAs. At the same time, it appears that the multilateral trading system continues to play a crucial role for both, although sometimes for different reasons. Essentially, for both, it remains important to maintain a multilevel engagement with its trading partners to tackle the global challenges in the most efficient fashion.

---

[71] Financial Times (2019) Trump's Angry Unilateralism Is a Cry of Pain. https://www.ft.com/content/7b9da60a-70b7-11e9-bf5c-6eeb837566c5. Accessed 2 Nov 2022.

[72] See, the reasons summarized, e.g., in: Murphy (2020).

4.2 TBT in the EU FTAs

This section aims to clarify the particular features of the TBT provisions in EU FTAs. It firstly maps the instruments that the EU is using to address technical barriers. Secondly, it describes the features of the main instruments: harmonization, mutual recognition, as well as innovative approaches, such as regulatory cooperation and good regulatory practices, and their interrelation with the WTO approach. Thirdly, it also reflects specifically on the interconnection between TBT and the environment, as well as TBT and digital goods.

4.2.1 Mapping the Instruments to Tackle TBT Across EU FTAs

Section 4.1.1 already touched upon the EU strategic intention to pursue a "deep" trade agenda in the context of a lack of substantial progress in multilateral trade negotiations. It referred to the 2006 EU's Global Europe agenda for trade agreements, which addressed issues of regulatory nature and even hinted to the concrete possible methods to deal with regulatory divergences:

> Instruments such as mutual recognition agreements, international standardisation and regulatory dialogues, as well as technical assistance to developing countries, will play an increasingly important role in promoting trade and preventing distorting rules and standards.[73]

It is important to note that the main emphasis in this study is on the EU "new generation FTAs". The "new generation" FTAs could be grouped into a category of their own as, in comparison to "first generation" FTAs, they have been negotiated after the 2006 EU Global Europe communication, which marked a shift towards a "deep" integration agenda in FTAs. The "new generation" FTAs, therefore, reflect the most modern approach by introducing a broader scope of commitments in comparison to previous agreements. Moreover, the "new generation" FTAs also differ from deep and comprehensive agreements (DCFTAs) and economic partnership agreements (EPAs), as the latter two categories, as a rule, are premised on distinctive strategic considerations, which impacts their design. The DCFTAs (with Ukraine, Georgia and Moldova) generally represent a certain form of integration into the EU single market imposing an obligation on European counterparts to unilaterally harmonize a significant part of their regulatory laws with the EU *acquis*, while the EPAs are mostly development-oriented and are targeted at poverty reduction in the African, Caribbean and Pacific (ACP) group of states and are very much focused on technical assistance cooperation. The exception is the EU-Japan EPA, the scope

[73] European Commission (2006) Global Europe: Competing in the World, p. 5. https://eur-lex.europa.eu/legal-content/EN/TXT/?uri=celex:52006DC0567. Accessed 2 Nov 2022.

of which is rather similar to the EU "new generation" FTAs. This approach also corresponds to the logic put into the 2017 report of the EU Commission on implementation of Free Trade Agreements, where it qualifies "new generation" FTAs, DCFTAs and EPAs into separate groupings.[74]

More specifically, this research is looking into the TBT chapters, regulatory cooperation chapters, sectoral annexes, as well as other relevant provisions of agreements that the EU concluded with the following partners: South Korea,[75] Singapore,[76] Vietnam,[77] Canada[78] and Japan.[79]

There are few main thematic sections that could be drawn from this analysis, the most crucial parts of which are addressed in this research:

- Harmonization and orientation towards international standards
- Mutual recognition
- Regulatory cooperation and good regulatory practices

This analysis also specifically addresses TBT provisions related to the protection of the environment and digital goods.

4.2.2 Harmonization and Orientation Towards International Standards

The common thread of "new generation" FTAs is the underlying orientation towards international standards. This is what differentiates this type of agreements from, for instance, DCFTAs. The TBT chapters of the latter are based on regulatory approximation, which implies incorporation of the relevant EU *acquis*.[80] This is achieved through references to specific EU regulations, annexed and subject to updates, which a partner country has to implement or incorporate in its domestic legal order.[81] This

---

[74] European Commission (2017) Report from the Commission to the European Parliament, the Council, the European Economic and Social Committee and the Committee of the Regions https://ec.europa.eu/transparency/regdoc/rep/1/2017/EN/COM-2017-654-F1-EN-MAIN-PART-1.PDF. Accessed 2 Nov 2022.

[75] Trade Agreement between the European Union and its Member States, of the one part, and the Republic of Korea, of the other part, L 127, 14 May 2011, pp. 6–1344.

[76] Free Trade Agreement between the European Union and the Republic of Singapore, OJ L 294, 14.11.2019, pp. 3–755.

[77] Free Trade Agreement between the European Union and the Socialist Republic of Viet Nam, OJ L 186, 12.06.2020, pp. 3–1400.

[78] Comprehensive Economic and Trade Agreement (CETA) between Canada, of the one part, and the European Union and its Member States, of the other part, OJ L 11, 14.02.2017, pp. 23–1079.

[79] Agreement between the European Union and Japan for an Economic Partnership, OJ L 330, 27.12.2018, pp. 3–899.

[80] Van Der Loo et al. (2014), p. 15.

[81] Van der Loo and Akhvlediani (2020), p. 4.

aspect is different in "new generation" FTAs, where the harmonization disciplines are based on international standards, however, we also see that these FTAs go beyond the WTO understanding of the "relevant international standards" by specifying particular standards developing bodies. They also contain stronger disciplines on alignment with international standards, specifically in the automotive sector.

4.2.2.1 The Role of the TBT Committee Decision Concerning "Relevant International Standards"

In general terms, in "new generation" FTAs, there is a continuation of the WTO approach stressing the importance of adherence to international standards. It could be seen in Table 4.1 that all of the agreements (except for the CETA and the EU-Singapore FTA) directly mention and reaffirm their commitments under the TBT Committee Decision on international standards. FTAs also include a commitment of the parties to provide an explanation (upon request) in case a party did not use a relevant international standard as a basis for its technical regulations and conformity assessment procedures.

At the same time, the developments have few aspects that go forward into the direction of further harmonization. These developments are reflected in Table 4.1 and are further described below.

4.2.2.2 Specific Fora as Relevant International Standard Developing Bodies

In contrast to a broad definition provided in the TBT Committee Decision on international standards, the "new generation" FTAs (except for the CETA) include references to the concrete fora, such as ISO, IEC and ITU. It could be assumed that this originates from the historical reliance of the EU on the work of these bodies, which is also reflected in EU internal law (Regulation 1025/2012) recognising ISO, IEC and ITU as the only "international standard developing organisations".[82]

Moreover, the way the European system of standardization is organized largely permits it to work in tune with international standard developing bodies. The European regional standard developing bodies—the European Committee for Standardization (CEN) and the European Committee for Electrotechnical Standardization (CENELEC) have a set of procedures built around the interaction with ISO and IEC. Despite CEN and CENELEC not being members of international standard developing bodies in their own right, (as is the case for national standard developing bodies of EU members), it is crucial that there is a system in place that allows for a high level of coordination between their work. The principles of cooperation

[82] Regulation No. 1025/2012 on European standardisation, OJ L 316/12, 14.11.2012, Art.1.9. See a similar observation in Romanchyshyna (2020), p. 55.

Table 4.1 "Relevant international standards" in EU FTAs

	EU-Korea FTA	EU-Singapore FTA	EU-Vietnam FTA	EU-Japan EPA	CETA
"relevant international standard"	TBT chapter Article 4.5.1: confirmation of obligations under the TBT Committee Decision on international standards. TBT chapter Article 4.4.1 (b):"where international standards have not been used as a basis, [a Party has] to explain on request to the other Party the reasons why such standards have been judged inappropriate or ineffective for the aim pursued".	No reference to the TBT Committee Decision. TBT chapter Article 4.6 (b): similarly, to EU-Korea, explanation upon request	Similar to EU-Korea (TBT chapter Articles 5.5, 5.4. (b))	Similar to EU-Korea (TBT chapter Article 7.6)	No reference to the TBT Committee Decision. Just a general incorporation of TBT Agreement's disciplines, including on international standards.
	References to specific standard developing bodies (in sectoral annexes), on the deliverables of which the parties have to base their own standards: • Automotive sector (Annex 2-C): WP.29 within the framework of the United Nations Economic Commission for Europe (UNECE), • Electronics sector (Annex 2-B): ISO, IEC, ITU.	References to specific standard developing bodies (in sectoral annexes): • Automotive sector (Annex 2-B): WP.29 • Electronics sector (Annex 4-A): ISO, IEC, ITU • Pharmaceuticals (Annex 2-C): WHO, OECD, ICH, PIC/S and GHTF	References to specific standard developing bodies: • Article 5.4, para. 1(b) of the TBT chapter: ISO, IEC, ITU • Automotive sector (Annex 2-B): WP.29 • Pharmaceuticals sector (Annex 2-C): WHO, OECD, ICH, PIC/S and the International Medical Device Regulators Forum (IMDRF)	References to specific standard developing bodies: • Article 7.6 of the TBT chapter: ISO, IEC, ITU, WP.29, as well as Codex Alimentarius Commissio, International Civil Aviation Organisation (ICAO), United Nations Sub-Committee of Experts on the Globally Harmonized System of Classification and Labelling of Chemicals	No definition of a relevant international standards or standardization bodies.

(continued)

Table 4.1 (continued)

	EU-Korea FTA	EU-Singapore FTA	EU-Vietnam FTA	EU-Japan EPA	CETA
	• In Pharmaceuticals sector (Annex 2-D): World Health Organization (WHO), the Organisation for Economic Co-operation and Development (OECD), the International Conference on Harmonisation (ICH), the Pharmaceutical Inspection Convention and Pharmaceutical Inspection Co-operation Scheme (PIC/S) and the Global Harmonization Task Force (GHTF)			(UNSCEGHS, International Council for Harmonisation of Technical Requirements for Pharmaceuticals for Human Use (ICH)	
	Article 4.3.2(d): "promoting and encouraging bilateral cooperation between their respective organisations, public or private, responsible for metrology, standardisation, testing, certification and accreditation."	TBT chapter Article 4.5.2: "each Party shall encourage its standardising bodies, as well as the regional standardising bodies of which they or their standardising bodies are Members, to cooperate with the relevant standardisation bodies of the other Party in international standardisation activities."	Similar to EU-Singapore (TBT chapter Article 7.6.2)	Similar to EU-Singapore. Also, references to international standards in the "Regulatory cooperation" chapter (Annex 3): bilateral cooperation in international standard developing bodies.	TBT chapter Article 4.3: general references to international standards and a need for cooperation: "...promoting and encouraging cooperation between the Parties' respective public or private organisations responsible for metrology, standardisation, testing, certification, etc."

between CEN and ISO and CENELEC and IEC are respectively depicted in the Vienna and the Frankfurt Agreements.[83] The ISO and IEC standards can be adopted as European standards with all respective legal consequences meaning that national members must withdraw conflicting standards. Also, in addition to adopting ISO and IEC standards *a posteriori*, CEN and CENELEC might align their own work in the process of standard's development (parallel work). The latter is an especially interesting case: In practice, it means the creation of parallel technical committees at regional and international level under ISO and IEC leadership, which entails information and expertise exchanges and ends up with parallel approval. Interestingly, the Vienna Agreement also foresees that in exceptional cases, the CEN leadership in standards development may also be accepted, which means that the main technical work could be performed at CEN and further approved by ISO.[84] The empirical evidence demonstrates a strong involvement of CEN and CENELEC within the process of international standards development. For CEN, out of 33% of adopted international deliverables, only 31% was adopted *a posteriori*, the remaining 57 and 12% were adopted as a result of parallel work either under ISO or CEN leadership respectively. The same is true for CENELEC: out of 72% of adopted IEC standards.[85]

This congruous work between the European level and international level of standardization is classified by Walter Mattli and Tim Büthe as an example of "institutional complementarities" that has a strategic dimension to it geared towards facilitation of global market access.[86] The basic consideration underpinning this argument is that the consolidated standardization system (CEN and CENELEC at the EU-wide level) helps to better translate the interests of EU stakeholders to the international arena and thereby has a wider impact on international standardization. This system permits to better aggregate various interests and then project national consensus on the international arena. Mattli and Büthe identify these complementarities as a strategic advantage of the European system.[87] Such state of the art respectively prompts the European system to prioritize standards development at the international level (as it is a way towards global impact).

---

[83] Agreement on Technical Cooperation between ISO and CEN (Vienna Agreement) (1991) https://isotc.iso.org/livelink/livelink/fetch/2000/2122/3146825/4229629/4230450/4230458/01__Agreement_on_Technical_Cooperation_between_ISO_and_CEN_(Vienna_Agreement).pdf?nodeid=4230688&vernum=-2. Accessed 2 Nov 2022; The IEC-CENELEC Frankfurt Agreement (1991). http://www.iec.ch/about/globalreach/partners/pdf/IEC-CENELEC_Frankfurt_Agreement%7B2016%7D.pdf. Accessed 2 Nov 2022.

[84] ISO. The Vienna Agreement FAQs (2016), p. 5. https://boss.cen.eu/media/CEN/ref/va_faq.pdf. Accessed 2 Nov 2022.

[85] See CEN and CENELEC. Work Programme (2022), p. 33. https://www.cencenelec.eu/media/CEN-CENELEC/News/Publications/2022/cen-cenelec_work_programme2022.pdf. Accessed 2 Nov 2022.

[86] Mattli and Büthe (2003), pp. 18–22.

[87] Ibid., p. 25.

The same is true with regard to the automotive sector, where the United Nations Economic Commission's for Europe (UNECE) World Forum for Harmonization of Vehicle Regulations (WP.29) is recognized as a relevant standard developing body. At the same time, the WP.29 has been historically influenced by the EU member states. It was founded in 1952 as a working party on automotive vehicles within the UNECE, the purpose of which was to promote pan-European economic integration. Only in 2000, it transformed into the world forum with the aim to "initiate and pursue actions aimed at worldwide harmonization".[88]

In addition, the EU-Singapore and EU-Vietnam FTAs, as well as the EU-Japan EPA, as we can see in Table 4.1, recognize as relevant a list of international bodies producing standards for the pharmaceuticals industry, such as the International Council for Harmonization of Technical Requirements for Pharmaceuticals for Human Use (ICH), the Pharmaceutical Inspection Convention and Pharmaceutical Inspection Co-operation Scheme, etc.

Moreover, as we can see in the EU-Singapore and EU-Vietnam FTAs, as well as in the EU-Japan EPA, there is a commitment for the parties to encourage cooperation between their relevant standardization bodies in international standardization activities. Although this provision is more of a "soft law" nature, it arguably could stimulate the work within the standardizing bodies and align their positions.

It is worthwhile mentioning that the EU's promotion of certain standard developing organizations meets with frustration on the part of the US, which was in fact one of the key proponents of the broad understanding of international standard developing bodies at the TBT Committee.[89] The US is concerned with this EU's limited reading of the TBT Committee Decision on international standards complaining that the EU is illegitimately trying to "reinterpret which standards should be deemed international".[90]

It is true that in some of the mentioned bodies the EU has a certain leverage. However, this fact hardly can be considered as reinterpretation of the understanding of international standards. The respective provisions do not limit the understanding of the term "international standard" and, as it was mentioned earlier, the TBT chapters and sectoral annexes of most of EU "new generation" FTAs refer to the general list of criteria under the TBT Committee Decision on international standards. At the same time, it could be argued that by additionally mentioning concrete international bodies, the EU reinforces international cooperation by making it more focused. This is an example of the EU model of regulatory influence mentioned by Joanne Scott, which is based on international orientation: Rather than seeking to export its own norms, it promotes the rules that have been internationally agreed

---

[88] See the UNECE website, Frequently Asked Questions. https://unece.org/faq. Accessed 2 Nov 2022.

[89] Delimatsis (2018), p. 281, footnote 31.

[90] United States Trade Representative (2020) 2020 National Trade Estimate Report on Foreign Trade Barriers, p. 179. https://ustr.gov/sites/default/files/2020_National_Trade_Estimate_Report.pdf. Accessed 2 Nov 2022.

upon.[91] Moreover, the EU FTAs (except for CETA) also transpose the TBT Committee Decision on international standards into the text of the agreements, which adds to the argument that the EU seeks to align with the WTO approaches including not only the text of the TBT Agreement, but also its further developments.

4.2.2.3 Harmonization of Standards and Conformity Assessment Procedures

When analyzing the EU "new generation" FTAs, it becomes evident that the specific harmonization disciplines are actually very limited. The approach comes in line with the strategy to follow international standards without specific references (electronics, pharmaceuticals sectors). One exception is the automotive sector, where all of the FTAs refer to a certain list of standards produced at UNECE.[92] Mostly, the sectoral provisions in EU "new generation" FTAs are focused on harmonizing the procedural methods of conformity assessment and regulatory cooperation between the parties.

4.2.2.3.1 Automotive Sector

The automotive sector is an instance where the harmonization requirements in EU FTAs have a concrete form. The respective provisions include requirements anchoring a legal obligation to follow the standards developed by the World Forum for Harmonisation of Vehicle Regulations (WP.29) within the framework of the United Nations Economic Commission for Europe (UNECE). As it can be seen in Table 4.2, in addition to recognizing WP.29 as a relevant standard developing body, all the analysed agreements, in relevant parts, refer to a list of UNECE standards. Even CETA, where WP.29 is not recognized explicitly, includes such an obligation on the part of Canada regarding a limited list of UNECE standards, as well as a commitment to continue further cooperation in terms of recognizing more UNECE standards, unless it harms North American integration.

It is relevant to mention the particular features of the global harmonization of vehicle regulations at the WP.29. Notably, the WP.29 administers two most significant agreements: the 1958 Agreement[93] and the 1998 Agreement.[94] The work

[91] Scott (2014), p. 87. See also Romanchyshyna (2020), p. 55.

[92] See also in Romanchyshyna (2020), p. 56.

[93] Agreement Concerning the Adoption of Harmonized Technical United Nations Regulations for Wheeled Vehicles, Equipment and Parts which can be Fitted and/or be Used on Wheeled Vehicles and the Conditions for Reciprocal Recognition of Approvals Granted on the Basis of these United Nations Regulations (1958). https://unece.org/trans/main/wp29/wp29regs. Accessed 2 Nov 2022.

[94] Agreement Concerning the Establishment of Global Technical Regulations for Wheeled Vehicles, Equipment and Parts which Can be Fitted and/or be Used on Wheeled Vehicles (1998). https://unece.org/DAM/trans/main/wp29/wp29wgs/wp29gen/wp29glob/tran132.pdf. Accessed 2 Nov 2022.

Table 4.2 Harmonization Requirements

	EU-Korea FTA	EU-Singapore FTA	EU-Vietnam FTA	EU-Japan EPA	CETA
Harmonization requirements	Automotive sector (Annex 2-C): Harmonization of regulations in accordance with the list of UNECE standards; Reaffirmation of validity of the type-approval certificates (based on equivalence of Korean and EU regulations).	Automotive sector (Annex 2-B): Harmonization of regulations in accordance with the list of UNECE standards; Recognition of certificates under the UNECE type approval system without additional testing and verification; Singapore might consider becoming a signatory of the 1958 Agreement.	Automotive sector (Annex 2-B): Harmonization of regulations in accordance with the list of UNECE standards; Recognition of certificates under the UNECE type approval system without additional testing and verification; Vietnam is encouraged to become a party to the UNECE 1958 Agreement.	Automotive sector (Annex 2-C): Harmonization of regulations in accordance with the list of UNECE standards; Recognition of certificates under the UNECE type approval system without additional testing and verification.	Automotive sector (Annex 4-A): Canada commits to uphold some international UNECE standards according to the list (caveat: Canada shall continue to recognize the relevant UNECE regulations, unless doing so would provide for a lower level of safety than the amendments introduced, or would compromise North American integration).
	Electronics sector (Annex 2-B): very limited harmonization disciplines with a simple mention of to follow international standards	Electronics sector (Annex 4-A): Similar to EU-Korea (Article 4.2)	No commitments	No commitments	No commitments
	Pharmaceuticals and medical devices sector (Annex 2-D): very limited and mostly aspirational provisions regarding ethnical business practices, following international standards, transparency	Pharmaceuticals and medical devices sector (Annex 2-C): similarly to the EU-Korea, very limited and mostly aspirational provisions	Pharmaceuticals and medical devices sector (Annex 2-C): similarly to the EU-Korea, very limited and mostly aspirational provisions.	Not applicable	Pharmaceuticals sector: No harmonization requirements.

regarding harmonization in such aspects as automotive safety, environment, or fuel efficiency under these agreements goes in parallel. However, there is a notable difference: The 1958 Agreement is more ambitious, as it also requires mutual recognition of type-approvals granted by its contracting parties. In practice, it means that as long as one contracting party accepts relevant and the most recent regulations under the 1958 Agreement, including the uniform performance oriented test provisions and administrative requirements, the certificates for a type of automotive products that its certification bodies issue, have to be also recognized by other parties, normally without additional testing. The list of contracting parties of the 1958 Agreement includes the EU, Japan, South Korea, Australia, Thailand, etc. The 1998 Agreement, on the other hand, does not have any administrative and mutual recognition requirements and, it is also less stringent in terms of implementation. The participation of countries in the work of WP.29 varies. It is worthwhile noting that the US, Canada, India and China are not signatories of the 1958 Agreement, but they contribute to the global harmonization of vehicle regulations within the framework of the 1998 Agreement.[95]

Apart from the general harmonization disciplines within WP.29, we see that the EU is also acting to promote the UNECE type approval system under the 1958 Agreement. The implementation of the European Commission's "Action plan for a competitive and sustainable automotive industry in Europe", where the 1958 Agreement is affirmed to be a market access tool, can be also seen in EU FTAs. In the EU-Korea, EU-Singapore, and EU-Vietnam FTAs, as well as in the EU-Japan EPA, the respective provisions reaffirm the above-mentioned type-approval system under the 1958 Agreement.[96] It is especially relevant in case of Singapore and Vietnam, since these countries have not signed the 1958 UNECE Agreement.[97] Under the respective FTAs, Singapore and Vietnam committed to harmonize their regulations towards UNECE standards and not to depart from the UNECE standards in the future. They also committed to accept the type approval certificates as valid without additional testing. Moreover, as we can see in Table 4.2, Singapore and Vietnam are also encouraged to sign the 1958 Agreement. For Korea and Japan, which are contracting parties of the 1958 Agreement, the reaffirmation of commitments also adds value, as in practice they only partially followed UNECE standards.[98] Here, it is

[95] Laurenza and Goyeneche (2017), p. 437.

[96] European Commission (2012).

[97] Romanchyshyna (2020), p. 56. The status of the agreements and the list of their contracting parties is available under the following links: https://www.unece.org/trans/main/wp29/wp29regs.html; https://www.unece.org/trans/main/wp29/wp29wgs/wp29gen/wp29glob_stts.html. Accessed 2 Nov 2022.

[98] See Romanchyshyna (2020), p. 56. See information on the practice of following the UNECE standards by Korea and Japan in European Commission (2017) Evaluation of the EU-Japan EPA, p. 2. https://trade.ec.europa.eu/doclib/docs/2018/july/tradoc_157115.pdf. Accessed 2 Nov 2022 http://trade.ec.europa.eu/doclib/docs/2017/july/tradoc_155720.pdf. Accessed 2 Nov 2022; Presentation of Fernando Perreu de Pinnick from DG Trade titled "The EU-Korea Free Trade Agreement. Motor Vehicles and Parts", prepared for the Seminar "EU-Korea FTA. Putting the FTA into

relevant to mention that the automotive sector provisions are subject to dispute settlement, the procedure of which, in case of the EU-Korea FTA and the EU-Japan EPA, have to be even accelerated for automotive sector disputes.[99]

4.2.2.3.2 Electronics and Pharmaceuticals Sectors

The state of play is a bit different in other areas that are explicitly addressed in EU FTAs—the electronics and pharmaceuticals sectors. Here, as we can see in Table 4.2, there is no harmonization in substance, except for a rather general commitment to follow international standards, as has been mentioned earlier. Instead, the focus is more on conformity assessment procedures and regulatory cooperation between the parties. The lack of formalized commitments does not mean, however, that the level of regulatory approximation between the parties at issue is lacking ambition. The regulatory dialogue in substantive terms is taking place at the level of international organizations mentioned in FTAs—IEC for electronics, WHO, OECD, ICH, etc. for pharmaceuticals. As we can see, there is no incentive to transpose the standards from these fora into the level of FTAs. One of the reasons could be the ever-changing character of standards in those areas. On the other hand, the very fact of inclusion of reference to these fora could lead to greater alignment with their work.

It is also worthwhile to note that the overall analysis of the "new generation" FTAs in terms of harmonization commitments demonstrates that the incentive to expand the sectoral disciplines is lacking, which could be related to the issue of "regulatory space" concerns. Instead, it appears that the EU practice goes more into the direction of promoting horizontal chapters on regulatory cooperation, which is non-binding and non-enforceable, but put a great emphasis on cooperation between the parties and their regulatory authorities.[100] This aspect is discussed in more detail in Sect. 4.2.4.

4.2.3 Mutual Recognition

As was mentioned in Sect. 3.5.1 of Chap. 3, the idea of mutual recognition is attractive, as, in contrast to harmonization, it is not directly aimed at creating a set of common rules. However, at the same time, it does not mean that it might be substantially easier to negotiate. Firstly, in order to better understand mutual

---

Practice", held on 20 June 2011 in Seul, South Korea. http://eeas.europa.eu/archives/delegations/south_korea/documents/eu_south_korea/fta_booklet_final_en.pdf. Accessed 2 Nov 2022.

[99] See Article 10 of Annex 2-C of EU-Korea FTA and Article 19 of Annex 2-C of EU-Japan EPA.

[100] Laurenza and Goyeneche (2017), p. 442.

recognition in the framework of EU "new generation" FTAs, it is important to clarify what is the place of mutual recognition in the EU legal system and what are the limits of mutual recognition, i.e., how (in which form) it can be addressed within a "new generation" FTA. This question is analysed in Sect. 4.2.3.1. Secondly, Sect. 4.2.3.2 analyses the mutual recognition provisions in EU "new generation" FTAs. Further, Sect. 4.2.3.3, with reference to the legal analysis in Chap. 3, reflects on whether the EU approach goes in line with the respective legal disciplines of WTO law.

4.2.3.1 The Limits of Mutual Recognition in EU "New Generation" FTAs

It has been already briefly mentioned in Sect. 3.5.1 of Chap. 3 that what is labelled in various sources as mutual recognition may represent different concepts.[101] This section reflects various definitions of mutual recognition and clarifies which type is possible within the framework of EU FTAs.

4.2.3.1.1 Mutual Recognition in the EU Internal Market and the EEA

First and foremost, it is due to clarify that mutual recognition in the context of the EU internal market and in relation to the European Economic Area (EEA) states (Norway, Iceland and Liechtenstein) is not similar to mutual recognition discussed in the framework of FTAs.[102] It is based on the principle that was firstly pronounced in the *Cassis de Dijon* case (1979) and was derived from the premises of "free movement": Once a product is lawfully produced and marketed in one member state, it shall be accepted to the markets of all other member states.[103] This type of mutual recognition is predicated not only on a high degree of regulatory compatibility and mutual trust, but also on common instruments for regulatory control and monitoring structures, a "well-developed regime beyond the member state level" including common rules, common supervision and market surveillance, administrative implementation and enforcement, and judicial review[104] This is what creates a level playing field within the internal market. To sum up on this matter, as mutual recognition in the EU internal market and the EEA is predicated on the idea of "free movement" rather than "free trade" and actually creates a "right of market

---

[101] See a comprehensive study on the spectrum of mutual recognition modalities in goods sectors in Correia de Brito et al. (2016).

[102] Romanchyshyna (2020b), p. 13.

[103] Pelkmans (2007), pp. 702–705. See a similar discussion in Romanchyshyna (2020b), p. 8.

[104] Ibid., p. 705.

access", it is a unique mechanism in itself that hardly could be replicated in the framework of an FTA.[105]

4.2.3.1.2 Mutual Recognition of Conformity Assessment

The form of mutual recognition that is practiced by the EU in trade relations outside the internal market is what is essentially classified as a "mutual recognition of conformity assessment"—recognition by parties of each others' authorities as competent to assess whether products satisfy the requirements of a relevant regulation. It does not create a "right to market", but facilitates market access based on certain conditions and, as a rule, it is only limited to certain sectors.

It is important to note that there is no one single model of mutual recognition of conformity assessment. Firstly, because conformity assessment methods are to a large extent based on risk assessment which would determine a more or less rigorous approach to certain sectors and products.[106] For instance, a supplier's declaration of conformity (SDoC) might be sufficient in certain cases, while in others a laboratory testing certificate from a third party is required.

Secondly, there are different models of mutual recognition depending on the level of engagement between the parties. In the EU classification, there are "traditional" and "enhanced" mutual recognition agreements. The following subparagraph clarifies the difference between the two.

"Traditional" and "Enhanced" MRAs

According to the 2004 EU Commission's Staff Working Paper, mutual recognition of conformity assessment is classified into "traditional" and "enhanced" types.[107]

Mutual recognition in its so-called "traditional" form is where parties do not cooperate on the content of rules and where the authorities only certify products according to the importing country's regulations different from domestic ones. Thus, the applicable regulations remain the same while market access is facilitated on account of avoiding duplicative testing, certifications and inspections. Also, providing possibilities for the approval procedures to be held in the exporting country implies more certainty for businesses and a reduced time to market.[108] The example of such recognition could be found in MRAs concluded by the EU, for instance, with

[105] Pelkmans (2007), p. 700; For a similar distinction, see also Eeckhout (2018) (differentiation between "market integration" and "trade liberalization"); See also Romanchyshyna (2020b), p. 13.

[106] See such considerations, e.g., in WTO (2018) Approaches to Conformity Assessment, Eighth Triennial Review. Submission from the European Union, G/TBT/W/462, 9.03.2018, para. 2.2.

[107] European Commission (2004).

[108] Romanchyshyna (2019). See also Correia de Brito et al. (2016), p. 22.

the United States, Japan, Australia and New Zealand.[109] However, the example of the 1998 EU-US MRA demonstrates that this type of mutual recognition is difficult to achieve. Recognition in some of the sectors proved to be simply unenforceable in practice.[110] Two main problems were a lack of trust between the institutions and insufficient regulatory compatibility.[111] In case the overall approaches of regulatory systems are too different, mutual recognition might not become a saving belt. In fact, in case of the US-EU MRA, the only sectors where mutual recognition succeeded were sectors with a high degree of convergence between the US and EU rules.[112]

Because of the aforementioned difficulties, the EU Commission in its 2004 Staff Working Paper marked a shift towards "enhanced" MRAs, i.e. MRAs predicated on a certain degree of regulatory compatibility.[113] Such compatibility could be ensured due to alignment with EU rules. This is the case, for instance, in the EU-Switzerland MRA: The second sentence of its Article 3.2 specifies that conformity reports have to indicate "conformity with the Community [EU] legislation".[114] In this category, one could also place the Agreements on Conformity Assessment and Acceptance of Industrial Products (ACAAs) which are concluded with the EU candidate and neighbouring countries.[115] In the Association Agreements (AAs) with Ukraine, for example, there is an explicit market access conditionality clause requiring Ukraine to accept the EU *acquis*,[116] the consistent interpretation of which is also ensured by the provision on the role of the European Court of Justice in the process of dispute settlement.[117] However, it is worth pointing out that in all those cases, the alignment with EU rules shows an apparent asymmetry within the decision-making process, as only EU members can adopt the regulations. We could assume that this kind of mutual recognition could be available in free trade agreements with power asymmetry.[118]

On the other hand, "enhanced" mutual recognition agreements can also be based on equivalence of regulations. As pointed out in the study conducted by the OECD,

---

[109] For an overview, see European Commission (2018) Trade Issues. . .Technical Barriers to Trade. Newsletter No.10, https://trade.ec.europa.eu/doclib/docs/2018/february/tradoc_156599.pdf. Accessed 3 Nov 2022.

[110] See on this matter., e.g., Ahearn (2009).

[111] Romanchyshyna (2019) The Post-TTIP Transatlantic Cooperation on Trade: Stepping up Conformity Assessment. EJIL:Talk! (blog of the European Journal of International Law). https://www.ejiltalk.org/the-post-ttip-transatlantic-cooperation-on-trade-stepping-up-conformity-assessment/. Accessed 3 Nov 2022.

[112] Ibid. See also Romanchyshyna (2020b), p. 11.

[113] European Commission (2004).

[114] Agreement between the European Community and the Swiss Confederation on Mutual Recognition in Relation to Conformity Assessment, OJ L114, 30.04.2002.

[115] Correia de Brito et al. (2016), p. 30. More on "enhanced" MRAs, see Romanchyshyna (2020b), p. 12.

[116] Van Elsuwege and Chamon (2019), p. 30.

[117] On the latter, see Article 322.2 of the EU-Ukraine Association Agreement.

[118] Romanchyshyna (2020b), p. 10.

such equivalence can be based on the adherence to the international standards and rules, or it might be the case that the parties agree, via screening of their relevant specific regulations, that the respective rules are equivalent. The EU-Switzerland MRA formally is an example of the latter, although, as was mentioned above, effectively Switzerland has to align to EU rules.

A relevant example of the former is the successful update by the EU and US of their mutual recognition agreements. After the mentioned failure of the US-EU MRA in a number of sectors, in 2004, the parties concluded a new MRA on marine equipment that relies on harmonization with International Maritime Organization's rules. Also, the negotiations on the pharmaceuticals sector finally succeeded following the EU's regulatory agencies joining the Pharmaceutical Inspection Co-operation Scheme, an international organization providing common rules for pharma inspections.[119] The use of international standards has long been favoured in facilitating technical barriers to trade. As it has been mentioned before, the WTO TBT Agreement even provides an obligation of Members to use the "relevant international standards" for their technical regulations (Article 2.4) and conformity assessment (Article 5.4). However, the practice of recognition agreements, which are only based on international standards, shows that they are concluded only in specific sectors with a comprehensive international regulatory framework implemented into the domestic legislation. The issue of trust between the certification authorities and modes to ensure the quality of the certification process also remain highly relevant in this type of "enhanced" MRAs.

4.2.3.2 Mutual Recognition in EU "New Generation" FTAs

Consistent with the clarification in the above sub-section, the type of mutual recognition that is addressed in EU "new generation" FTAs is mutual recognition of conformity assessment. There are few elements that are prominent in the EU approach, which follow from the below excerpt from the EU statement at the 2018 WTO Triennial Review of the TBT Agreement:

> a joint commitment to choose the least-burdensome procedure on basis of risk assessment and GRP principles to ensure fitness for purpose; the reference to existing multilateral schemes (e.g. ILAC, IAF) where positive assurance of conformity is required; sector-specific provisions such as use of UNECE-type approval certificates for motor vehicles or supplier's declaration of conformity (SDoC) for some sectors, e.g. electronics; and, where appropriate, integration of existing bilateral MRAs into FTAs.[120]

Firstly, it is clear from this excerpt (and also confirmed by the practice of "new generation" FTAs) that addressing mutual recognition in FTAs is not incidental, but

[119] Romanchyshyna (2019).

[120] WTO Committee on Technical Barriers to Trade (2018) Eighth Triennial Review of the Operation and Implementation of the Agreement on Technical Barriers to Trade under Article 15.4. G/ TBT/ 41, 19.11.2018, para. 4.7.

is a part of the EU current approach. Before, it was addressed through separate MRAs. Secondly, as was the case with MRAs, the approach to conformity assessment is sector-specific and depends on many factors, including risk assessment which can help identify the least burdensome procedure. Thirdly, the EU intends to incorporate international mechanisms into the accreditation process of certification bodies, which is expected to elevate the level of quality of certification and trust between certification authorities. For reference, the International Laboratory Accreditation Cooperation (ILAC) and International Accreditation Forum (IAF), referred to in the above excerpt, are the international quality network on accreditation[121] of conformity assessment bodies. The ILAC is the body for laboratory accreditation and IAF accredits the certification bodies in the field of management systems, personnel and products. They operate mutual recognition arrangements between national accreditation bodies based on certain standards of their quality, such as ISO/IEC standards and related ILAC and IAF guidance documents.[122]

The use of international accreditation mechanisms has long been discussed at the TBT Committee as a way to facilitate conformity assessment.[123] As for the EU, it states that it accepts the ILAC and IAF accreditation system as long as there is also an MRA or an FTA in place that refers to those instruments.[124]

In EU "new generation" FTAs, we see the realization of the EU approach mentioned above. First and foremost, the conformity assessment mechanisms are very sector-specific. For instance, in the automotive sector, the system of mutual recognition (which could be classified as "enhanced" type) relies heavily on harmonization with UNECE standards in the sector. As it was already mentioned above, the parties to the respective agreements (except for Canada) recognize the type-approval system under the UNECE 1958 Agreement, under which the certificates granted by authorities of the parties for the types of vehicle parts are mutually recognized and which therefore releases the producers from the burden of obtaining additional certification in the country of imports. Here, there is a link to extensive harmonization disciplines at the UNECE listed in the FTAs text, the application of which is a condition for mutual recognition.

The sector-specific provisions are also based on risk assessment. In the electronics sector, the EU-Korea and EU-Singapore FTAs, provide for the acceptance of recognition of suppliers' declarations of conformity (SDoC) with regard to electric safety and electromagnetic compatibility. This method is designed for products that are of lower risk and do not necessarily require third-party certification. At the same time, however, it is necessary that the producers test the products they are intending

[121] "Accreditation" was defined in Sect. 2.2.3 of Chap. 2.

[122] World Trade Organization (2012), p. 180; Correia de Brito et al. (2016), p. 25.

[123] WTO Committee on Technical Barriers to Trade (2017) Indicative List of Approaches to Facilitate Acceptance of the Results of Conformity Assessment. G/TBT/1/Rev.13, 8.03.2017, p. 52.

[124] WTO Committee on Technical Barriers to Trade (2019) Thematic Session on Conformity Assessment Procedures, G/TBT/GEN/278, 5.12.2019, para. 1.2.

to self-certify at the testing laboratories located within the importing country.[125] Therefore, one could suggest that it comes down to mutual recognition of the parties' laboratories and mutual trust that the laboratories would perform the similar quality of work. These aspects of mutual recognition are very much related to the specifics of the sectors, level of risk arising from the products in question, which permits to ease the certification burden. There is no single approach to sector-specific obligations.[126]

It is relevant to note that CETA includes an attempt to have a more unified approach towards conformity assessment, although just in respect of "traditional" mutual recognition, without harmonization or equivalence of substantive provisions. It includes the Protocol on the mutual acceptance of the results of conformity assessment, which is, in fact, a "traditional" MRA, although it could be argued that it represents a new model, as its sector coverage is the broadest in comparison to all other EU MRAs and aims to include other sectors in the future. This Protocol also uses innovative methods with regard to accreditation—the use of ILAC and IAF, which was mentioned as part of the EU approach to conformity assessment before.

4.2.3.2.1 CETA Protocol on the Mutual Acceptance of the Results of Conformity Assessment

The Protocol on the mutual acceptance of the results of conformity assessment (Protocol) is in fact a modification of the EU-Canada MRA dating back to 1998. It has the broadest sectoral coverage in comparison to all other MRAs: eleven sectors, including electrical and electronic equipment, radio and telecommunications terminal equipment, toys and machinery, some of which were not previously within the scope of the MRA or were not operational.[127] Moreover, the parties envisage to have a dynamic regulatory dialogue to expand its scope for additional sectors ("living agreement").[128]

As it represents a "traditional" type of mutual recognition agreement, which does not foresee cooperation on substance of rules, the trust between authorities is especially relevant (positive assurance is necessary that the other party's authorities can provide the same quality of testing and certification). The Protocol heavily relies

[125] See on acceptance of supplier's declaration of conformity in Annex 2-B (Article 3 (b)) of EU-Korea and Annex 4-A (Article 4.2) of EU-Singapore. The suppliers' declarations of conformity have to be based on test reports from other party's testing laboratory.

[126] See similar conclusions in Van Damme (2020), p. 232.

[127] Annex 1 to the CETA Protocol on mutual acceptance of the results of conformity assessment. See the analysis on CETA Protocol's coverage in Pelkmans (2015), p. 34.

[128] Article 2 of the Protocol. Initial sectors for further expansion are contained in Annex 2 to the Protocol.

on accreditation to build this confidence.[129] The parties agree to mutually recognize their accreditation bodies: the Standards Council Canada (SCC) and EU's accreditation bodies in each Member state. Additional level of trust is ensured by the accreditation body's mandatory membership in international quality networks—ILAC and IAF.[130] These efforts allow for conformity assessment bodies to be designated at home without the need for additional approval in the exporting country. Overall, it could be considered as innovative approach in terms of improving the quality of testing and certification and building trust between the parties.

4.2.3.3 Mutual Recognition in EU FTAs and the WTO Approach to TBT

Another question that is worth looking into is whether the EU approach to mutual recognition in FTAs goes in line with the WTO rules and principles. In Sect. 3.5 of Chap. 3 the legal analysis highlighted that mutual recognition, which has exclusionary membership risks to be framed as going against the respective WTO disciplines. The preferential regime in this case is hinged upon the membership status and not the objective criteria, which might go against the foundations of the non-discrimination requirements (Articles 2.1 and 5.1.1. of the TBT Agreement and Article I of the GATT), as well as the requirement for trade measures to be not more trade restrictive than necessary (Articles 2.2, 5.1.2 of the TBT Agreement and paragraph E of Annex 3 "Code of Good Practice" of the TBT Agreement). Based on this reasoning, only when respective regional rules provide access to the possibility of recognition for other WTO Members, they could be viewed as WTO-compliant.[131]

A special concern is related to the model of mutual recognition with restrictive rules of origin. Such provisions would increase intra-regional trade at the expense of imports from third countries.[132] However, mutual recognition, which does not provide rules of origin limitations could also run contrary to the TBT Agreement's provisions (Sect. 3.5 of Chap. 3).

In the practice of EU FTAs, we see that neither of the disciplines on mutual recognition in mentioned agreements include restrictive rules of origin. In fact, the only rules of origin restriction in the framework of mutual recognition with EU we could find in former versions of MRAs with Australia and New Zealand. However, these agreements have also been recently amended.[133] It is also worth to note that CETA specifically highlights that it does not restrict products of a specific origin. It

[129] See comments of the EU and Canada's representatives in: WTO Committee on Technical Barriers to Trade (2017) Thematic Session on Conformity Assessment Procedures, G/TBT/GEN/213, 5.04.2017, para. 4.

[130] Article 12.2(l) of the Protocol.

[131] Bartels (2005), pp. 701, 709; Trachtman (2006), p. 16.

[132] Chen and Matoo (2008), p. 840.

[133] Correia de Brito et al. (2016), p. 31.

is important that the CETA Protocol (Article 9) explicitly states that the procedure for mutual recognition is not limited to products originating in the parties: products coming from other countries can also be tested by the authorities on both sides of the Atlantic. Hence, it confirms a lack of origin-based bias.[134]

However, as highlighted before, the very fact that there is no practical possibility of other WTO Members to benefit from mutual recognition could be recognized as inconsistent with the WTO provisions. In fact, scholars have been repeatedly bringing to light the problematic WTO legality of the mutual recognition agreements between EU and other countries under the WTO law: for example, mutual recognition under the EC-Turkey CU or MRA between the US and EU.[135] In this respect, a suggestion to clarify recognition provisions of the TBT Agreement (Sect. 3.5.5 of Chap. 3), could be instrumental in ensuring a greater openness and transparency of recognition regimes.

4.2.4 *Innovative Approaches: Regulatory Cooperation and Good Regulatory Practices*

Another crucial aspect of the EU approach to TBT in "new generation" FTAs is use of regulatory cooperation and good regulatory practices. It follows that putting emphasis specifically on such provisions rather than developing new sectoral annexes is the new trend in the EU approach.[136] It reflects an innovative approach to tackling the regulatory challenges in a dynamic manner and by addressing internal regulatory inefficiencies. The most recent agreements dedicate specific chapters to regulatory cooperation and good regulatory practices, which also allow for a more integrated cross-sectoral approach to cooperation on regulatory issues.

4.2.4.1 Regulatory Cooperation

Regulatory cooperation provisions could be found in the TBT chapters, the sectoral annexes, as well as specific regulatory cooperation chapters in the most recent FTAs, such as EU-Japan EPA and CETA.

The "new generation" FTAs provisions build on the WTO approach when it comes to regulatory cooperation. Some aspects of the WTO approach are also given consideration. For instance, prominently, the FTAs analyzed incorporate the rule established by the TBT Committee that the reasonable period of time for other WTO

[134] See also Romanchyshyna (2020), p. 58.

[135] For the former, see Bartels (2005), and, for the latter, Mathis (1998).

[136] Laurenza and Goyeneche (2017), p. 442.

Members to make written comments to the new regulation's draft should be 60 days.[137]

What the regulatory cooperation provisions in EU FTAs are putting emphasis on is the sustained dialogue between the parties and focused cooperation. This is maintained by, first of all, putting in place the institutional structure (Table 4.3). As we see in Table 4.3, all the "new generation" FTAs include a certain institutional framework, through which the parties can maintain a focused dialogue on regulatory matters. This could be viewed as an element of a "living agreement". The example where such focused dialogue actually led to a positive result could be the EU-Korea Automotive Working Group, in the framework of which, in 2016, Korea agreed to further harmonize its regulations with international standards. The EU Commission underscored that this account proves that the implementation structure provides an effective vehicle to address trade barriers.[138]

Moreover, the TBT horizontal and sectoral provisions also contain supporting disciplines which strengthen cooperation. For instance, as we see in Table 4.3, these are the commitments to strengthen future cooperation by information exchanges, commitment in some of the FTAs to consider requests regarding recognition of technical regulations as equivalent, etc. What particularly attracts attention are the provisions encouraging the parties' regulatory and standardization authorities to cooperate, the examples of which are given in line 3 of Table 4.3. This creates a framework for the bottom-up engagement, without direct involvement of the governments. Such a framework for future cooperation at different levels could be actually a new way to go forward in terms of a "deep" trade agenda and have more compatibility in terms of disciplining technical barriers to trade.

4.2.4.1.1 Regulatory Cooperation Chapters

The regulatory cooperation chapters in the EU-Japan EPA and CETA similarly focus on the framework for regulatory exchange. In terms of structure, these provisions often go together with the provisions on good regulatory practices, and they apply to a variety of areas. For instance, for CETA, those are TBT, SPS, services, trade and sustainable development, etc.[139] It appears that the parties envisage it as an additional platform to undertake cooperation activities.

The regulatory cooperation chapters also contain an institutional structure,[140] as well as a list of cooperation activities, from information exchanges to cooperation on

---

[137] See. e.g., Article 4.4, para. 1 (f) of the EU-Korea FTA.

[138] European Commission (2017) Report on Trade and Investment Barriers, COM(2017), p. 27. https://trade.ec.europa.eu/doclib/docs/2017/june/tradoc_155642.pdf. Accessed 3 Nov 2022.

[139] Article 21.1 of the CETA.

[140] See provisions on Regulatory Cooperation Forum and contact points in CETA (Articles 21.6, 21.9) and on Committee on Regulatory Cooperation and contact points in EU-Japan EPA (Article 18.14–18.15).

Table 4.3 Regulatory cooperation provisions in TBT chapters and sectoral annexes of EU "new generation" FTAs

	EU-Korea FTA	EU-Singapore FTA	EU-Vietnam FTA	EU-Japan EPA	CETA
Institutional structure	Appointing TBT Coordinators to facilitate implementation of the TBT chapter, as well as working parties on sectoral cooperation. (Article 4.10 of the TBT chapter)	Committee on Trade in Goods is responsible for implementation of the chapter. Also, the parties established contact points, as well as working groups on sectoral cooperation (Article 4.12 of the TBT chapter)	Contact points responsible for implementation of the chapter; in the automotive sector – joint work within the Committee on Trade in Goods (Article 5.12 of the TBT chapter)	Contact points and the Specialized Committee on TBT (Article 7.13 of the TBT chapter)	Committee on Trade in Goods (Article 4.7.2 of the TBT chapter)
General clause on strengthening future cooperation	Article 4.3 of the TBT chapter indicates a number of methods, such as an exchange of information and experiences, promoting promoting and encouraging bilateral cooperation between the regulatory authorities, etc. On request, a party shall also give positive consideration for cooperation proposals of the other party.	Similar to EU-Korea FTA (Article 4.3 of the TBT chapter). Also, Article 4.7.4: On conformity assessment: non-binding commitment to engage in consultations with regard to regulatory cooperation in sectors and explain reasons for declining such requests.	Future cooperation provisions essentially similar to EU-Korea and EU-Singapore FTAs. Also, Article 5.4 (recognition of equivalence request): A party may request another party's recognition of equivalence of its technical regulations. It makes a request in writing. A party which does not agree shall provide to the other part the reasons for its decision	Future cooperation between standardizing bodies bilaterally or in the framework of international standardizing bodies (Article 6.4 of the TBT chapter). On conformity assessment: consider joining international arrangements for facilitation of acceptance of CA results Article 7.5.2 (recognition of equivalence request): similar to EU-Vietnam FTA	Commitment to work more closely in future, including through cooperation within the standardizing bodies (Article 4.3 of the TBT chapter). Article 4.4 of the TBT chapter (recognition of equivalence request): similar to EU-Vietnam and EU-Japan. Extensive provisions on future cooperation on conformity assessment (extension of the list of products under the CETA Protocol), etc.

Cooperation between the authorities	Article 4.3. (d) of the TBT chapter: promoting and encouraging bilateral cooperation between respective organisations, public or private, responsible for metrology, standardisation, testing, certification and accreditation. Article 5 (Annex 2-D of the TBT chapter) For the Working Group on Pharmaceutical Products and Medical Devices the parties shall provide for adequate participation of officials of agencies or departments responsible for health care or other matters and regulations Article 2.3 (Annex 2-B): The Parties shall ensure that their standard-setting bodies participate in the development of international standards in the ISO, IEC and ITU, and commit to consult with a view to establishing common approaches.	Article 4.4.2(d) of the TBT chapter: Encouraging cooperation between their respective bodies, whether public or private, that are responsible for metrology, standardisation, testing, certification and accreditation. Article 2.4 (Annex 4-A): The Parties shall encourage their standard-setting bodies to participate in the development of international standards in the ISO, IEC and ITU, and to consult within the framework of those international standard-setting bodies, with a view to establishing common approaches.	Article 5.5.2 of the TBT chapter: the parties shall encourage cooperation between their standardization bodies in international standardisation activities. That cooperation may be undertaken in international standardising bodies or at regional level.	Article 7.6.4 of the TBT chapter: " encourage standardising bodies to cooperate in international standardising activities. Such cooperation may take place in international standardising bodies of which both parties or standardising bodies of both parties are members. Such bilateral cooperation could aim, inter alia, at promoting the development of international standards, facilitating the development of common standards in areas of shared interest, in particular as regards new products or technologies." Article 7.12.3(d): ensuring efficient interaction and cooperation of their respective regulatory authorities at international, regional or national level	Article 4.3 of the TBT chapter: promoting and encouraging cooperation between the respective public or private organisations responsible for metrology, standardisation, testing, certification and accreditation, market surveillance or monitoring and enforcement activities; and, in particular, encouraging their accreditation and conformity assessment bodies to participate in cooperation arrangements that promote the acceptance of conformity assessment results.

international standards and harmonization and mutual recognition.[141] It is envisaged that the regulatory cooperation, could also take place at the level of regulatory authorities. The EU-Japan EPA, for instance, provides a framework for cooperation between the regulatory authorities of the parties, which would include (a) a possibility of developing common guidelines, principles, recognition of equivalence, as well as (b) bilateral cooperation in international fora, including through joint initiatives and proposals.[142]

Reflecting on the benefits of horizontal regulatory cooperation chapters, one might pinpoint the possibilities of cross-sectoral cooperation.[143] Potentially, this could contribute to a more integrated approach in terms of priorities across different areas. In particular, as it is described in the following section, it could help integrate the environmental objectives into the area of regulatory policies.

4.2.4.1.2 "Living Agreement"

An important aspect of regulatory cooperation is the decision-making powers within the FTAs' institutional structure: forums, committees, working parties, etc. This institutional structure is especially elaborate in CETA. Importantly, CETA provides that its bodies have the power to adopt decisions binding on the parties.[144] This creates a certain dynamism in addressing regulatory measures reflecting the dynamic nature of globalization, which often demands targeted and quick decision-making.[145]

At the same time, it is also worth noting that there are some democratic concerns related to such delegation of decision-making powers to the FTAs' bodies. For instance, Wolfgang Weiss questions the legitimacy of the rulemaking function of the CETA bodies. In particular, he argues that it could undermine the role of the European Parliament.[146] Those concerns are legitimate in view of the limited role the European Parliament plays in the FTAs' implementation stage. However, it appears to be more of a concern with regard to the EU internal processes, rather than a flaw of the institutional structure and decision-making in CETA. It is important to pinpoint that CETA includes provisions where recourse to domestic procedures is explicitly required—Article 26.3.2 provides that the CETA joint committee's decisions are binding subject to "completion of any necessary internal requirements", and Article 30.2.2 notes that a decision to amend CETA protocols and annexes has to be approved by the parties according to their "respective internal requirements…". It

[141] See, e.g., CETA (Article 21.4).

[142] Article 18.13 of the EU-Japan EPA.

[143] Bull et al. (2015), p. 13.

[144] See Articles 26.1, para.4. (e), 26.3 (CETA Joint Committee), Article 26.2, para.4 (specialized committees) of the CETA.

[145] Repasi (2017), p. 90.

[146] Weiss (2018), p. 544.

is for the parties to determine by themselves which internal procedures are relevant in this regard in order to create a right balance and to guarantee the democratic process.

It is important to mention that regulatory cooperation does not necessarily aim to achieve such close forms of integration, as harmonization and mutual recognition. The very existence of a sustained dialogue between the parties and their regulatory authorities, ongoing communication and information exchanges, could in the long run lead to substantial functional regulatory convergence.[147]

When drawing an interim conclusion about regulatory cooperation in EU "new generation" FTAs, it is worth to note that although the obligations are defined in quite a detailed manner, the cooperation still remains voluntary. In principle, the respective provisions only set out a platform and legal instruments for facilitation of regulatory cooperation.[148] As we see from the provisions on the parties' regulatory authorities both in TBT and regulatory cooperation chapters, some of this cooperation is to be undertaken at the level of the regulatory and standardization bodies. Such framework for future cooperation at different levels could be actually a new way to go forward in terms of "deep" trade agenda and have more compatibility in terms of disciplining technical barriers to trade.

4.2.4.2 Good Regulatory Practices

Another aspect, which prominently stands out in EU "new generation" FTAs is good regulatory practices, which, as it has been clarified in Sect. 2.3.2.8 of Chap. 2, deal with improving the quality of domestic regulatory process. These provisions relate to making the regulatory procedures of each party more transparent, predictable and comprehensible.[149] They seek to "ensure rationality, democratic accountability and the rule of law in the domestic regulatory process", which in turn "promises to reduce the adverse effects of domestic regulations on international trade without overly interfering with the right of individual states to regulate".[150]

It is worth to note that the regulatory cooperation chapters in CETA and the EU-Japan EPA take a leap forward in terms of addressing good regulatory practices provisions. Other FTAs also mention some elements of good regulatory practices, but in quite an obscure manner, for instance, the EU-Korea FTA and the EU-Singapore FTA, in the chapters dealing with transparency, mention that the parties subscribe to the principles of "good administrative behaviour" without detailing what that means.[151]

---

[147] Bull et al. (2015), p. 8.

[148] See similar conclusions in Van Damme (2020), p. 216.

[149] Ibid., p. 215.

[150] Lin and Liu (2018), p. 151.

[151] Article 12.7 of EU-Korea FTA and 13.7 of EU-Singapore FTA.

The EU-Japan EPA and CETA are more specific, as they include specifically dedicated horizontal disciplines on good regulatory practices, which are parts of the regulatory cooperation chapters. These chapters ensure a certain baseline standard for regulatory management across all areas covered by the agreements.[152]

The EU-Japan EPA is especially comprehensive. It includes a whole section on good regulatory practices detailing the following instruments:

- Early information on planned regulations
- Public consultations
- Impact assessment
- Retrospective evaluation
- Public consultations and comments
- Exchange of information on good regulatory practices.[153]

Along with this list of good regulatory practices, the EU-Japan EPA also details a number of factors that have to be considered, for instance, for the impact assessment—the nature and significance of the intended measure; any feasible alternatives thereto; how the options under consideration relate to the relevant international standards, etc.[154] A more stringent approach is taken with respect to retrospective evaluation: the parties' authorities "shall" maintain mechanisms to promote retrospective evaluation, and they "shall" make publicly available their results.[155]

The regulatory cooperation chapter in CETA similarly refers to some of the good regulatory practices, such as impact assessment, ex-post evaluation, and stakeholders engagement, but without going into much detail.[156] It is also worthwhile to note that CETA uses good regulatory practices as instruments for further cooperation between the parties to achieve greater convergence. For instance, it encourages the parties to perform joint impact assessments, exchange information on implementation and enforcement, etc.[157]

Although the provisions on good regulatory practices remain voluntary, and they are also explicitly carved out from the dispute settlement disciplines,[158] their very inclusion signals the parties' realization how important good regulatory disciplines are for trade barriers' prevention. It demonstrates the commitment to streamline the quality of the regulatory processes. This could also signal the angle of future development for the "deep" trade agenda in the area of TBT cooperation.

---

[152] See a general characteristics of these chapters in: Kauffmann and Saffirio (2021), p. 13.

[153] See sub-section 2 of chapter 18 of EU-Japan EPA.

[154] Article 18.8 of EU-Japan EPA.

[155] Article 18.9 of the EU-Japan EPA.

[156] See Articles 21.4, 21.8, 21.8 of CETA.

[157] Articles 21.4(g)(i), 21.4(m). See a similar argument specifically with respect to ex-post evaluation in: Bellmann and Van der Ven (2020), p. 34.

[158] See, e.g., Article 18.19 of EU-Japan EPA.

4.2.5 *TBT and Environmental Considerations*

Another aspect that is important in relation to the EU approach to TBT in "new generation" FTAs is the strong emphasis on addressing the sustainable development agenda. As it was mentioned before, the TBT measures are often aimed at protecting important societal values, including the environment, thus, addressing environmental considerations via TBT disciplines is a highly relevant issue in trade agreements.

The EU is a prominent actor in framing its external trade agenda in pursuit of non-trade values, including sustainable development. The EU Commission's reflection paper on "Harnessing Globalisation" envisaged international trade as a means to re-affirm global social and environmental protection standards.[159] Likewise, a recent "Strategic Plan 2020-2024" of the EU Commission puts a particular emphasis on the trade policy's support for a broader push for sustainable development and internationally set standards.[160]

These objectives also find their way in FTAs, first and foremost, by means of including specific trade and sustainable development chapters. Trade and sustainable development chapters require adherence to international labour and environmental standards.[161] Moreover, they include a non-regression clause, according to which the parties are restricted from weakening environmental and labour protection to promote trade and investment.[162] To a certain extent, it circumscribes the parties' right to regulate in ways that would not harm the sustainable development agenda.[163]

Notably, in CETA, the trade and sustainable development chapter goes a bit further into a direction of positive commitments. Article 24.9 provides that the parties agree to "make every effort to facilitate and promote trade and investment in environmental goods and services, including through addressing the reduction of non-tariff barriers related to these goods and services". Specifically, the parties agree to pay attention to those goods and services that are relevant to climate change mitigation and renewable energy.

Although most of the provisions related to the environment represent more of a soft law instrument, it could be assumed that they might be relevant in terms of interpreting the interrelation between trade liberalization and legitimate policy considerations by tilting the tip of the scales more in favour of measures which have sustainable development considerations in mind. Similarly, Isabelle Van Damme suggests that this "may result in more progressive interpretations and applications of identical obligations under . . . trade agreements as compared to the available practice under the TBT Agreement".[164]

---

[159] European Commission (2017).

[160] European Commission, Strategic Plan 2020–2024. https://trade.ec.europa.eu/doclib/docs/2020/november/tradoc_159104.pdf. Accessed 3 Nov 2022.

[161] See, e.g., Article 13.5.2 of the EU-Korea TSD chapter.

[162] See, e.g., Article 13.7 of the EU-Korea TSD chapter; Article 24.5, para.1 of CETA.

[163] Van Damme (2020), p. 233.

[164] Ibid.

Additional instruments in "new generation" FTAs, which could play part in promoting the objectives of sustainable development are the regulatory cooperation and good regulatory practices provisions. As it has been already briefly mentioned before, a specific feature of regulatory cooperation in the EU-Japan EPA and CETA is that it is refers to specifically dedicated chapters with cross-cutting disciplines for a variety of sectors and areas. More so, it is notable that both the EU-Japan EPA and CETA mention environment as one of the areas of cooperation.[165] The EU-Japan EPA also articulates that the parties, in any case, shall not be prevented from defining their own level of protection, inter alia, with regard to setting the rules of regarding the protection of the environment.[166] The CETA regulatory chapter goes even further by listing among its key principles "high levels of protection for. . .the environment".[167]

Moreover, the EU-Japan EPA also makes a reference to environmental protection in its good regulatory practices section suggesting to consider along the economic effects, also environmental, social, public health, and safety effects.[168] Incorporating environmental considerations into the regulatory impact assessment could be one of the instruments to ensure that the trade liberalization disciplines in trade agreements do not create a situation where a less stringent standard is used as a common denominator for regulatory convergence.[169]

It also has to be noted that the existing disciplines on good regulatory practices and regulatory cooperation in EU FTAs are not ideal in terms of protecting the environment. These disciplines could be more pronounced in advancing this goal, such as to be more elaborate in including environmental objectives into the regulatory impact assessment. More specifically, Christoph Bellmann and Colette van der Ven suggest to include circular economy and energy efficiency considerations into the impact assessment exercise.[170] They provide an example of the EU Sustainability Impact Assessment (SIA) issued in the process of negotiating trade agreements, which includes, for instance, circular economy concerns, and they argue that such a practice could be also integrated into the horizontal chapters on regulatory cooperation and good regulatory practices.[171] Some critics express a concern that without a set of environment-specific disciplines, the regulatory cooperation risks to be biased towards trade facilitation.[172]

[165]Article 21.1 of the CETA; Article 18.3.1 of the EU-Japan EPA mentions that the section on regulatory cooperation "applies to regulatory measures issued by the regulatory authority of a Party in respect of any matter covered by this Agreement". Trade and sustainable development is a matter "covered", as it is referred to in chapter 16 of the EU-Japan EPA.

[166]Article 18.1.2 of the EU-Japan EPA.

[167]Article 21.2.2 of CETA.

[168]Article 18.8.2(c) of the EU-Japan EPA.

[169]Bellmann and Van der Ven (2020), p. 50.

[170]Ibid., pp. 48–49.

[171]Ibid., p. 48.

[172]See, e.g., Meyer-Ohlenhof et al. (2016), p. 12.

However, it should be also pointed out that the mentioned references to the protection of the environment in the CETA and EU-Japan EPA's regulatory cooperation and good regulatory practices already represent a positive trend. As it was mentioned before, these chapters apply horizontally to multiple areas of cooperation in contrast to the previous approach, where specific cooperation provisions were set only in relation to specific areas. It could be suggested that these chapters connect different concerns, such as liberalizing the technical barriers to trade and protecting the environment, better than under the previous approach, where trade agreements include separate chapters on the environment. However, since the parties have quite a large freedom in terms of drawing the agenda of future regulatory cooperation, it would be up to the parties to create a more environmentally friendly agenda in the course of the regulatory cooperation.

4.2.6 TBT and Digital Products

Digital products are more often discussed within the framework of services and IP regulation because of their intangible nature. However, as it has been mentioned in Sect. 3.6.1 of Chap. 3, they become more and more relevant for TBT regulation. Some of the digital products, such as artificial intelligence solutions, medical internet technologies, etc., are embedded into physical objects, and, therefore, their technical requirements, which set product characteristics or related production methods, can be viewed as TBT measures. Moreover, it has been long disputed whether purely digital products can be classified as goods or services.[173] If digital products are classified as goods, regulations with regard to their technical characteristics could be also viewed as TBT measures. It is not the intention of this sub-section to review all disciplines in relation to digital products in EU FTAs, however, some issues deserve particular attention, as they have relevance for domestic regulation of digital products, which might essentially amount to TBT measures.

The substantive disciplines on TBT are in fact quite limited. The EU-Japan EPA, for instance, provides the following with regard to domestic regulation: "Each party shall ensure that all its measures of general application affecting electronic commerce are administered in reasonable, objective and impartial manner".[174] CETA largely follows the same pattern on this matter by providing that "the parties recognize importance of clarity, transparency and predictability of their domestic regulatory frameworks in facilitating, to the maximum extent possible, electronic commerce".[175] There are somewhat more specific issues in areas of particular concern. Both CETA and the EU-Japan EPA contain a general declaration to maintain transparency and effectiveness of consumer protection and the importance

[173] See, e.g., Voon (2007), p. 6.

[174] Article 8.74 of the EU-Japan EPA.

[175] Article 16.5(a) of CETA.

of personal data protection.[176] Moreover, according to CETA, "when doing so [the parties should] take into consideration international standards of data protection of relevant international organizations of which both parties are members."[177]

The limited scope of substantive disciplines is supplemented by the focused regulatory cooperation requirements. In addition to the general disciplines, there are specific provisions in CETA and the EU-Japan EPA to spur focused cooperation on the issues of electronic commerce.[178] As it has been mentioned above, these "living agreement" disciplines could lead to furthering the goal of regulatory convergence on this emerging issue.

4.3 TBT in US FTAs

This section looks into the US approach to negotiating TBT in free trade agreements. As it was mentioned in Sect. 4.1.2, the US has been actively pursuing bilateral and regional negotiations as a complement to the existing rules of the multilateral trading system, to better reflect the realities of global commerce.

This section concerns the most recent US FTAs, in particular, recently renegotiated US-Korea FTA (KORUS FTA), as well as United States-Canada-Mexico Agreement (USMCA, formerly known as NAFTA).[179] It describes the features of the main instruments that the US is using, namely, harmonization, equivalence, mutual recognition and other conformity assessment methods, and innovative approaches on regulatory cooperation and good regulatory practices. It also reflects specifically on the interconnection between TBT and environment, as well as TBT and digital goods. This section also includes certain relevant comparisons with the EU approach discussed in the previous section.

4.3.1 KORUS FTA and USMCA

Before going into detail with regards to substantive legal obligations on TBT in the KORUS FTA and USMCA, it is worthwhile to give a bit of background on the respective disciplines of these agreements.

The KORUS FTA was originally signed in 2007 and was recently updated in 2018. Its TBT provisions are quite limited in scope in terms of obligations that go

---

[176] Article 16.4 of CETA, Article 8.78 of the EU-Japan.

[177] Article 16.4 of CETA.

[178] Articles 8.80 of the EU-Japan EPA and 16.6 of CETA.

[179] Agreement between the United States of America, the United Mexican States, and Canada, 7.01.2020; Free Trade Agreement between the United States of America and the Republic of Korea, 30.06.2007.

beyond the existing WTO rules, but they do set some key priorities that the US has in this area. Also, some of the provisions are specifically tailored to the bilateral context, such as automotive sector liberalization.

USMCA was signed in 2018 and represents a renegotiation of NAFTA, the agreement between US, Canada and Mexico which dates back to 1993. USMCA contains quite far-reaching disciplines on TBT, most of which has become the result of the NAFTA renegotiation and thus represent the most recent approach. The new USMCA relies more on the WTO TBT Agreement and the subsequent TBT Committee practice. Also, a significant amount of provisions was taken from the former Trans-Pacific Partnership (TPP), which seems logical, as the TPP draft embodied the most deep and comprehensive US approach on many areas at the time.[180]

With regard to the structure of the TBT provisions, in the KORUS FTA, they are included in the chapter on TBT (chapter 9), transparency (chapter 21), as well as the attached annexes establishing the TBT Committee and the Automotive Working Group, and the so-called "confirmation letters" on specific regulatory issues regarding the automotive sector. In USMCA, except for the dedicated TBT chapter (chapter 11), there is also a separate chapter on sectoral provisions (chapter 12 that includes provisions on chemicals, cosmetics, ICT products, energy performance standards, medical devices and pharmaceuticals), chapter on good regulatory practices (chapter 28), as well as a side letter from Mexico to the United States on auto safety standards.

4.3.2 *Harmonization and Orientation Towards International Standards*

There are few key aspects of the US approach to the harmonization of TBT rules. First and foremost, similarly to the EU approach described in the previous section, it heavily relies on the international standards and promotes the parties' cooperation with respect to their development. However, there are some nuances when it comes to the understanding of the term "relevant international standard", which reflects the key differences between the EU and US standardization systems. Secondly, for the sake of greater alignment, USMCA suggests to consider other party's standards as a second-best in case of a lack of a relevant international standard. Thirdly, USMCA also contains some limited sector-specific provisions where a greater harmonization between the parties has to take place. These points are discussed, in turn, in the subsections below.

[180] Gantz (2020).

Table 4.4 Regulatory cooperation and good regulatory practices chapters in CETA and the EU-Japan EPA

	CETA	EU-Japan
Regulatory cooperation	Article 21.6: Regulatory Cooperation Forum; Article 21.9: contact points Articles 21.4 and 21.7: List of possible regulatory cooperation activities, including exchange of information, considering mutual recognition, comparing data collection practices, etc.	Article 18.4: Committee on Regulatory Cooperation; Article 18.5: contact points Article 18.12: each party may propose regulatory cooperation activities, which the other party shall consider. Article 18.13: framework of cooperation between the parties' regulatory authorities
Good regulatory practices	Article 21.4(iv): The parties endeavour to exchange experiences with regard to a variety of instruments, including impact assessment, risk assessment, compliance and enforcement strategies; 24.4 (g)(i): conducting joint risk assessment and impact assessment 24.2. (o): conducting post-implementation reviews of regulations and policies Article 21.8: Consultation with stakeholders and other interested parties, such as academia, think tanks, NGOs, consumers, and businesses.	Article 18.6: Early information on planned regulatory measures Article 18.7: Public consultations Article 18.8: Impact assessment Article 18.9: Retrospective evaluation Article 18.10: Opportunity to submit comments Article 18.11: Exchange of information on good regulatory practices

4.3.2.1 Treatment of International Standards

The analyzed US trade agreements strongly emphasize on need to follow international standards. Similarly to the EU approach, the KORUS FTA and USMCA contain a reference to the TBT Committee Decision on international standards. Therefore, the US agreements also elevate the status of the TBT Committee decision to a binding obligation. Moreover, both agreements contain provisions that imply further cooperation of the parties in the framework of international standardizing bodies. Additionally, USMCA, similarly to most of the EU agreements, requires that the party, which does not use a relevant international standard, explains the reasons for not doing so. Likewise, it requires that the parties make periodic reviews for consistency with international standards. The respective disciplines are described in Table 4.4.

From Table 4.4, it also becomes apparent that USMCA further develops the rules concerning international standards. In particular, it articulates that "each party shall apply no additional principles or criteria other than those in the TBT Committee Decision [on international standards]", and clarifies further that "criteria that are not relevant to determining whether a standard is an international standard include: (a) the domicile of the standards body; (b) whether the standards body is non-governmental or inter-governmental; and (c) whether the standards body limits participation to delegations." It also adds that that the parties cannot grant preferences to standards developed through the process inconsistent with the TBT Committee Decision on international standards and the process which "treats persons of any of the parties less favorably than persons whose domicile is the same as the standardization body".[181]

Such emphasis on the TBT Committee Decision on international standards could be explained by the particular features of the US standardization system, which is fundamentally different from the one of the EU, as it was described in the previous section. The US standardization system is deeply rooted in the historical development of its market—fragmented and competition-based, with significant power to regulate granted to the sub-federal level. It is based on a logic that is very distinct from the European and its premise is that "no single method of standards development can satisfy the needs of all sectors".[182] Thus, there is a variety of standard developing bodies (around 600[183]) that may be established in the form of private consortia, non-governmental organizations such as professional associations or scientific institutes, or public bodies. Not even is there a requirement for standardization to be their main area of activity.

A certain level of structure to the standardization activities of standards developing bodies is introduced by the American National Standards Institute (ANSI), which is a non-governmental membership-based organization providing a certain level of coordination. This organization, however, in contrast to the CEN and CENELEC's position in the EU, could hardly be claimed an overarching structure for all standardization activities in the US. The standards developing bodies it accredits, subject to a defined high equality requirements, co-exist with a manifold of other standards setters from business, academia, and industry associations, which may compete with accredited standard developing bodies if the industries find them relevant.

It is also important to point out that some of the US-domiciled standard developing bodies have an open membership and a global reputation, such as the American Society for Testing and Materials (ASTM), the Institute of Electrical and Electronics Engineers (IEEE), the American Society for Mechanical Engineers (ASME). It gives rise to the US' claim that these standard developing bodies have an international status producing standards with global application on a par with the ISO and the IEC, especially given the fact that they satisfy the requirement for international standard developing bodies identified in the TBT Committee Decision on international standards. In fact, a variety of participants may take part in the work of these bodies. This fact is often referred to by the US when criticizing the European standardization system, which does not provide the same level of openness.

We could see these particular features being manifested in the US trade agreements with a specific articulation of broad criteria for international standardizing

[181] See Article 11.4 of USMCA.

[182] American National Standards Institute. Overview of the US Standardization System. https://www.standardsportal.org/usa_en/standards_system.aspx. Accessed 3 Nov 2022.

[183] Ibid.

bodies without mentioning specific fora. Here, it is important to note that, in fact, a broad definition by the TBT Committee was pushed by the United States, dissatisfied that the EU dominated the international standards development at the ISO and the IEC.[184] Up to now, the US remains concerned by the EU's practice of inclusion of specific standards developing bodies, stating that by doing so, the EU is illegitimately trying to "reinterpret which standards should be deemed international".[185] Such position is understandable given that the European model provides more possibilities to work in tune with ISO and IEC due to internal coherence allowing to channel the consolidated national consensus into the international field. It is more complicated in the fragmented US system, where it is harder to reach consensus internally. The empirical evidence collected by Walter Mattli and Tim Büthe confirm this statement by showing that because of the institutional structure for participation at ISO and IEC, US companies are less involved into the work of the ISO and the IEC than European ones and it is more difficult for them to project any consolidated stance at the international level.[186]

Except for this general understanding of the sources of "relevant" international standards , the US and the EU positions on international standards are not starkly different. They both aim to promote them by building on the TBT Agreement. It is worthwhile mentioning that USMCA even contains some references to the specific international fora (Table 4.5), but, mostly, it relates to coherence with regards to the terminology, or the specific fora are mentioned as an example where parties could cooperate.

4.3.2.2 Consideration of the Other Party's Standards

Apart from harmonization with international standards, USMCA also stimulates harmonization between its parties in cases when there is no international standard that could meet the legitimate objectives of the respective regulations. This is quite a rare type of harmonization.[187]

The mechanism, according to Article 11.5.4 of USMCA, is the following: a party suggesting its own standard has to bring it to the attention of another party who is planning to implement a measure. This must be done at the stage when a regulation is planned or when it is published for comments. If the party implementing a measure refuses to use the proposed standard, it has to explain the reasons for that in a written document that is publishes at the same time when a final version of the regulation is issued. A similar mechanism is set in the sector-specific annexes. For instance,

---

[184] Delimatsis (2018), p. 281, footnote 31.

[185] United States Trade Representative (2020) 2020 National Trade Estimate Report on Foreign Trade Barriers, p. 179. https://ustr.gov/sites/default/files/2020_National_Trade_Estimate_Report.pdf. Accessed 2 Nov 2022.

[186] Mattli and Büthe (2003), p. 40.

[187] Bellmann and Van der Ven (2020), p. 24.

Table 4.5 International standards in the KORUS FTA and USMCA

	KORUS FTA	USMCA
"Relevant international standard"	Article 9.1 of the TBT chapter refers to the Decision of the WTO Committee	Article 11.4: "To determine whether there is an international standard. . .each Party shall apply the TBT Committee Decision on International Standards. Each Party shall apply no additional principles or criteria other than those in the TBT Committee Decision on International Standards. . . . For greater certainty, criteria that are not relevant to determining whether a standard is an international standard include: (a) the domicile of the standards body; (b) whether the standards body is non-governmental or intergovernmental; and (c) whether the standards body limits participation to delegations. No Party shall accord any preference to the consideration or use of standards that are developed through processes that: (a) are inconsistent with the TBT Committee Decision on International Standards; or (b) treat persons of any of the Parties less favorably than persons whose domicile is the same as the standardization body." Article 11.5.3: "If the Party has rejected an international standard that was brought to its attention, issue a written explanation wherever practicable." Article 11.5.2(a)(i): "[Each Party shall] periodically review technical regulations and conformity assessment procedures in order to: (i) examine increasing alignment with relevant international standards, including by reviewing any new developments in the relevant international" Sectoral provisions: Article 12.A.4.6(a): [The Parties recognise as potential area of cooperation] – implementation of the United Nations System for Classification and Labelling of Chemicals (GHS)

(continued)

Table 4.5 (continued)

	KORUS FTA	USMCA
		Article 12.B.6: on labelling of cosmetic products: recognition of importance and aligning with the International Nomenclature Cosmetic Ingredient (INCI) Article 12.E.4.2 on medical devices: "The Parties shall seek to collaborate to improve alignment. . . through work in relevant international initiatives, such as those aimed at harmonization, including the International Medical Device Regulators Forum, as well as regional initiatives that support those international initiatives. . ." Article 12.F.5.10: "Each Party shall review the safety, effectiveness, and quality information submitted to the applicant requesting marketing authorization in a format that is consistent with the specifications set forth in the Common Technical Document of the International Conference on Harmonization of Technical Requirements for Registration of Pharmaceuticals for Human Use.
Cooperation in international standard developing bodies	Article 9.4: Alignment with international standards is mentioned among other possible measures of joint cooperation	Article 11.4.4.: "The Parties shall cooperate with each other to ensure that international standards, guides and recommendations that are likely to become the basis for technical regulations do not create unnecessary obstacles to international trade." Sectoral provisions: Article 12B4.1 and 12B4.2 on cosmetics: "The Parties shall seek to collaborate to improve the alignment of their respective regulations and regulatory activities for cosmetic products through work in relevant international initiatives. . ., such as those aimed at harmonization, as well as regional initiatives that support those international initiatives; In developing or implementing regulations on cosmetic products, the Parties shall consider relevant scientific or

(continued)

Table 4.5 (continued)

	KORUS FTA	USMCA
		technical guidance documents developed through international collaborative efforts. Article 12.F.4 on pharmaceuticals: "The Parties shall seek to collaborate to improve alignment of regulatory activities for pharmaceutical products through the work in relevant international initiatives."

Article 12.A.4.5 on chemical products provides that "[e]ach party, when developing, modifying, or adopting a measure concerning chemical substances..., shall endeavor to consider how a measure adopted by another party could inform its decision making".[188]

4.3.2.3 Other Harmonization Disciplines

Other harmonization disciplines in USMCA are sector-specific and differ in terms of scope and mandatory force.

4.3.2.3.1 Energy Performance

In the area of energy performance, the parties to USMCA agreed to "endeavor" to harmonize their standards and test procedures within 8–9 years (Article 12.D.4.2). Although this provision pertains to soft law, as it does not have a mandatory force, it is clear that, by including such an obligation, the parties undertook a positive commitment to focus their regulatory cooperation efforts in the future to achieve a result where regulations would be harmonized.

4.3.2.3.2 ICT Goods That Use Cryptography and Telecommunication Equipment

There are few important aspects in terms of regulation of ICT goods which reflect the current developments and the concerns associated with this sector and which have been included into USMCA. They represent very issue-specific alignment.

First aspect relates to the ICT goods that use cryptography. Concerned by unauthorized technology transfer and theft of business confidential information, USMCA parties included the provision, which prohibits that any party requires a

[188] See similar provision in Article 12B4.2 on cosmetics.

producer or supplier of a good (a) to transfer or provide access to proprietary information, including disclosing particular technology, algorithm, (b) partner with a person in its territory, or (c) use or integrate a particular algorithm or cipher.[189]

The other provision concerns trade facilitation with the use of new technology. In particular, when it comes to equipment subject to electromagnetic compatibility and radio frequency, the parties shall be allowed to use electronic labels containing information about the equipment.[190]

4.3.2.3.3 Automotive Sector

The automotive sector contains stronger and more binding commitments both in USMCA and the KORUS FTA.

At the outset, it is important to understand that in the automotive sector, US regulations substantively differ from UNECE standards discussed in the previous section on the EU approach, as it has been mentioned before. The US has not signed the 1958 Agreement on mutual recognition of type approval for auto parts and maintained its own standards instead.[191] It does engage with the UNECE in relation to the most recent 1998 Agreement to maintain a certain level of coherence with the work at the international level, however, because it hasn't signed the 1958 Agreement, its level of integration with the UNECE standards is much lower. This manifests itself in trade agreements.

It could be observed that in the KORUS FTA, as well as in USMCA, the US promotes its own home-grown standards on auto vehicles. In USMCA, Mexico affirmed that some of its regulations on technical requirements of car parts, such as on tyres, braking lights, reverse lights, etc., incorporate the US Federal Motor Vehicle Safety Standards.[192]

The KORUS FTA uses a somewhat different mechanism, which is essentially equivalence that is addressed in the next subsection, but is also briefly described here for the sake of completeness of the automotive sector analysis. The KORUS FTA deals with two major issues—Korean safety standards and emission requirements. It allows the US exporters to sell on the Korean market by only complying with the US federal safety standards (subject to certain quota), as well as the US emission standards.[193] A concern could be made here that such equivalence is origin-based and is not derived from the quality criteria.

---

[189] Article 12.C.2.2 of USMCA.

[190] Article 12.C.4.5 of USMCA.

[191] Moguen-Toursel (2007), pp. 7–8.

[192] See Mexico-US Side Letter on Auto Safety Standards, 20.11.2018, annexed to USMCA. See also Lovells (2019).

[193] See Confirmation Letter (Specific Autos Regulatory Issues), annexed to the TBT Chapter of the KORUS FTA; Briefly described in US Congressional Research Service (2021) U.S.-South Korea (KORUS) FTA. https://fas.org/sgp/crs/row/IF10733.pdf. Accessed 3 Nov 2022.

In addition to instruments that essentially promote the US standards, it is still relevant to point out that working within the UNECE in relation to the 1998 Agreement is also part of the US trade agenda. We could see it being articulated in the KORUS FTA, which states that the parties shall cooperate bilaterally, including within the framework of the UNECE WP.29 to harmonize standards for motor vehicle environmental performance and safety (Article 9.7).

Overall, the US approach to harmonization mostly goes in line with WTO disciplines, in particular, with respect to multiple references to WTO law and practice on international standards. A slight concern could be raised with respect to the automotive sector. Firstly, promoting its own US standards in relation to Mexico does not square well with the idea of multilateralism and the requirement for the countries' regulations to be based on international standards. However, it does not mean that it would directly violate WTO provisions: for that there must be a set of conditions, such as an availability of a relevant international standard, and/or standards at issue being more restrictive than necessary. Secondly, the equivalence requirement in the KORUS FTA appears to be solely based on the origin of the imported products and not the quality characteristics of the respective US regulations, which does not go in line with the equivalence disciplines of the TBT Agreement. However, as it follows from Sect. 2.3.2.6 of Chap. 2, the equivalence disciplines, being of soft law nature, provide a significant discretion for the WTO Members in terms of their design.

4.3.3 Equivalence

Continuing the topic of equivalence, it is important to note that the general equivalence obligation is also contained in the horizontal provisions of USMCA. Equivalence, in fact, is a dominant approach to liberalization in most US FTAs.[194] Article 11.5.7 of USMCA contains the following mechanism, which, as stated in this article, furthers the goal of Article 2.7 of the TBT Agreement on equivalence: "a Party shall, on request of another Party, provide the reasons why it has not or cannot accept a technical regulation of that Party as equivalent to its own. The Party to which a request is made should provide its response within a reasonable period of time".

This requirement could be generally viewed as a continuation of the WTO approach as it builds on the respective disciplines. Moreover, it incorporates a suggestion, in Sect. 3.5.5 of Chap. 3 to clarify the meaning of Article 2.7 in order to provide a mechanism for equivalence requests.

[194] Alshareef (2019), p. 449.

4.3.4 *Mutual Recognition and Other Conformity Assessment Methods*

The US tackles conformity assessment facilitation in its trade agreements in multiple ways. The overall approach is to provide national treatment for third-party conformity assessment bodies, which is quite different from the EU approach. The sector-specific sections of the US agreements also refer to mutual recognition.

4.3.4.1 National Treatment of Third-Party Conformity Assessment Bodies

Both the KORUS FTA and USMCA contain a national treatment provision for conformity assessment bodies, which perform third-party mandatory conformity assessment.[195] For instance, the KORUS FTA states the following:

> Each party shall accredit, approve, license, or otherwise recognize conformity assessment bodies in the territory of the other party on terms no less favourable than those it accords to conformity assessment bodies in its territory. Where a Party… refuses to accredit, approve, license, or otherwise recognize a body assessing conformity … in the territory of the other Party, it shall, on request of the other Party, explain the reasons for its decision.[196]

Also, to make this requirement operational, the KORUS FTA requires the parties to publish accreditation, licensing or approval criteria, which determine whether a conformity assessment body is competent to be recognized.[197]

This builds on the TBT Agreement's provision (Article 6.4), where it encourages the WTO Members to allow participation of conformity assessment bodies of other Members in their conformity assessment procedures "under conditions no less favourable than those accorded to bodies located in their territories or the territory of any other country". Therefore, the US approach elevates the level of this provision to a legal obligation.

The USMCA goes even further to clarify the extent of this obligation, by prescribing a set of additional provisions. For instance, conformity assessment bodies cannot be required to be located in the territory of the recognizing party or operate an office; they should be allowed to use subcontractors; the procedure for conformity assessment bodies' recognition has to be transparent.[198]

It follows from the KORUS FTA and USMCA that the parties retain a possibility to decline recognition of conformity assessment bodies, but such decision has to be

[195] More on this in: Alshareef (2019), p. 440.

[196] Article 9.5.3 of the KORUS FTA. See a similar obligation in Article 11.6 of USMCA.

[197] Article 9.5.4 of the KORUS FTA.

[198] See Article 11.6 of USMCA.

well-motivated and formally explained to the party, whose conformity assessment bodies are seeking recognition.[199]

Interestingly, to elevate the level of trust between the parties' accreditation authorities and their technical competence, USMCA also provides that the parties have to facilitate and encourage their authorities to rely on mutual or multilateral recognition arrangements and consider approving accreditation bodies that are signatories of the international quality networks - ILAC and ILAF. However, in contrast to the CETA Protocol, which also addresses ILAC and ILAF, the membership of accreditation bodies in these networks is not mandatory.

Overall, the US approach for conformity assessment in trade agreements is very different in comparison to the EU approach, where the level of integration in terms of conformity assessment is much lower. This is related to the differences in the internal systems of conformity assessment. In the EU, all third-party conformity assessment procedures have to be performed by "notified bodies", which need to be established in the EU, while the US does not include in its FTAs the establishment criteria for the conformity assessment bodies.[200] As it has been mentioned before, USMCA specifically emphasizes that establishment cannot be a reason for denying the possibility for conformity assessment bodies to be recognized. The particularities of the EU conformity assessment is, in fact, viewed as a trade barrier for the US.[201]

4.3.4.2 Mutual Recognition

US trade agreements also include references to the mutual recognition of conformity assessment in some areas.

In the area of electromagnetic compatibility, USMCA provides that the parties agree to mutually accept the suppliers' declarations of conformity in case the declarations in question are based on tests from accredited laboratories.[202]

In the area of telecommunications equipment, USMCA refers to two previously negotiated mutual recognition agreements: between the US and Mexico and between the US and Canada.[203] Therefore, USMCA elevated these MRAs to the status of FTA obligation, making them more enforceable. On a separate note, it is important to mention that the MRAs in question shall not contain any rules of origin for the products and limitations on the nationality of the supplier of the telecommunication

---

[199] See. e.g., Articles 11.6.4, 11.6.11 of USMCA.

[200] United States Trade Representative (2020) 2020 National Trade Estimate Report on Foreign Trade Barriers, p. 179. https://ustr.gov/sites/default/files/2020_National_Trade_Estimate_Report.pdf. Accessed 2 Nov 2022.

[201] Ibid.

[202] Article 12.C.2.3 of USMCA.

[203] Article 12.C.4 of USMCA.

equipment. Similarly to CETA, USMCA highlights explicitly that there shall be no such limitations.[204]

In addition, both USMCA and the KORUS FTA refer to the APEC Mutual Recognition Arrangement for Conformity Assessment of Telecommunications Equipment (APEC TEL MRA).[205] While USMCA only "encourages" parties to implement the arrangement, the KORUS FTA contains a binding commitment stating that the parties "shall take steps" to implement the Phase II of the APEC TEL MRA and that no later than 5 years after the KORUS FTA enters into force, Korea has to publish the respective changes to its legislation. This represents quite an open approach, as all 21 APEC members could use this instrument between each other, by declaring their will in the exchange of letters.[206]

4.3.5 Innovative Approaches: Regulatory Cooperation and Good Regulatory Practices

A more innovative approach towards resolving regulatory divergences could be seen in provisions on regulatory cooperation and good regulatory practices, which are contained in the dedicated TBT chapters of the KORUS FTA and USMCA.

Except for the TBT-specific provisions, USMCA also includes a horizontal chapter on good regulatory practices. Although this chapter, except for good regulatory practices, also contains references and highlights the relevance of regulatory cooperation,[207] its main focus is still on good regulatory practices. As explained by Celine Kauffmann and Camila Saffirio, this could be due to the fact that the US already has comprehensive regulatory cooperation platforms, such as the Canada-US Regulatory Cooperation Council (RCC), and the High Level Regulatory Cooperation Council between (HLRCC) between the US and Mexico.[208]

The following subsections discuss, in turn, the regulatory cooperation and good regulatory provisions relevant for the TBT, which are contained both in the TBT chapters of the KORUS FTA and USMCA, as well as the chapter on good regulatory practices of USMCA. They also include two tables: Table 4.6 highlights the regulatory provisions in the TBT chapters of the KORUS FTA and USMCA, while Table 4.7 is on the good regulatory practices chapter of USMCA.

---

[204] Ibid.

[205] Article 9.5.5 of the KORUS FTA and Article 12.C.4.2 of USMCA.

[206] Correia de Brito et al. (2016), p. 33.

[207] See, e.g., Article 28.2.1 of USMCA: "[g]ood regulatory practices are fundamental to effective regulatory cooperation".

[208] Kauffmann and Saffirio (2021), p. 17.

Table 4.6 Regulatory cooperation provisions in TBT chapters of the KORUS FTA and USMCA

	EU-Korea FTA	USMCA
Institutional structure	Article 9.8, Annex 9-A: Committee on Technical Barriers to Trade Article 9-B: Automotive working group	Article 11.11: Committee on Technical Barriers to Trade; Article 11.12: contact points
General provisions on strengthening future cooperation	Article 9.4: the parties shall promote trade facilitative initiatives on particular issues and sectors. A party shall consider sector-specific proposals of the other party Article 9.6: a party shall allow persons of the other party to participate in the development of standards, technical regulations and conformity assessment procedures, if this process is open to public	Article 11.9: the parties shall consider sector-specific proposals of another party to facilitate conformity assessment facilitation. Article 11.9.3: the parties shall work to develop common standards and conformity assessment procedures in sectors of mutual interest Article 11.7.1: a party shall allow persons of the other party to participate in the development of standards, technical regulations and conformity assessment procedures. Article 11.9.3: the parties shall work to develop common standards and conformity assessment procedures in sectors of common interest Article 11.10: a party may request the other party to engage in technical discussions and information exchanges Article 11.8: clarifies that the "reasonable interval" between the publication of a measure and its entry into force should be at least 6 months
Cooperation between the authorities	Article 9.5(e): conformity assessment bodies of the parties may enter into voluntary recognition arrangements	Article 11.9(a): the parties recognize a possibility for mutual and multilateral recognition arrangements to facilitate conformity assessment Article 11.11.3(f): TBT Committee should encourage cooperation between the non-governmental bodies in the parties' territory

4.3.5.1 Regulatory Cooperation

The provisions on regulatory cooperation in US agreements somewhat resemble the disciplines of the EU trade agreements discussed earlier, but also have their own specific features.

Table 4.7 Good regulatory practices (and regulatory cooperation) chapter of USMCA

Good regulatory practices	Article 28.18: Committee on Good Regulatory Practices Article 28.3: regulatory oversight by central regulatory coordinating bodies Article 28.4: Each party shall maintain the internal processes for consultation, coordination, and review Article 28.5: Regulations need to be based on reliable and high quality information, including scientific, economic data, etc. Public surveys have to be based on sound statistical methodologies Transparency provisions, such as early planning and publishing of proposed regulations (Article 28.6), publicly available website (Article 28.7), transparency within the process of regulations' development, including that the text of the regulation shall be published along with impact assessment (in any) and explanation of its objectives (Article 28.9), publication of regulations (Article 28.12), publication of information about the regulatory process (Article 28.14), annual report on significant regulations (Article 28.16), etc. Article 28.8: Use of plain language in regulations Article 28.10: Possibility to consult expert advisory groups and transparency of this process Article 28.11: Regulatory impact assessment Article 28.13: Retrospective review Article 28.14: Opportunities for interested persons to submit proposals on improvement of regulations
Regulatory cooperation	Article 28.17: the parties should encourage their respective authorities to engage into regulatory cooperation activities with relevant counterparts; the parties intend to work together in bilateral and trilateral cooperation fora

The TBT chapters, as it could be seen in Table 4.6, provide for an institutional structure, through which the parties are aiming to strengthen their joint work to facilitate trade by reducing technical barriers. Similarly to the EU FTAs mentioned above, they are created to maintain a sustained dialogue and focused cooperation between the parties, and could be viewed as elements of a "living agreement". This mechanism is supplemented by other general provisions on strengthening cooperation, such as the consideration for sector-specific proposals, engaging in information exchange and technical discussions, etc.

The USMCA's TBT chapter codifies some of the WTO practice and clarifies WTO provisions. For instance, it provides that the reasonable period of time for parties to make comments on the new regulation could be at least 60 days, which follows the previous TBT Committee practice.[209] Also, USMCA stipulates that the "reasonable interval" between the publication of a measure and its entry into force, mentioned only vaguely in Articles 2.12 and 5.9 of the TBT Agreement, should be at least 6 months.[210]

[209] Article 11.7.4 of USMCA codifying the rule elaborated by the WTO Committee; WTO TBT Committee, Decisions and recommendation adopted by the WTO Committee on Technical Barriers to Trade since 1 January 1995, G/TBT/1/Rev.13, 8.03.2017, Section 5.3.1.8, p. 27.

[210] Article 11.8 of USMCA.

Similarly to the EU FTAs, the analyzed agreements also refer to the cooperation at the level of the parties' regulatory authorities. The TBT chapters of the KORUS FTA and USMCA refer to cooperation between the conformity assessment bodies (Table 4.6). USMCA provides more broadly that the parties should encourage their authorities to engage with relevant counterparts (Table 4.7).[211]

The USMCA, in its chapter on good regulatory practices, also mentions that the parties shall cooperate at international bilateral and trilateral fora,[212] which essentially refers to the cooperation platforms that already exist between the US, Mexico, and Canada outside the scope of the free trade agreement. By doing so, USMCA provides additional legitimacy to these settings.

The regulatory cooperation platforms—the RCC between the US and Canada and the HLRCC between the US and Mexico—are essentially the fora that bring together the central regulatory bodies of the participating countries to develop sectoral initiatives in order to stimulate regulatory alignment.[213] They are, in fact, quite unique mechanisms, as they involve dialogue directly between the regulators on sector-specific issues, while most of RTA regulatory cooperation mechanisms are primarily driven by trade authorities. Such a setting proved to be beneficial: according to evidence on the pharmaceutical, automotive and IT sectors, the RCC had quite successful results.[214] Another positive feature of the RCC is that it provides opportunities for stakeholders, such as businesses and consumers, to comment on technical and strategic documents of its action plan.[215]

All in all, the regulatory cooperation in the analyzed trade agreements goes further than the respective WTO disciplines, and, similarly to the regulatory cooperation in EU FTAs, provides a platform for continuous process of engagement between the parties in order to reach alignment in areas of interest. USMCA specifically refers to the cooperation directly between the regulatory authorities of the parties (an instrument that is also mentioned in EU FTAs), and it refers to an elaborate institutional structure for such cooperation.

4.3.5.2 Good Regulatory Practices

At the outset, it is worth noting that the good regulatory practices disciplines as parts of trade governance at the regional and multilateral levels, in fact, originate in US administrative law (including public consultations, regulatory impact assessment, inter-agency coordination, and administrative review), elaborated further by transgovernmental networks, such as the OECD and the APEC.[216]

---

[211] Article 28.17 of USMCA.

[212] Article 28.17 of USMCA.

[213] Heyden (2013), p. 18; Steiger (2012), p. 113.

[214] See this account in: Gray (2015), p. 40.

[215] Heyden (2013), p. 18.

[216] Lin and Liu (2018), pp. 152, 160.

Some elements of good regulatory practices, such as notice, comment, and review mechanisms were already included into NAFTA and were further diffused to subsequent trade agreements, including the KORUS FTA. USMCA inherited this scope too. Moreover, it incorporated the ambitious scope of good regulatory practices from the TPP draft, which was the first to include a separate chapter on those issues.

The KORUS FTA had already built on some NAFTA disciplines in terms of scope of coverage. In its transparency chapter, it detailed the procedure for publishing the proposed regulations in the official journal, mandated to explain the rationale of the proposed regulation and to address the substantive comments received during the comments period.[217]

The USMCA, building on the TPP template, went further with its horizontal chapter on good regulatory practices, as it can be seen in Table 4.7. In particular, USMCA disciplines include elaborate provisions on the impact assessment, retrospective review of regulations, ensuring stakeholders' engagement, including by duly publishing the regulations and allowing for the time for comments.

Although it is notable that many of the regulatory practices provisions in USMCA are quite similar as in CETA and the EU-Japan EPA, there are some notable differences. First and foremost, USMCA's good regulatory practices chapter has a binding nature. While CETA and EU-Japan include best effort language, USMCA has a binding language providing that the chapter stipulates "specific" requirements with respect to good regulatory practices. Also, the regulatory cooperation chapter in USMCA is subject to the dispute settlement, even though to a limited extent: "to address a sustained or recurring course of action or inaction" inconsistent with the chapter.[218] Secondly, USMCA includes a number of provisions that go beyond what CETA and the EU-Japan EPA provide, such as, an obligation of the parties to provide an annual report on significant regulations; a standard for information on which the regulations have to be based: it needs to be reliable and of high quality; transparency of the process of seeking advice from the expert advisory groups, etc.

4.3.6 TBT and Environmental Considerations

It has been mentioned in in the context of the EU approach that the "new generation" FTAs put more emphasis on environmental concerns in comparison to the WTO approach. The US FTAs analyzed here, especially USMCA, largely follow the same pattern.

At the outset, it is important to note that the United States is also one of the main advocates of strengthening environmental protection in the international arena.

[217] Article 21.1.3 and 21.1.4 of the KORUS FTA; See this account also in: Lin and Liu (2018), pp. 152, 163.

[218] Article 28.20 of USMCA. See Kauffmann and Saffirio (2021), pp. 19–20.

Environmental disciplines were already included in NAFTA and, in 2007, the US Congress and the president's administration set up a bipartisan agreement on trade policy, where the protection of the environment was identified as one of the core issues for pursuing bilateral and regional free trade agreements. Therefore, all future FTAs had to include environmental provisions.[219] The most recent policy of the US administration not only confirms this direction, but also proclaims that environmental policy is one of the main priorities and has to be pursued from multiple perspectives, through bilateral and multilateral engagement.[220]

In more concrete terms, similarly to the EU "new generation" FTAs, the US FTAs contain specifically dedicated chapters on the environment, where they require adherence to international environmental standards.[221] They also include non-regression clauses, according to which the parties shall not derogate from environmental laws in order to encourage trade and investment.[222]

Similarly to the respective discipline of CETA, the environmental chapter in USMCA goes further into a direction of positive obligations. Its article 24.24. provides that "[t]he parties shall strive to facilitate and promote trade and investment in environmental goods and services" and the Environmental Committee "shall consider issues related to trade in environmental goods.. . . including issues identified as potential non-tariff barriers to trade." It goes a bit further than CETA in stating that the parties "shall cooperate in international fora in ways to further facilitate and liberalize global trade in environmental goods and services, and may develop cooperative projects on environmental goods and services to address current and future global environmental challenges".[223] Similarly to the conclusion made in respect of CETA, such a provision might be relevant for the interpretation of the interrelation between trade liberalization and legitimate policy considerations when it comes to environmental goods. It could make a finding on the acceptability of a more favorable treatment for such goods less controversial.

Another important aspect is regulatory cooperation and good regulatory practices, which are used to promote environmental objectives. It is worthwhile to note that the introductory provision to USMCA's chapter on good regulatory practices and cooperation states that the purpose of regulatory cooperation is "to promote economic growth, while maintaining or enhancing standards of public health and safety and environmental protection".[224] More specifically, some of the good regulatory practices could have a significance in keeping the environmental concerns high on the agenda while pursuing regulatory action. For instance, regulatory impact assessment shall include a consideration of feasible alternatives and the associated

[219] Kennedy (2009), p. 543.

[220] United States Trade Representative (2021) 2021 Trade Policy Agenda and 2020 Annual Report, pp. 1–3.

[221] See Articles 20.2 of the KORUS FTA and 24.8 of USMCA.

[222] Articles 23.3.2 of the KORUS FTA and 24.4.3 of USMCA.

[223] Article 24.24 of USMCA.

[224] Article 28.1 of USMCA.

environmental costs.[225] In case of projects that have a significant effect on the environment, the parties have to conduct the assessment of environmental impacts of these projects to avoid or minimize the possible negative impact.[226] Other good regulatory practices, such as stakeholders' participation, could also contribute to a greater awareness of the public about the planned measures and could become vehicles through which the environmental groups could have a better access to the debate on the environmental effects of the proposed regulations. As it was put by Christoph Bellmann and Colette van der Ven, those kind of provisions provide a structure for a political commitment to advance environmental objectives.[227]

4.3.7 TBT and Digital Products

Similarly to the EU approach, regulation of digital goods that has relevance for the TBT regulation, is also addressed in the framework of USMCA, although in a more elaborate fashion.

In substance, there are few key disciplines. The general provision states that the parties shall "endeavor to avoid unnecessary regulatory burden on electronic transactions".[228] Moreover, there is an obligation to maintain a legal framework on electronic transactions consistent with the principles of the UNCITRAL Model Law on Electronic Commerce 1996.[229] A set of specific provisions address consumer protection and data privacy.[230] In particular, on data privacy, the parties recognize the authority of a number of international recommendations. For instance, the parties should take into consideration the APEC Privacy Framework and OECD Recommendation of the Council concerning Guidelines governing the Protection of Privacy and Transborder Flows of Personal Data. Also, the parties recognize the APEC Cross-Border Privacy Rules system as a valid mechanism to facilitate cross-border information transfers while protecting personal information.[231] Another set of disciplines concerns the technology side of the digital products regulation. For instance, USMCA forbids data localization requirements,[232] and transfer of source code and algorithm as a condition for import, distribution or sale of a certain digital good.[233]

---

[225] Article 28.11.2(c) of USMCA.

[226] Article 24.7 of USMCA.

[227] Bellmann and Van der Ven (2020), p. 35.

[228] Article 19.5.2(a) of USMCA.

[229] Article 19.5.1.

[230] Articles 19.7 and 19.8 of USMCA.

[231] Article 19.8 of USMCA.

[232] Article 19.12 of USMCA.

[233] Article 19.16 of USMCA.

It is also worth pointing out that the digital goods concerns have been also specifically addressed in sectoral TBT provisions (on ICT products), which demonstrates the growing relevance of digital products concerns for the TBT regulation in particular. The respective provisions, inter alia, forbid the requirement to disclose particular technology or algorithm with respect to the ICT goods that use cryptography.[234]

4.4 Multilateralizing Regional Cooperation

This section builds on the discussion in Sect. 3.6 of Chap. 3 on the multilateral approaches to TBT liberalization, which argues that, despite the WTO limitations in addressing the regulatory agenda, there might be ways to go forward on this issue, for example, via plurilateral agreements, or by strengthening the deliberation function of the WTO. It was also mentioned that the approaches in regional trade agreements could serve as an inspiration for future multilateral disciplines. This section also draws from the previous two sections of this Chapter, which discuss the TBT provisions in the US and EU FTAs, and endeavors to identify approaches in these FTAs, which could serve as such an inspiration, taking into account the limitations of the WTO system.

The structure of this section is the following. Section 4.4.1 discusses entrenched regulatory differences as an impediment to cooperation and suggests few less contentious options for moving forward. Section 4.4.2 analyses issues of the multilateral dimension, where there could be a possibility of bringing cooperation to the multilateral level.

4.4.1 Focusing on Possibilities, Rather Than Impediments

4.4.1.1 Entrenched Regulatory Differences as an Impediment to Cooperation

It is quite clear that where regulatory traditions and underlying practices are different, it might not be expected that they could be easily transformed. On the example of the US and the EU FTAs analyzed in the previous sections, we could see how such systemic differences could impede further cooperation. In particular, it has been discussed in the previous sections that the EU and the US have a different perspective with regard to the understanding on what constitutes international standards and the designation and operation of conformity assessment bodies. This essentially translates into the respective provisions of their trade agreements. For instance,

[234] Article 12.C.2.2 of USMCA.

many EU FTAs include an understanding that ISO, IEC, and ITU are relevant international standardizing bodies, thereby recognizing their primal authority, while USMCA specifically points out that there could be no other criteria for international standardizing bodies than those identified in the TBT Committee Decision on international standards. On conformity assessment, USMCA provides that the parties shall not provide less favorable conditions to conformity assessment bodies that are not located in their territory, while in the EU, mandatory third party conformity assessment has to be performed only by the bodies located in its territory. The most pronounced example is perhaps the automotive sector, where the US and EU standards differ substantively. As the EU standards are widely based on the UNECE standards elaborated by the UNECE WP.29, many of the EU trade agreements also contain a reference to this setting. Moreover, in some of the agreements, the requirement to consider the UNECE standards and the associated conformity system architecture goes beyond a mere soft law provision. The US, on the other hand, promotes references to its homegrown standards. Also, it is worthwhile to note that the US actually considers the mentioned particularities of the EU regulatory system and the EU approach in trade agreements with specific references to particular standardizing bodies a trade barrier.[235] Those issues were largely discussed as problematic within the negotiations of the Transatlantic Trade and Investment Partnership (TTIP).[236]

These are examples of issues that could hardly be subject to the multilateral agenda due to their contentious character. While in RTA settings, the EU and US could advance their interests by including their own approaches with smaller and/or likeminded trading partners, it is could hardly be achieved at the multilateral level, even in the framework of a plurilateral agreement, as it would face opposition.

4.4.1.2 Going Forward on Less Contentious Issues

One option to go forward might include strengthening the enforcement of disciplines that already exist in the TBT agreement. For instance, it could be done with regards to the adherence to the international standards. One might draw an inspiration from the US and EU FTAs, which provide in relevant parts that the parties have to explain, on request, why they did not use a "relevant international standards". The TBT Committee could clarify the Members' obligation to respond to such requests. Likewise, the Members could also clarify the mechanism for equivalence requests, as it is provided in USMCA and as it was suggested earlier in Sect. 3.5.5 of Chap. 3.

Another option could be to develop a common understanding on best practices with regard to conformity assessment. Such a proposal has recently been tabled by

[235] United States Trade Representative (2020) 2020 National Trade Estimate Report on Foreign Trade Barriers, p. 178. https://ustr.gov/sites/default/files/2020_National_Trade_Estimate_Report.pdf. Accessed 2 Nov 2022.

[236] See, e.g., Jacques Pelkmans (2015).

the European Union for the TBT Committee Ninth Triennial Review, where it suggests to develop a "recommendation that sets a number of general principles on good practices on conformity assessment and some practical elements on how conformity assessment procedures should be designed by regulators."[237] It could be imagined that such guidelines could include some of the mechanisms from the US and EU FTAs, such as the risk assessment approach, promotion of suppliers' declarations of conformity where appropriate, recognition of the ILAC and ILAF as valid conformity assessment quality networks, etc.

A more contentious suggestion could be to conclude mutual recognition agreements within the framework of the WTO. Such agreements could be concluded between some of the Members (on a plurilateral basis). Although the participation of other Members in such arrangements should in any case be subject to conditions, such arrangement would be more transparent than any of the RTA mutual recognition provisions, or MRAs.

4.4.2 Multilateral Dimension of Substantive Cooperation

Section 3.6 of Chap. 3 discussed the reasons why multilateral cooperation on technical barriers to trade could be an optimal solution when it comes to the issues of global concern. There are two main contexts for such cooperation: it is either related to the protection of the global public good, such as the protection of the environment, or it deals with sectors, which are affected by rules of multiple jurisdictions and where the regulations are less entrenched, such as digital goods.[238] On both areas, where they are interconnected with trade, RTAs have become the primary vehicle to move forward global trade regulation. It could be suggested that the RTAs approach might be used as a basis for further multilateral action.

4.4.2.1 Environmental Concerns

On environmental protection, RTAs contain some important solutions that could also be envisaged at the multilateral level. One of these solutions relates to environmental goods and has quite a nascent form in CETA and USMCA, which provide that the parties agree to make efforts to promote trade in environmental goods through reduction of non-tariff barriers related to those goods. The problem with this solution, if it gets further development in RTAs, is that it might risk running

[237] WTO Committee on Technical Barriers to Trade (2021) Proposals on Conformity Assessment, Transparency, and COVID-19, Ninth Triennial Review, Submission from the European Union, G/TBT/W/736, 1.02.2021, paras.1.1–1.2.

[238] Bollyky (2017), p. 4.

inconsistent with the WTO TBT Agreement's provisions. It could raise a question on the relevance of the production methods: whether it is justified to provide preferential treatment for products produced in an environmentally-friendly manner. Depending on the context, it might raise the issue of "likeness" between such products, with, for instance, products produced with the use of fossil fuels, as well as whether the preferential treatment is applied even-handedly, whether it is really connected with the objective of environmental protection. The answers might not be straightforward. That is why the multilateral agreement on non-tariff measures on environmental goods might be a better option, as it would constitute a broad-based consensus that liberalization of environmental goods has to be a priority. Such an agreement could take the form of an open plurilateral agreements, to which all the WTO Members could easily subscribe to. Moreover, within the scope of these plurilateral agreements, the Members could also come up with the sector specific understandings in order to make the initiative more concrete.

Another solution is related to advancing good regulatory practices, and in this specific context—promoting environmental considerations within their scope. One could see that the EU-Japan EPA and USMCA mention the environment as one of the considerations for impact assessment. This aspect could also be further developed and receive an active promotion at the multilateral level. It might be suggested that the strengthened deliberative role of the TBT Committee could include discussion and a review of the implementation of such good regulatory practices by the Members.

In addition, developing and least developed countries could also benefit more from the capacity building initiatives to strengthen their administrative procedures for this purpose. In this regard, as it has been mentioned in Sect. 3.6.2.2 of Chap. 3, it would be beneficial if the WTO cooperated with other international organizations on environmental protection, as well as Multilateral Development Banks and other capacity building projects, which could help in terms of technical assistance.[239]

Regulatory cooperation could also provide a structure for a political commitment to advance environmental objectives.[240] The suggestion here could be to include environmental considerations as a regular item into the TBT Committee agenda, so that when working on recommendations and best practices on how to deal with technical barriers to trade, WTO Members would take environmental concerns as one of the main principles for such solutions.

4.4.2.2 Digital Goods

It has been mentioned in Sect. 3.6.2.1 of Chap. 3 that the negotiations on e-commerce, including digital goods, is already a subject of the open plurilateral agreement negotiations at the WTO. What is lacking is consistent regulatory

[239] Gari (2020), p. 54.

[240] Bellmann and Van der Ven (2020), p. 35.

framework for such goods. In this respect, CETA, the EU-Japan EPA, and USMCA could provide guidance on how to move forward to certain specific issues.

It is relevant to point out that the EU-Japan EPA, CETA, and USMCA include "limited requirements that potentially discipline technical barriers", as it was pointed out by Canada in its submission to the Ninth Triennial Review of the TBT Committee.[241] This is the requirement for reasonable, impartial, transparent and clear regulation and administration of the area of digital products in the EU-Japan EPA and CETA, as well as the requirement to try to avoid unnecessary regulatory burden for electronic transactions in USMCA.

Going forward, and, following the suggestion made by Canada at the Ninth Triennial Review, it might be beneficial to "clearly specify that intangible digital products are covered by the obligations in the TBT provisions", or "to replicate TBT provisions in digital agreements".[242] The TBT Agreement's disciplines could fill in the gaps in the global regulatory framework for digital goods with its provisions on non-discrimination, necessity, and international standards.

At the same time, it is also important to note that such issues as privacy and data protection, obligation not to require the disclose of a source code and algorithms, as well as data localization would certainly remain contentious regulatory issues, on which the EU and the US, for instance, do not have a consensus. Those issues are at the intersection of goods, services and IP regulations, and they have to be considered separately.

4.4.2.3 Regulatory Cooperation and Good Regulatory Practices

As it was described in the previous sections, the inclusion of regulatory cooperation and good regulatory practices into the "new generation" EU and US FTAs represents an innovative approach and is a new trend in global trade regulation. The existing WTO framework does include regulatory cooperation disciplines, through the deliberation in the TBT Committee, however, it could also learn from some of the more advanced mechanisms of the RTAs.

First, it could be suggested that the structure of the institutional framework for regulatory cooperation could serve as an inspiration for framework plurilateral agreements, which, according to Thomas Bollyky and Petros Mavroidis, could include a set of baseline rules and goals for cooperation, pursuant to which the parties would be able to collaborate on topic-specific emerging issues, coupled

[241] WTO Committee on Technical Barriers to Trade (2021) Proposals on Conformity Assessment, Environment and Climate Change, Transparency, Digital Products, and Micro, Small, and Medium-Sized Enterprises (MSMEs), Ninth Triennial Review, Submission from Canada, G/TBT/W/745, 28.04.2021, para. 4.3.

[242] Ibid., para. 4.4.

together with a mechanism for monitoring and reporting.[243] This is essentially an idea of a "living agreement", which is extended and adapted continuously.

Secondly, the regulatory cooperation disciplines could also serve as inspiration for extending the deliberation function of the WTO. Regulatory cooperation in the most recent RTAs is cross-sectoral. It could cover many issues and include concerns from the perspectives of different domains. The WTO TBT Committee could also benefit from such varied expertise, and per Gabriel Gari and Bernard Hoekman suggestion, it could connect better with the stakeholders—Members' officials responsible for regulatory policy, in addition to the trade officials, who usually take part in the committee deliberations.[244]

Good regulatory practices, especially the most elaborate provisions in the EU-Japan EPA and USMCA, could also find their way into the WTO. The list of good regulatory practices already exists in the form of a recommendation of the TBT Committee.[245] However, it is quite short and less elaborate than the good regulatory practices in the RTAs. Moreover, it could be also suggested to make good regulatory practices a regular part of the TBT Committee agenda and to install the review function of the TBT Committee regarding the Members' progress in implementing them. As it has been already mentioned before in the context of strengthening of the provisions on the environmental protection, this has to be supplemented by comprehensive capacity building programs along with other international organizations and development funds.

4.5 Conclusion

The above analysis demonstrated how the EU and US transitioned from reliance on the negotiations at the multilateral level to addressing the "deep" trade agenda in their trade agreements. It showed different forms of navigating cooperation on TBT: from some forms of regulatory alignment to strengthened regulatory cooperation. This arsenal of methods might move forward the global regulatory governance in response to the changing paradigms of global commerce and could also serve as an inspiration for future multilateral disciplines.

[243] Bollyky and Mavroidis (2017), p. 27.

[244] Gari (2020), p. 53; Hoekman (2019), p. 387.

[245] WTO Committee on Technical Barriers to Trade (2015) Decisions and Recommendations. G/TBT/1/Rev.12, 21.01.2015, p. 6.

References

Books and Book Chapters

Cooper R (2003) Comment to Jeffrey Schott, "Free Trade Agreements: Boon or Bane of the World Trading System?". In: Schott J (ed) Free Trade Agreements – US strategies and priorities. Institute for International Economics, Washington DC, pp 20–24

De Burca G (2013a) EU external trade relations: the governance mode of foreign policy. In: Van Vooren B, Blockmans S, Wouters J (eds) The EU's role in global governance: the legal dimension. Oxford University Press, Oxford, pp 39–58

De Burca G (2013b) Europe's "raison d'etre". In: Kochenov D, Amtenbrink F (eds) European Union's shaping of the international legal order. Cambridge University Press, Cambridge, pp 21–37

Garcia-Duran P (2016) The bilateralism/multilateralism debate and European Trade Policy. In: Garcia-Duran P, Millet M (eds) Different glances at EU trade policy. Barcelona Centre for International Affairs, Barcelona, pp 23–32

Gari G (2020) Narrowed Down Utopia: adjusting the WTO to a changing trade environment. In: Kolski Lewis M et al (eds) A post-WTO international legal order. Utopian, Dystopian and other scenarios. Springer, Cham, pp 37–55

Heydon K, Woolcock S (2009) The rise of bilateralism: comparing American, European and Asian approaches to preferential trade agreements. United Nations University Press, Hong Kong

Larik J (2011) Much more than trade: the common commercial policy in a global context. In: Evans M, Koutrakos P (eds) Beyond the established legal orders: policy interconnections between the EU and the rest of the world. Hart Publishing, Oxford, pp 13–46

Melo Araujo B (2016) The EU Deep Trade Agenda: law and policy. Oxford University Press, Oxford

Romanchyshyna I (2020) Tackling technical barriers to trade in EU "New Generation" FTAs – an example of open, competing or conflicting regionalism? In: Weiss W, Furculita C (eds) Global politics in EU Free Trade Policy. Springer, Cham

Twitchett K (ed) (1976) Europe and the World: the external relations of the common market. St. Martin's Press, New York

Van Damme I (2020) Technical barriers to trade in the new generation of EU Trade Agreements. In: Hahn M, Van Der Loo G (eds) Law and practice of the common commercial policy. Brill, Leiden, pp 206–234

Van Vooren B (2013) The EU's financial transaction tax: shaping global financial governance in its own image? In: Kochenov D, Amtenbrink F (eds) The European Union's shaping of the international legal order. Cambridge University Press, Cambridge, pp 328–348

Journal Articles

Alshareef S (2019) Technical standards liberalization in FTAs of the United States, the European Union and China. J World Trade 53(3):433–454

Bartels L (2005) The legality of the EC mutual recognition clause under the WTO law. J Int Econ Law 8(3):691–720

Bergsten F (2002) A Renaissance for US Trade Policy. Foreign Aff 81(6):86–98

Biden J (2020) Why America must lead again: rescuing U.S. foreign policy after trump. Foreign Aff 99(1):64–76

Bollyky T, Mavroidis P (2017) Trade, social preferences and regulatory cooperation. The new WTO-think. J Int Econ Law 20(1):1–30

Bown C (2017) Mega-regional trade agreements and the future of the WTO. Global Pol 8(1): 107–112
Bradford A (2015) Exporting standards: the externalization of the EU's regulatory power via markets. Int Rev Law Econ 42:158–173
Brewster R (2018) Analyzing the trump administration's international trade strategy. Fordham Int Law J 42(1):1419–1430
Bull R, Mahboubi N et al (2015) New approaches to international regulatory cooperation: the challenge of TTIP, TPP, and mega-regional trade agreements. Law Contemp Probl 78(1):1–29
Chen M, Matoo A (2008) Regionalism in standards: good or bad for trade. Can J Econ 41(3): 838–863
Cho S (2001) Breaking the barrier between regionalism and multilateralism: a new perspective on trade regionalism. Harv Int Law J 42(2):419–465
Damro C (2012) Market power Europe. J Eur Publ Policy 19(5):682–699
Delimatsis P (2018) Global standard-setting 2.0: how the WTO spotlights ISO and impacts the transnational standard-setting process. Duke J Comp Int Law 28(273):273–326
Foulon M (2021) Turbulent Trade: Europe and Biden Challenge. ETH Zurich Policy Persp 9(1):1–4
Gray B (2015) Upgrading existing regulatory mechanisms for transatlantic regulatory cooperation. Law Contemp Probl 78(31):31–48
Hoekman B (2019) Urgent and important: improving WTO performance by revisiting working practices. J World Trade 53(3):373–394
Kennedy K (2009) The Status of the Trade-Environment-Sustainable Development Triad in the Doha Round Negotiations and in Recent U.S. Trade Policy. Indiana Int Comp Law Rev 19(3): 529–552
Laurenza E, Goyeneche F (2017) Regulatory cooperation in Free Trade Agreements: perspectives from the automotive and information and communication technology sectors. Global Trade Cust J 12(11/12):433–444
Lin C-F, Liu H-W (2018) Regulatory rationalization clauses in FTAs: a complete survey of the US, EU and China. Melbourne J Int Law 19(1):149–177
Manners I (2002) Normative power Europe: a contradiction in terms? J Common Mark Stud 40(2): 235–258
Mathis J (1998) Mutual recognition agreements. Transatlantic parties and the limits to non-tariff barrier regionalism in the WTO. J World Trade 32(6):5–31
Mattli W, Büthe T (2003) Setting international standards. Technological rationality or primacy of power? World Polit 56(1):1–42
Maull H (1990) Germany and Japan: the new civilian powers. Foreign Aff 69(5):91–106
Pelkmans J (2007) Mutual recognition in goods. On promises and disillusions. J Eur Publ Policy 14(5):699–716
Repasi R (2017) Dynamisation of international trade cooperation. Powers and limits of joint committees in CETA. Quest Int Law 41:73–95
Romanchyshyna I (2020b) Mutual recognition as a method to deal with regulatory divergence: what is its reach in EU FTAs? Global Trade Cust J 15(1):6–14
Scott J (2014) Exterritoriality and territorial extension of EU law. Am J Comp Law 62(1):87–125
Steiger D (2012) Institutions for regulatory cooperation in "New Generation" Economic and Trade Agreements. Legal Iss Econ Integr 39(1):109–112
Tellis A (2015) The geopolitics of TTIP and TPP. Adelphi Series 54(450):93–120
Weiss W (2018) Delegation to treaty bodies in EU agreements: constitutional constraints and proposals for strengthening the European Parliament. Eur Const Law Rev 14:532–566

Official Documents

European Commission (2004) Commission staff working paper: priorities for bilateral/regional trade activities in the field of mutual recognition agreements for industrial products and related technical dialogue, SEC (2004)1072. European Commission

European Commission (2012) Communication "CARS2020 action plan for a competitive and sustainable automotive industry in Europe. European Commission

European Commission (2015) Trade for all. Towards a more responsible trade and investment policy. European Commission

European Commission (2017) Reflection paper on harnessing globalization. European Commission

Lamy (2004) Trade policy in the Prodi Commission 1999–2004: an assessment. European Commission

United States Trade Representative (2021) 2021 Trade Policy Agenda and 2020 Annual Report

World Trade Organization (2012) World Trade Report. WTO

Other Articles

Evenett S, Meier M (2007) An Interim Assessment of the US Trade Policy of "Competitive Liberalization". University of St. Gallen Discussion Paper No. 207-18. https://papers.ssrn.com/sol3/papers.cfm?abstract_id=985521. Accessed 1 Nov 2022

Gantz D (2020) The USMCA: Updating NAFTA by Drawing on the Trans-Pacific Partnership. Arizona Legal Studies Discussion Paper No.10-06, Mexico Center, Rice University's Baker Institute for Public Policy. https://ssrn.com/abstract=3542536. Accessed 3 Nov 2022

Moguen-Toursel M (2007) Emergence and Transfer of Vehicle Safety Standards: Why We Still Do not Have Global Standards? Business and Economic History Online Vol 5. Center for Historical Research at Ohio State University, pp 7–8. https://thebhc.org/sites/default/files/moguen-toursel.pdf. Accessed 3 Nov 2022

Romanchyshyna I (2019) Standards as Transatlantic Trade Barriers: Is there a Future for the EU-US Regulatory Cooperation? Geneva Jean Monnet Working Papers. https://papers.ssrn.com/sol3/papers.cfm?abstract_id=3490517. Accessed 1 Nov 2022

Trachtman J (2006) Embedding Mutual Recognition at the WTO, p. 16. https://ssrn.com/abstract=923903 or https://doi.org/10.2139/ssrn.923903. Accessed 1 Nov 2022

Van der Loo G, Akhvlediani T (2020) Catch Me if You Can: Updating the Eastern Partnership Association Agreements and DCFTAs. CEPS "3DCFTAs" project. https://www.ceps.eu/wp-content/uploads/2020/05/GVDL-and-TA-Updating-AA-DCFTAs.pdf. Accessed 2 Nov 2022

Van Der Loo G, Van Elsuwege P, Petrov R (2014) The EU-Ukraine Association Agreement: Assessment of an Innovative Legal Instrument. EUI Working Papers LAW 2014/09

Voon T (2007) A New Approach to Audiovisual Products at the WTO: Rebalancing GATT and GATS. Melbourne Law School, Legal Studies Research Paper No.244, p. 6. https://ssrn.com/abstract=1012213. Accessed 3 Nov 2022

Woolcock S (2007) European Union Policy towards Free Trade Agreements. ECIPE Working Paper, No, 03/2007, European Centre for International Political Economy (ECIPE), Brussels

Woolcock S (2019) The Role of the European Union in the International Trade and Investment Order. Dahrendorf Forum IV Working Paper, London School of Economics, p 3. https://www.dahrendorf-forum.eu/wp-content/uploads/2019/04/EU-international-trade-investment.pdf. Accessed 3 Nov 2022

Research Papers of International Organizations and Research Institutions

Ahearn R (2009) Transatlantic Regulatory Cooperation: Background and Analysis. US Congressional Research Service. https://fas.org/sgp/crs/row/RL34717.pdf. Accessed 3 Nov 2022

Bellmann C, Van der Ven C (2020) Greening Regional Trade Agreements on non-tariff measures through technical barriers to trade and regulatory cooperation. OECD Publishing, Paris

Bollyky T (2017) The role of regulatory cooperation in the future of the WTO. RTAs Exchange. International Centre for Trade and Sustainable Development (ICTSD) and the Inter-American Development Bank (IDB)

Correia de Brito A et al. (2016) The Contribution of Mutual Recognition to International Regulatory Co-operation. OECD Regulatory Policy Working Papers. OECD Publishing, Paris, p 22. https://doi.org/10.1787/5jm56fqsfxmx-en. Accessed 1 Nov 2022

Eeckhout P (2018) Future Trade Relations between the EU and the UK: Options for Brexit. Study for the European Parliament, INTA Committee, Directorate General for External Policies. http://www.europarl.europa.eu/RegData/etudes/STUD/2018/603866/EXPO_STU(2018)603866_EN.pdf. Accessed 2 Nov 2022

Heyden J (2013) The Canada-U.S. Regulatory Cooperation Council. OECD International Regulatory Cooperation: Case Studies, Vol.2: Canada-US Cooperation, EU Energy Regulations, Risk Assessment and Banking Supervision. OECD Publishing, Paris

Kauffmann C, Saffirio C (2021) Good regulatory practices and cooperation in Trade Agreements: a historical perspective. OECD Regulatory Policy Working Papers. OECD Publishing, Paris

Meyer-Ohlenhof N et al (2016) Regulatory Cooperation under CETA: Implications for Environmental Policies, The Ecologic Institute. https://www.ecologic.eu/sites/default/files/publication/2016/2586-regulatorische-kooperation-greenpeace-ceta.pdf. Accessed 3 Nov 2022

Murphy J (2020) Why American Business Needs the WTO. US Chamber of Commerce, https://www.uschamber.com/series/above-the-fold/why-american-business-needs-the-wto. Accessed 2 Nov 2022

Pelkmans J (2015) TTIP: Opportunities and Challenges. Technical Barriers to Trade including Standards Study for the European Parliament, Committee on the Internal Market and Consumer Protection, IP/A/IMCO/2014-14

US Congressional Research Service (2021) US – South Korea (KORUS) FTA. https://fas.org/sgp/crs/row/IF10733.pdf. Accessed 3 Nov 2022

Van Elsuwege P, Chamon M (2019) The Meaning of Association under EU Law, Study on the Law and Practice of EU Association Agreements. European Parliament's Policy Department for Citizens' Rights and Constitutional Affairs. https://www.europarl.europa.eu/thinktank/en/document/IPOL_STU(2019)608861. Accessed 3 Nov 2022

Chapter 5
Conclusion

As per the research question described in the introduction, this study analyzed the interrelation between cooperation on technical barriers to trade (TBT) in RTAs and the WTO system. In particular, it examined whether the TBT facilitation methods in RTAs go in line with the respective WTO approach, and whether, drawing from the RTAs experience, the WTO could improve its TBT-related disciplines and institutional procedures.

Chapter 2 provided a context for this study. It began by examining the issue of increasing relevance of technical barriers to trade, which creates a need for strengthened global trade regulation in this area. In view of the changing realities of global commerce, production and distribution processes are being unbundled across countries via global value chains (GVCs), facilitated through rapid technological growth modifying the channels of communication, manufacturing and trade leading to greater interconnectedness between countries, which creates a demand for closer cooperation on regulatory matters. TBT have a particular significance, as they are by far the most widely used type of non-tariff measures affecting goods having the most profound effects in terms of trade value and product coverage. They inhibit trade in various ways: from differences in regulations of product design and packaging that may induce producers to establish separate production lines for different jurisdictions, to burdensome, duplicative and unnecessary procedures for testing and certification that also generate additional costs and disincentivize exporters to open new markets.

This context calls for action at the international level. Because of the link between trade and regulation, more and more regulatory issues are addressed specifically within the context of trade agreements. It is fair to assume that regulatory measures, including TBT, would represent an avenue where future trade liberalization efforts will be focusing on.

At the same time, cooperation on technical barriers to trade should not only concern the aspect of trade liberalization per se. Another issue relevant in the context of the changing paradigms of global commerce is the expanded regulatory need to

I. Romanchyshyna, *Technical Barriers to Trade in "New Generation" RTAs and in the WTO Agreements*, EYIEL Monographs - Studies in European and International Economic Law 29, https://doi.org/10.1007/978-3-031-25791-9_5

protect consumers, the environment and other societal values. Increasing production and trade elevate sensitivities in these areas and create more risks of weakening of the respective levels of protection. Therefore, it is clear that future trade agreements also have to address those public policy issues in a more comprehensive manner.

Chapter 2 then included an analysis of the existing multilateral trade regulation on technical barriers to trade, as well as regulation established within RTAs. It pinpointed that in the past the GATT/WTO system used to adapt to new realities: While it was initially mostly focused on tariffs and other border measures, along the way it incorporated a progressive agenda on other trade-related issues, including on TBT. However, now there are substantive constraints to moving the system forward. Most importantly, they are associated with the way the WTO system is built, in particular, the fact that agreements have to be adopted as a "single undertaking" by consensus of all WTO Members and eventually be binding and enforceable by dispute settlement. While such an ambitious approach could work in the past in relation to tariff liberalization, now, with a large number of WTO Members with different priorities and different levels of development, it is particularly challenging and is not always desirable.

The gap between the limits of the WTO toolbox to address the challenges of the globalised commerce and the countries' ever-increasing need to move forward with further trade liberalization prompts WTO Members to conclude between each other trade agreements with "deep" integration provisions. This raises the question on whether such agreements could be a complement to the process of global integration or rather create fragmentation of the global trade governance.

Chapter 3 was dedicated to the discussion on regionalism and multilateralism, which has been ongoing since the creation of the GATT/WTO system. It explored the question on whether TBT cooperation in RTAs goes in line with WTO rules, including on regional integration, as well as how WTO approach could adapt to address TBT in a more comprehensive fashion.

As it was noted in the historical account of the interrelation between the WTO and RTAs, the regional exception clause was envisaged from the very beginning when the GATT/WTO system was created. Article XXIV of the GATT was expected to provide a leeway for WTO Members to pursue trade deals with some of the other Members even when it could run contrary to the MFN principle. It came from the conviction that RTAs would not largely compromise the multilateral ideas, but rather complement its goals, as both the multilateral system, as well as regional trade agreements have a common enemy—domestic trade barriers that excessively burden international trade. However, with time RTAs proliferated at a great pace becoming essentially a major driver of global trade governance. While the first wave of RTAs appeared to be largely non-threatening for the envisaged development of the multilateral project, more recent RTAs cause some concerns in this respect, especially taking into consideration the fact that after the Uruguay Round multilateral trade negotiations at the WTO stalled.

At the same time it is fair to note that when it comes to the TBT cooperation methods in RTAs, one has to keep in mind that their effects for outsiders are not similar to the effect of tariffs meaning that the classic theory of regionalism built on the study of tariffs, which to a large extent blasts RTAs, would be less relevant. It appears that overall, in comparison to tariffs, the TBT provisions in RTAs could have positive static and dynamic effects for global welfare, as their benefits might be less exclusive. For instance, countries outside the preferential area might still benefit from one unified standard, which creates greater predictability and could help scale the production faster.

However, despite that TBT cooperation methods in RTAs tend to have less exclusive effects than tariff preferences, there are still some concerns associated with their use. In particular, in RTAs, the design of methods chosen to deal with technical barriers could reflect the preferences of the exclusive group of countries. It might be difficult to efficiently tackle a broad range of issues of multilateral dimension, such as the environmental protection and economic development, especially in a manner that would be inclusive with regard to a multitude of interests at the international arena. The relevant provisions of RTAs may lock in certain regulatory solutions that do not reflect a broad consensus between the WTO Members. For instance, as harmonization in RTAs could be based on the approaches of the participating parties (mainly from the developed world, as those issues are more likely to appear on their agenda), other countries, especially developing and least developed ones, could find themselves in a disadvantage.

Further, Chap. 3 analyzed the legal dimension of the interconnection between TBT in RTAs and the WTO. It focused specifically on harmonization and mutual recognition, as these methods achieve a greater level of integration exclusively between the parties and might cause some concerns with regard to the outsiders of such agreements or arrangements. In essence, mutual recognition with exclusive membership might run afoul of the WTO disciplines, in particular, the disciplines of the GATT and the TBT Agreement on non-discrimination, as well as the TBT Agreement's obligation for measures to be not more trade restrictive than "necessary". Also, it appears that although Article XXIV of the GATT could potentially be applicable to the inconsistencies arising from mutual recognition in RTAs (if to interpret Article XXIV in the evolutionary manner meaning that technical barriers, in principle, could be covered), there is little chance it could be used as a defence for TBT Agreement's violations. It appears that a lack of references in the TBT Agreement to Article XXIV might be intentional and that the TBT Agreement's approach towards preferential deals is effectively different from Article XXIV GATT, in a way that calls for a greater openness of such deals.

At the same time, Chap. 3 also clarified that although the respective WTO provisions have a preference for "open" recognition regimes, this "openness" is not enforceable. The Chapter included a proposal to create a mechanism at the WTO to ensure that the motivation behind recognition regimes is based on legitimate considerations. This could be done through clarifying the procedure for recognition of equivalence, as it was done by the SPS Committee in relation to sanitary and phytosanitary measures. Essentially, the SPS Committee decision provides that the importing WTO Member has to clearly identify the appropriate level of protection that the relevant measure is aimed to ensure, while the exporting Member has to provide a reasonable access to the importing Member to inspect its facilities in order to determine the equivalence between the two measures. It could be imagined that a clearer mechanism of equivalence consideration could also benefit the Members in the context of TBT measures and would provide the outsiders of mutual recognition agreements, in the best case scenario, with a potential for their own measures to be considered for recognition, or, in the worst case scenario, with an additional level of transparency in the respective regulations of the parties to a mutual recognition agreement.

Chapter 3 also delved into the issue of a potential transfer of the RTAs agenda to the multilateral level, given the RTAs' limits. It recognized that there have to be sufficiently meaningful reasons for the parties to bring their cooperation to the multilateral level instead of giving preference to other means, such as RTAs, or unilateral actions. Building on the existing academic literature, WTO committees documents, and other studies, the Chapter suggested that multilateral cooperation would be especially relevant in areas involving global public goods, such as the protection of the environment, as well as in sectors dominated by global value chains and where the regulatory paradigms are less entrenched, such as sectors involving goods embedding new technologies. The options for multilateralizing cooperation are limited given a number of constraints for negotiations at the WTO described earlier. All possible mechanisms that could be imagined would require a proactive role of the main international trade players in an effort to revitalize the multilateral agenda.

One of the possible solutions could be to move from a consensus-based single undertaking approach to negotiations to the option of concluding plurilateral agreements on specific issues between a sub-set of WTO Members. The plurilateral agreements date back to the GATT Tokyo Round, where the first TBT provisions were negotiated (later evolved into the TBT Agreement) and applied only to some of the GATT contracting parties. These provisions appeared at the time when regulation of non-tariff measures has become an extremely relevant issue, but the GATT contracting parties could not all agree how to tackle it. This experience could be instrumental in creating the model of cooperation on regulatory issues at the WTO, as similar dynamics are present nowadays. The plurilateral agreements could be approached through two models: exclusive plurilateral agreements and open plurilateral agreements (the latter are sometimes called the "critical mass agreements"). The difference between these models is that under open plurilaterals the benefits are extended to all WTO Members on an MFN basis, while exclusive plurilateral agreements do not extend their benefits to the outsiders. Both models have their pros and cons. While open plurilaterals directly benefit all WTO Members, they could create a free rider problem, the risks from which would limit the ambition of any such deals. As for the exclusive plurilaterals, they would not create such a problem, but to be added to the WTO legal architecture, they have to be approved by consensus of all WTO Members, making the procedure too complex.

Both models of plurilateral engagement might be useful to move forward on the regulatory agenda depending on the issues at stake. The open plurilaterals could be useful in case the participating members would represent a large share of the global trade ("critical mass"). It could be also imagined that they might be relevant for issues of global concern to promote a common understanding on certain issues among a large group of countries, such as treatment of environmental goods, or subjecting digital goods to the provisions of the TBT Agreement.

The exclusive plurilateral agreements might take more sophisticated forms tailor-made to specific concerns of certain WTO Members. To practically implement such deals, a suggestion could be made to amend the consensus requirement and to provide instead clear principles limiting the use of plurilateral, as well as a number of assurances to the outsiders of such agreements that they would not be disadvantaged, e.g., if they decide to sign such agreements, they would be given the same conditions as the original signatories. Also, as suggested by some of the scholars, plurilateral agreements could include an "aid-for-trade" component, which would assist the least developed countries in improving their regulations and conformity assessment procedures.

Another possible option for multilateral cooperation could take the form of strengthening the deliberative function of the WTO. The WTO already has a structure of committees where trade officials from Members engage on variety of issues. Still, more could be done to advance this institutional structure to help promote regulatory coherence. For instance, committees could engage better with regulators, industries, civil society groups, in addition to trade officials, who usually take part in deliberations. They could reinforce cooperation with international organizations dealing with non-tariff measures, such as OECD and APEC, as well as with Multilateral Development Banks and other capacity building instruments that could help in terms of technical assistance to least developed countries. Furthermore, the WTO could implement a platform, which would closely analyze and discuss the initiatives adopted at the level of regional trade agreements. This has already been implemented in WTO bodies on an ad-hoc basis. The suggestion would be to make it a regular item on the agenda of committees in order to better understand which approaches work in practice and could be potentially multilateralized.

Chapter 4 focused more specifically on TBT provisions in free trade agreements of the EU and the US as major rule makers in the area of TBT. It demonstrated how the EU and US transitioned from reliance on the negotiations at the multilateral level to addressing the "deep" trade agenda in their trade agreements. It showed different forms of navigating cooperation on TBT: from some forms of regulatory alignment to strengthened regulatory cooperation. It noted that mutual recognition within such agreements does not always go in line with the WTO rules and principles. Also, harmonization and equivalence disciplines mostly promote the interests of a more powerful partner. Nevertheless, for the most part, US and EU FTAs move forward the global regulatory governance in response to changing paradigms of global commerce and could also serve as an inspiration for future multilateral disciplines.

When comparing the US and EU approaches, Chap. 4 brought to the attention that in some of areas, these approaches are substantively different. On the example of the US and the EU trade agreements one could see how such systemic differences could impede further cooperation. In particular, the EU and the US have a different perspective with regard to the understanding on what constitutes international standards and with regard to the designation and operation of conformity assessment bodies. These differences translate into the respective provisions of their trade agreements. For instance, many EU FTAs include an understanding that ISO, IEC, and ITU are relevant international standardizing bodies, thereby recognizing their primal authority, while USMCA specifically points out that there could be no other criteria for international standardizing bodies than those identified in the WTO TBT Committee Decision on international standards. On conformity assessment, USMCA contains a rule that the parties shall not provide less favorable conditions to conformity assessment bodies that are not located in their territory, while in the EU, mandatory third party conformity assessment has to be performed only by the bodies located in its territory. Due to their contentious character, these issues could hardly be subject to the multilateral agenda. While the EU and the US could advance their interests by including their own approaches into trade agreements with smaller and/or likeminded trading partners, it could hardly be achieved at the multilateral level, even in the framework of a plurilateral agreement, as it would face opposition from countries following a different approach.

On the other hand, some of the approaches in the EU and US trade agreements are quite similar. It is more constructive to analyze those approaches, taking into consideration that they could serve as an inspiration for future multilateral rules. As it was mentioned before, when it comes to future multilateral rules, there are two main contexts for cooperation: it is either related to the protection of the global public good, such as the protection of the environment, or it deals with sectors, which are affected by rules of multiple jurisdictions and where the regulations are less entrenched, such as digital goods.

On environmental protection, the US and EU trade agreements contain some important solutions that could also be envisaged at the multilateral level. One of these solutions relates to environmental goods. CETA and USMCA provide that the parties agree to make efforts to promote trade in environmental goods through reduction of non-tariff barriers related to those goods. While a further development of this solution in trade agreements could risk being found inconsistent with the TBT Agreement's provisions, the multilateral agreement on non-tariff measures on environmental goods might be a better option, as it would constitute a broad-based consensus that liberalization of environmental goods has to be a priority. Such an agreement could take the form of an open plurilateral agreement, to which all the WTO Members could easily subscribe to. Moreover, within the scope of this plurilateral agreement, the Members could also come up with the sector specific understandings in order to make the initiative more concrete.

Another solution on the interconnection between TBT and the environment in EU and US trade agreements is related to advancing regulatory cooperation and good regulatory practices, and in this specific context—promoting environmental considerations within their scope. One could see that the EU-Japan EPA and USMCA mention the environment as one of the considerations for impact assessment. This aspect could also be further developed and receive an active promotion at the multilateral level. It might be suggested that the strengthened deliberative role of the TBT Committee could include discussion and review of the implementation of such good regulatory practices by the WTO Members. Also, drawing from the EU and US trade agreements' experience of including environmental consideration into a regular regulatory cooperation agenda, suggestion here could be made to include environmental considerations as a regular item into the TBT Committee agenda, so that when working on recommendations and best practices on how to deal with technical barriers to trade, WTO Members would take environmental concerns as one of the main principles for such solutions.

Another area where the multilateral agenda on TBT could draw from the EU and US RTAs agenda is the area of digital goods. The EU-Japan EPA, CETA, and USMCA include provisions that potentially discipline technical barriers. This is the requirement for reasonable, impartial, transparent and clear regulation and administration of the area of digital products in the EU-Japan EPA and CETA, as well as the requirement to try to avoid unnecessary regulatory burden for electronic transactions in USMCA. Going forward, and, following the suggestion made by Canada at the TBT Committee's Ninth Triennial Review, it might be beneficial to "clearly specify that intangible digital products are covered by the obligations in the TBT provisions", or "to replicate TBT provisions in digital agreements". The TBT Agreement's disciplines could fill in the gaps in the global regulatory framework for digital goods with its provisions on non-discrimination, necessity, and international standards.

Furthermore, the WTO framework could benefit from learning from some of the advanced mechanisms for regulatory cooperation and good regulatory practices in EU and US RTAs. The inclusion of these mechanisms into the "new generation" EU and US trade agreements represents an innovative approach and is a now a new trend in global trade regulation. First, it could be suggested that the structure of the institutional framework for regulatory cooperation could serve as an inspiration for framework plurilateral agreements at the WTO, which could include basic rules and goals for cooperation, pursuant to which the parties would be able to collaborate on topic-specific emerging issues. This is essentially an idea of "living agreements", which are extended and adapted continuously. Secondly, the regulatory cooperation disciplines could also serve as an inspiration for extending the deliberation function of the WTO. Regulatory cooperation in the most recent EU and US trade agreements is cross-sectoral. It could cover many issues and include concerns from different domains. The WTO TBT Committee could also benefit from such varied expertise. It could introduce cross-committee meeting, as well as involve various stakeholders, in additional to trade officials.

Good regulatory practices, especially the most elaborate provisions in the EU-Japan EPA and USMCA, could also find their way into the WTO. The list of good regulatory practices already exists in the form of a recommendation of the TBT Committee. However, it is quite short and less elaborate than the good regulatory practices in the EU and US RTAs. Moreover, it could also be suggested to make good regulatory practices a regular part of the TBT Committee agenda and to install a review function of the TBT Committee regarding the Members' progress in implementing them. This has to be supplemented by comprehensive capacity building programs along with other international organizations and development funds.

All in all, the unifying idea behind the findings is that both the RTAs and the WTO are important components in disciplining technical barriers. At the moment, because of a number of political and legal constraints, the process of further cooperation at the WTO is stalled, which makes RTAs a central pillar in setting the agenda of international trade governance. This research does not see this trend from a negative perspective, but it suggests that, because of the RTAs limitations, the most optimal way forward would be to have a parallel work on TBT cooperation at the WTO, which is a more inclusive forum, and could tackle issues of multilateral significance in a more efficient and comprehensive manner.

Bibliography

International Agreements

Agreement Establishing the World Trade Organization (Marrakesh Agreement), 1994
Agreement on Technical Barriers to Trade, 1994
General Agreement on Tariffs and Trade, 1994
General Agreement on Trade in Services, 1994
Agreement on the Application of Sanitary and Phytosanitary Measures, 1994
Trade Agreement between the European Union and its Member States, of the one part, and the Republic of Korea, of the other part, OJ L 127, 14.05. 2011, p. 6-1344
Free Trade Agreement between the European Union and the Republic of Singapore, OJ L 294, 14.11.2019, p. 3-755
Free Trade Agreement between the European Union and the Socialist Republic of Viet Nam, OJ L 186, 12.06.2020, p. 3-1400
Agreement between the European Union and Japan for an Economic Partnership, OJ L 330, 27.12.2018, p. 3-899
Comprehensive Economic and Trade Agreement (CETA) between Canada, of the one part, and the European Union and its Member States, of the other part, OJ L 11, 14.02.2017, p. 23-1079
Agreement between the United States of America, the United Mexican States, and Canada, 7.01.2020
Free Trade Agreement between the United States of America and the Republic of Korea, 30.06.2007
Vienna Convention on the Law of Treaties, 1969
General Interpretative Note to Annex IA of the Marrakesh Agreement, Annex IA of the Marrakesh Agreement establishing the World Trade Organization, 1994
Treaty on European Union, 26 October 2012, OJ C326/13
Agreement on Technical Barriers to Trade ("Standards Code"), 1979. http://www.worldtradelaw.net/tokyoround/standardscode.pdf.download. Accessed 1 Nov 2022
WTO (1979) Decision on Differential and More Favourable Treatment, Reciprocity and Fuller Participation of Developing Countries, 28.11.1979. https://www.wto.org/english/docs_e/legal_e/enabling1979_e.htm. Accessed 1 Nov 2022
Understanding on Interpretation of Article XXIV of the General Agreement on Tariffs and Trade, para. 2 (1994). https://www.wto.org/english/tratop_e/region_e/region_art24_e.htm#understanding. Accessed 3 Nov 2022

I. Romanchyshyna, *Technical Barriers to Trade in "New Generation" RTAs and in the WTO Agreements*, EYIEL Monographs - Studies in European and International Economic Law 29, https://doi.org/10.1007/978-3-031-25791-9

WTO Protocol of Accession of the People's Republic of China, WT/L/432, 23.11.2001

Agreement Concerning the Adoption of Harmonized Technical United Nations Regulations for Wheeled Vehicles, Equipment and Parts which can be Fitted and/or be Used on Wheeled Vehicles and the Conditions for Reciprocal Recognition of Approvals Granted on the Basis of these United Nations Regulations (1958). https://unece.org/trans/main/wp29/wp29regs. Accessed 2 Nov 2022

Agreement Concerning the Establishment of Global Technical Regulations for Wheeled Vehicles, Equipment and Parts which Can be Fitted and/or be Used on Wheeled Vehicles (1998). https://unece.org/DAM/trans/main/wp29/wp29wgs/wp29gen/wp29glob/tran132.pdf. Accessed 2 Nov 2022

Agreement between the European Community and the Swiss Confederation on Mutual Recognition in Relation to Conformity Assessment, OJ L114, 30.04.2002

Official Documents of Issued by Governments and International Institutions

European Commission (2006) Global Europe: Competing in the World

European Commission (2015) Trade for All. Towards a more Responsible Trade and Investment Policy

European Commission (2017a) Reflection Paper on Harnessing Globalization

WTO Committee on Sanitary and Phytosanitary Measures (2001) Decision on the Implementation of Article 4 of the Agreement on the Application of Sanitary and Phytosanitary Measures, G/SPS/19, 2001, reviewed in 2004

WTO, Committee on Technical Barriers to Trade, Decisions and Recommendations (2015) G/TBT/1/Rev.12, 21.01.2015

ISO and IEC (2004) ISO/IEC Guide 2. Standardisation and Related Activities

ISO/IEC Guide 2:1991: General Terms and Their Definitions Concerning Standardization and Related Activities (1991)

ISO/IEC Guide 2:2004: General Terms and Their Definitions Concerning Standardization and Related Activities (reviewed version of the 1991 Guide), 2004. https://www.iso.org/standard/39976.html. Accessed 1 Nov 2022

GATT (1963) Kennedy Round of Trade Negotiations - Forthcoming Meetings, GATT/873

WTO, Doha WTO Ministerial Declaration, WT/MIN(01)/DEC/1, 20.11.2001

WTO, EU Proposal TN/MA/W/93/Rev.1 and Add.1, 15.09.2009

WTO, EU Proposal TN/MA/W/129, 7.12.2009

WTO, US Proposal TN/MA/W/105/Rev.2, 15.09.2009

WTO, Argentina and Brazil Proposal TN/MA/W/135, 04.02.2010

WTO, EU Proposal TN/MA/W/118/Rev.1, 4.12.2009

WTO, Brazil EU and India's Proposals TN/MA/W/136, 15.03.2010

WTO Committee on Technical Barriers to Trade (2017a) Decisions and Recommendation Adopted by the WTO Committee on Technical Barriers to Trade since 1 January 1995, G/TBT/1/Rev.13, 8.03.2017

WTO Committee on Technical Barriers to Trade (2000) Second Triennial Review of the Operation and Implementation of the Agreement on Technical Barriers to Trade, Annex 4: Decision of the Committee on Principles for the Development of International Standards, Guides and Recommendations with Relation to art. 2, 5 and annex 3 of the Agreement," G/TBT/9, 13. 11

WTO (2012) Summary Report of the TBT Workshop on Regulatory Cooperation between Members, G/TBT/W348, 14.02.2012

WTO Committee on Technical Barriers to Trade (2009) Fifth Triennial Review, G/TBT/26, 13.11.2009

US Department of State (1946-1947) Preliminary Proposals for an ITO, In: US Department of State, American Trade Proposals – A Series of Articles Looking Toward a World Conference on Trade, US Government Printing Office, Washington DC

United States Tariff Commission (1947) Analysis – Geneva Draft of Charter for an International Trade Organization, Washington D.C.

United Nations Conference on Trade and Employment (1947-1948) Havana Final Act and Related Documents. https://www.wto.org/english/docs_e/legal_e/havana_e.pdf. Accessed 1 Nov 2022

WTO Committee on Technical Barriers to Trade (2021a) Proposals on Conformity Assessment, Environment and Climate Change, Transparency, Digital Products, and Micro, Small, and Medium-Sized Enterprises (MSMEs), Ninth Triennial Review, Submission from Canada, G/TBT/W/745, 28.04.2021

GATT (1990) Communication from the European Community, No. MTN.GNG/NG14/W42, 9.07.1990

United States Trade Representative (2021) 2021 Trade Policy Agenda and 2020 Annual Report

European Commission (2017b) Report from the Commission to the European Parliament, the Council, the European Economic and Social Committee and the Committee of the Regions https://ec.europa.eu/transparency/regdoc/rep/1/2017/EN/COM-2017-654-F1-EN-MAIN-PART-1.PDF. Accessed 2 Nov 2022

Regulation No. 1025/2012 on European standardisation, OJ L 316/12, 14.11.2012

Agreement on Technical Cooperation between ISO and CEN (Vienna Agreement) (1991). https://isotc.iso.org/livelink/livelink/fetch/2000/2122/3146825/4229629/4230450/4230458/01__Agreement_on_Technical_Cooperation_between_ISO_and_CEN_(Vienna_Agreement).pdf?nodeid=4230688&vernum=-2. Accessed 2 Nov 2022

The IEC-CENELEC Frankfurt Agreement (1991). http://www.iec.ch/about/globalreach/partners/pdf/IEC-CENELEC_Frankfurt_Agreement%7B2016%7D.pdf. Accessed 2 Nov 2022

United States Trade Representative (2020) 2020 National Trade Estimate Report on Foreign Trade Barriers. https://ustr.gov/sites/default/files/2020_National_Trade_Estimate_Report.pdf. Accessed 2 Nov 2022

European Commission (2012) Communication "CARS2020 Action Plan for a Competitive and Sustainable Automotive Industry in Europe

European Commission (2017c) Evaluation of the EU-Japan EPA, p 2. https://trade.ec.europa.eu/doclib/docs/2018/july/tradoc_157115.pdf. Accessed 2 Nov 2022

WTO (2018) Approaches to Conformity Assessment, Eighth Triennial Review Submission from the European Union, G/TBT/W/462, 9.03.2018

European Commission (2004) Commission Staff Working Paper: Priorities for Bilateral/Regional Trade Activities in the Field of Mutual Recognition Agreements for Industrial Products and Related Technical Dialogue, SEC(2004)1072

WTO Committee on Technical Barriers to Trade (2018) Eighth Triennial Review of the Operation and Implementation of the Agreement on Technical Barriers to Trade under Article 15.4. G/TBT/ 41, 19.11.2018

WTO Committee on Technical Barriers to Trade (2017b) Indicative List of Approaches to Facilitate Acceptance of the Results of Conformity Assessment. G/TBT/1/Rev.13, 8.03.2017

WTO Committee on Technical Barriers to Trade (2019) Thematic Session on Conformity Assessment Procedures, G/TBT/GEN/278, 5.12.2019

WTO Committee on Technical Barriers to Trade (2017c) Thematic Session on Conformity Assessment Procedures, G/TBT/GEN/213, 5.04.2017

European Commission (2017d) Report on Trade and Investment Barriers, COM(2017), p. 27. https://trade.ec.europa.eu/doclib/docs/2017/june/tradoc_155642.pdf. Accessed 3 Nov 2022

European Commission, Strategic Plan 2020-2024. https://trade.ec.europa.eu/doclib/docs/2020/november/tradoc_159104.pdf. Accessed 3 Nov 2022

WTO Committee on Technical Barriers to Trade (2021) Proposals on Conformity Assessment, Transparency, and COVID-19, Ninth Triennial Review, Submission from the European Union, G/TBT/W/736, 1.02.2021

WTO Cases

Panel Report, Australia – Certain Measures Concerning Trademarks, Geographical Indications and Other Plain Packaging Requirements Applicable to Tobacco Products and Packaging, WT/DS435/R, WT/DS441/R WT/DS458/R, WT/DS467/R, 28 June 2018 (Australia – Tobacco Plain Packaging)

Panel Report, United States – Measures Concerning the Importation, Marketing and Sale of Tuna and Tuna Products, WT/DS381/R, 13 June 2012 (US – Tuna II (Mexico))

Panel Report, United States – Certain Country of Origin Labelling (COOL) Requirements, WT/DS384/R, WT/DS386/R, 23 July 2012 (US – COOL)

Panel Report, United States – Certain Country of Origin Labelling (COOL) Requirements, Recourse to Article 21.5 by Canada and Mexico, WT/DS384/RW WT/DS386/RW, 20 October 2014 (US – COOL (Article 21.5 – Canada and Mexico))

Panel Report, United States – Measures Concerning the Importation, Marketing and Sale of Tuna and Tuna Products, Recourse to Article 215 of the DSU by Mexico, WT/DS381/RW/Corr.1, 22 April 2015 (US – Tuna II (Mexico) (Article 21.5 – Mexico))

Panel Report, European Communities – Measures Prohibiting the Importation and Marketing of Seal Products, WT/DS400/R, WT/DS401/R / and Add.1, 18 June 2014 (EC – Seal Products)

Panel Report, United States – Measures Affecting the Production and Sale of Clove Cigarettes, WT/DS406/R, 24 April 2012 (US – Clove Cigarettes)

Panel Report, European Communities – Trade Description of Sardines, WT/DS231/R and Corr.1, 23 October 2002 (EC – Sardines)

Panel Report, European Communities – Measures Affecting Asbestos and Asbestos-Containing Products, WT/DS135/R and Add.1, 5 April 2001 (EC – Asbestos)

Panel Report, Russia – Measures Affecting the Importation of Railway Equipment and Parts thereof, WT/DS499/R, 30 July 2018 (Russia – Railway Equipment)

Panel Report, Canada – Certain Measures Affecting the Automotive Industry, WT/DS139/R, WT/DS142/R, 19 June 2000 (Canada – Autos)

Panel Report, United States – Definitive Safeguard Measures on Imports of Circular Welded Carbon Quality Line Pipe from Korea, WT/DS202/R, 8 March 2002 (US – Line Pipe)

Appellate Body Report, United States – Measures Concerning the Importation, Marketing and Sale of Tuna and Tuna Products, WT/DS381/AB/R, 13 June 2012 (US-Tuna II (Mexico))

Appellate Body Report, United States – Measures Affecting the Production and Sale of Clove Cigarettes, WT/DS406/AB/R, 24 April 2012 (US – Clove Cigarettes)

Appellate Body Report, European Communities – Measures Affecting Asbestos and Asbestos-Containing Products, WT/DS135/AB/R, 5 April 2001 (EC – Asbestos)

Appellate Body Report, United States – Measures Concerning the Importation, Marketing and Sale of Tuna and Tuna Products, WT/DS381/AB/R, 13 June 2012 (US – Tuna II (Mexico))

Appellate Body Report, United States – Certain Country of Origin Labelling (COOL) Requirements, WT/DS384/AB/R, WT/DS386/AB/R, 23 July 2012 (US – COOL)

Appellate Body Report, United States – Certain Country of Origin Labelling (COOL) Requirements, Recourse to Article 21.5 of the DSU by Canada and Mexico, WT/DS384/AB/RW, WT/DS386/AB/RW, 18 May 2015 (US – COOL (Article 21.5 – Canada and Mexico))

Appellate Body Report, Russia – Measures Affecting the Importation of Railway Equipment and Parts thereof, Russia – Railway Equipment, WT/DS499/AB/R, 4 February 2020 (Russia – Railway Equipment)

Appellate Body Report, Australia – Certain Measures Concerning Trademarks, Geographical Indications and Other Plain Packaging Requirements Applicable to Tobacco Products and Packaging, WT/DS435/AB/R, WT/DS441/AB/R, 9 June 2020 (Australia – Tobacco Plain Packaging)

Appellate Body Report, United States – Measures Affecting the Cross-Border Supply of Gambling and Betting Services, WT/DS285/AB/R, 20 April 2005 (US – Gambling)

Appellate Body Report, Colombia – Measures Relating to the Importation of Textiles, Apparel and Footwear, WT/DS461/AB/R, 7 June 2016 (Colombia – Textiles)

Appellate Body Report, European Communities – Measures Prohibiting the Importation and Marketing of Seal Products, WT/DS400/AB/R, WT/DS401/AB/R, 18 June 2014 (EC – Seal Products)

Appellate Body Report, China – Measures Affecting Trading Rights and Distribution Services for Certain Publications and Audiovisual Entertainment Products, WT/DS363/AB/R, 19 January 2010 (China – Publications and Audiovisual Products)

Appellate Body Report, European Communities – Trade Description of Sardines, WT/DS231/AB/R, 23 October 2002 (EC – Sardines)

Appellate Body Report, United States – Import Prohibition of Certain Shrimp and Shrimp Products, WT/DS58/AB/R, adopted 6 November 1998 (US – Shrimp)

Appellate Body Report, United States – Import Prohibition of Certain Shrimp and Shrimp Products, Recourse to Article 21.5 of the DSU by Malaysia, WT/DS58/AB/RW, 21 November 2001 (US – Shrimp (21.5))

Appellate Body Report, China – Measures Related to the Exportation of Rare Earths, Tungsten, and Molybdenum, WT/DS431/AB/R, WT/DS432/AB/R, WT/DS433/AB/R, 29 August 2014 (China – Rare Earths)

Appellate Body Report, Turkey – Restrictions on Imports of Textile and Clothing Products, WT/DS34/AB/R, 19 November 1999 (Turkey –Textiles)

Appellate Body Report, Peru – Additional Duty on Imports of Certain Agricultural Products, WT/DS457/AB/R, 20 July 2015 (Peru – Agricultural Products)

Appellate Body Report, Canada – Certain Measures Affecting the Automotive Industry, WT/DS139/AB/R, WT/DS142/AB/R, 19 June 2000 (Canada – Autos)

Appellate Body Report, United States – Standards for Reformulated and Conventional Gasoline, WT/DS2/AB/R, 20 May 1996 (US – Gasoline)

Appellate Body Report, United States – Definitive Safeguard Measures on Imports of Circular Welded Carbon Quality Line Pipe from Korea, WT/DS202/AB/R, 8 March 2002 (US – Line Pipe)

Appellate Body Report, European Communities – Regime for the Importation, Sale and Distribution of Bananas, WT/DS27/AB/R, 25 September 1997 (EC – Bananas III)

Appellate Body Report, Canada – Certain Measures Concerning Periodicals, WT/DS31/AB/R, 30 July 1997 (Canada – Periodicals)

Appellate Body Report, Korea – Definitive Safeguard Measure on Imports of Certain Dairy Products, WT/DS98/AB/R, 12 January 2000 (Korea – Dairy)

Appellate Body Report, Appellate Body Report, Argentina – Safeguard Measures on Imports of Footwear, WT/DS121/AB/R, 12 January 2000 (Argentina – Footwear)

Appellate Body Report, United States – Definitive Safeguard Measures on Imports of Certain Steel Products, WT/DS248/AB/R WT/DS249/AB/R WT/DS251/AB/R WT/DS252/AB/R WT/DS253/AB/R WT/DS254/AB/R WT/DS258/AB/R WT/DS259/AB/R, 10 November 2003 (US – Steel Safeguards)

Other Sources

Slany W et al (eds) (1956) Foreign Relations of the United States 1955-1957. United States Government Printing Office, Washington DC

Lamy P (1999) Speech 99/132. https://europa.eu/rapid/press-release_SPEECH-99-132_en.htm. Accessed 2 Nov 2022

Lamy P (2004) Trade Policy in the Prodi Commission 1999-2004: An Assessment. https://pascallamyeu.files.wordpress.com/2016/11/1999_2004_pl_legacy_e.pdf. Accessed 2 Nov 2022

Lamy P (2003) Speech 03/514. https://europa.eu/rapid/press-release_SPEECH-03-514_en.htm. Accessed 2 Nov 2022

WTO News, Talks Suspended. Today there are Only Losers, July 2006. https://www.wto.org/english/news_e/news06_e/mod06_summary_24july_e.htm. Accessed 2 Nov 2022

Financial Times (2019) Trump's Angry Unilateralism Is a Cry of Pain.https://www.ft.com/content/7b9da60a-70b7-11e9-bf5c-6eeb837566c5. Accessed 2 Nov 2022

ISO. The Vienna Agreement FAQs (2016). https://boss.cen.eu/media/CEN/ref/va_faq.pdf. Accessed 2 Nov 2022

CEN and CENELEC. Work Programme (2022). https://www.cencenelec.eu/media/CEN-CENELEC/News/Publications/2022/cen-cenelec_work_programme2022.pdf. Accessed 2 Nov 2022

Presentation of Fernando Perreu de Pinnick from DG Trade titled "The EU-Korea Free Trade Agreement. Motor Vehicles and Parts", prepared for the Seminar "EU-Korea FTA. Putting the FTA into Practice", held on 20 June 2011 in Seul, South Korea. http://eeas.europa.eu/archives/delegations/south_korea/documents/eu_south_korea/fta_booklet_final_en.pdf. Accessed 2 Nov 2022

Romanchyshyna I (2019) The Post-TTIP Transatlantic Cooperation on Trade: Stepping up Conformity Assessment. EJIL:Talk! (blog of the European Journal of International Law).https://www.ejiltalk.org/the-post-ttip-transatlantic-cooperation-on-trade-stepping-up-conformity-assessment/. Accessed 3 Nov 2022

European Commission (2018) Trade Issues…Technical Barriers to Trade. Newsletter No10, https://trade.ec.europa.eu/doclib/docs/2018/february/tradoc_156599.pdf. Accessed 3 Nov 2022

American National Standards Institute. Overview of the US Standardization System. https://www.standardsportal.org/usa_en/standards_system.aspx. Accessed 3 Nov 2022

Lovells H (2019) Automotive in Mexico. https://www.lexology.com/library/detail.aspx?g=925665e3-9a0f-4bfc-af4c-28288ae3eee6. Accessed 3 Nov 2022

Printed by Printforce, the Netherlands